WORKSHOPS IN COMPUTING
Series edited by C. J. van Rijsbergen

*Also in this series*

AI and Cognitive Science '89, Dublin City University, Eire,
14–15 September 1989
A. F. Smeaton and G. McDermott (Eds.)

Specification and Verification of Concurrent Systems, University of
Stirling, Scotland, 6–8 July 1988
C. Rattray (Ed.)

Semantics for Concurrency, Proceedings of the International
BCS-FACS Workshop, Sponsored by Logic for IT (S.E.R.C.), University
of Leicester, UK, 23–25 July 1990
M. Z. Kwiatkowska, M. W. Shields and R. M. Thomas (Eds.)

Functional Programming, Proceedings of the 1989 Glasgow
Workshop, Fraserburgh, Scotland, 21–23 August 1989
K. Davis and J. Hughes (Eds.)

Persistent Object Systems, Proceedings of the Third International
Workshop, Newcastle, Australia, 10–13 January 1989
J. Rosenberg and D. Koch (Eds.)

J. E. Nicholls (Ed.)

# Z User Workshop

Proceedings of the Fourth Annual
Z User Meeting
Oxford, 15 December 1989

**Springer-Verlag London Ltd.**

J. E. Nicholls, MA
Oxford University Programming Research Group,
8–11 Keble Road,
Oxford, UK

ISBN 978-3-540-19627-3

British Library Cataloguing in Publication Data
Z User Meeting (4th; 1989; Oxford, England)
  Z the users workshop Oxford, 1989: proceedings of the fourth annual Z User
Meeting, 15 December, 1989, Oxford.– (Workshops in computing)
  1. Computer systems.Programming languages:Z language
  I. Title  II, Nicholls, J. E. (John Edward) *1928–*    005. 133
ISBN 978-3-540-19627-3      ISBN 978-1-4471-3877-8 (eBook)
DOI 10.1007/978-1-4471-3877-8

Library of Congress Cataloging-in-Publication Data
Z User Workshop (4th:1989: Oxford, England)
Proceedings of the Fourth Annual Z User Meeting, 15 December 1989,
Oxford/J.E. Nicholls (ed.)
  p.cm. – (Workshops in computing)
Includes bibliographical references and index.
ISBN 978-3-540-19627-3
1. Z (Computer program language)–Congresses.  I. Nicholls, John E.  II. Title.
III. Series.
QA76.73.Z2Z2    1989
005.13′3–dc20                                                    90-41955
                                                                    CIP

2128/3916–543210   Printed on acid-free paper

# Preface

The mathematical concepts and notational conventions we know of as Z were first proposed around 1981. Its origins were in line with the objectives of the PRG – to establish a mathematical basis for programming concepts and to verify the work by case studies with industry. Hence among early Z users some were from academic circles, with interests in the mathematical basis of programming; others came from industry and were involved with pilot projects and case studies linked with the Programming Research Group.

Four years ago we had the first Z User Meeting, a fairly modest affair with representatives more or less equally divided between academia and industry. At the first meeting there were, as in this meeting, a variety of technical papers, reports of work in progress and discussions. A number of people from industry came along, either because they had begun to use Z or were curious about the new direction. In the discussion sessions at the end of the meeting, there were calls from attendees for the establishment of a more stable base for the notation, including work on its documentation and standards. Many of these requests have now been satisfied and the notation is now being proposed for standards development.

Since 1986, there has been a steady growth in the number of Z users and a corresponding increase in the publication of technical papers and reports of work with Z. For this year's meeting we felt it was time to have a more formal arrangement for preparing and presenting these papers. It is therefore a pleasure to introduce this collection of papers, the first published Proceedings of a Z User Meeting. The papers originally presented at the meeting have been revised, updated and prepared for publication in a permanent form.

There have been two events marking what may be called the consolidation of Z. The first was the publication in 1987 of the book of Case Studies edited by Ian Hayes. The second occurred prior to this meeting in 1989 with the publication of the Z Reference Manual by Mike Spivey. These two books have established a precise description of the notation and a sampler of methods that show how it may be used.

The topics presented at the meeting included new work on the theory of Z, the design of tools and environments, and descriptions of its practical application in industrial projects. It is specially important for potential users to hear of the experiences of other users, and we welcome those who have documented their experiences of work with Z. If they seem to some observers to leave many questions unanswered, it is because these experiences are of intense interest to those carrying out research on Z, and those contemplating a decision about its use.

The meeting was organised by a Programme Committee who helped in planning the meeting and refereeing the papers. Members of the Committee were as follows:

**Jonathan Bowen, PRG Oxford**
**Dr David Duce, RAL Chilton**
**Professor Pat Hall, Brunel University**
**Tim Hoverd, Logica Cambridge**
**Peter Lupton, IBM UK Laboratories Hursley**
**John Nicholls, PRG Oxford (Chairman)**
**Dr Chris Sennett, RSRE Malvern**

I should like to acknowledge support by the SERC on the Software Engineering project.

December 1989                                                John Nicholls
                                                    Oxford University PRG

# Contents

# Opening address:
# The state of use of Formal Methods

Brian Oakley, CBE
Chairman, Logica Cambridge Ltd

## Why do we need Formal Methods?

It is very nice to be opening this conference, here in Oxford, the very home, if not the birthplace, of Z. Of course some of you will say that the pleasure really comes from the euphoria of having got away from Cambridge.

This time last year Martin Thomas of Praxis opened this conference by giving a quotation from Brian Oakley. I will return the compliment by quoting the Chairman of Praxis: "Mathematical Methods have a fundamental role to play in improving the certainty of computer system development." Perhaps being more cynical than Martin I might be tempted to rephrase that to "Mathematical Methods have a fundamental role to play in reducing the uncertainty of computer system development.". But basically we are at one in recognising the key importance of the work dependent on these mathematical methods.

Before looking at the current state of employment of Formal Methods it seems worth reminding ourselves just *why* we need Formal Methods. One approach to that question is to consider what a traditional professional engineer, say a member of one of the great Victorian engineering institutions, would think of those upstarts who earn their living by programming computers; those scoundrels who dare to call themselves software "engineers"! In the first place the traditional engineer would be very doubtful at the term "engineering" being applied to a process that did not produce an artifact – a bridge, a road, an engine – at the end. However this is a matter of perception and of course there are well established examples of engineering disciplines that do not lead to end products that one can see and touch – heating engineers, audio engineers, for example – even if in these examples the traditional engineer then tends to shift attention from the intangible end product to the hardware system that produces the end product. Software engineering produces the manuals – the music manuscript rather than the audio amplifier – except in the rather special case of CAD design for VLSI chips.

A much more substantial complaint of the traditional engineer, and one that is much harder to answer, is that there is a great deal of very badly engineered software out there in use. It's like the early days of structural engineering – pre Tay Bridge disaster days – where one learnt the limits of the trade by building an even larger unsupported arch and then backed off a bit, when building the next one, if the previous one collapsed. Who ever heard of a respectable engineer who sent out products with faults in them? Well, don't answer that! Software lacks the equivalent of Bowes diagrams, lacks component reuse, lacks tolerancing and quality approval processes, lacks proof, beyond the existence proof that it works for one set of input conditions, that it can cope with input parameters across its specification limits. Indeed, though I doubt if the traditional engineer has thought this out, if Moore's law says that the potential complexity on a chip doubles every year, and this has been going on for the last 25 years and more, and is still going on, we know that for a system with only a relatively modest number of variable inputs the output combinations are theoretically so astronomical in number as to be untestable by the "try them all" approach.

Which, of course, is where Formal Methods come in. There is a small pamphlet published some years ago with the title – I speak from memory – "Software building *is* an Engineering discipline" – author one Tony Hoare. Perhaps it is that author's more recent work that has led to the substantiation of that proud acclaim. It was the same Tony Hoare who defined Formal Methods as the "use of mathematically vigorous notations and techniques to specify unambiguously and to reason about computational process". All current emphasis and, even, hype on the use of Formal Methods for Safety Critical software tends to disguise the fact that the overwhelming reason for using Formal Methods is because it improves the quality of software in all aspects of that word. It reduces the chances of errors, and it improves the likelihood that what is built actually meets the requirement. Reducing ambiguity, improving communication between customer and supplier is a very important aspect of the benefit – though I suppose that really requires the customer to understand logical notations to get the full benefit. Incidentally there is ample proof that it helps to reduce the problems of uncertainty in communication between members of a team. This will become increasingly important as modern communications make it feasible to have software development teams widely scattered round the world. The use of formal methods undoubtedly leads to improved productivity, as the case of the Inmos T800 transputer dramatically illustrates. And our traditional engineer will welcome the evidence that it leads to true reuse, always a function of good engineering if only because it leads to better reliability and less uncertainty in time scales and costs.

## Limitations of Formal Methods

It should not be necessary to say a word of warning about the limitations of Formal Methods to this audience. After all it is early days in the development. But there has been such hype that it seems worth reminding ourselves that there are severe limitations. The specification, after formal checking, may be internally consistent, but there is no way of saying that it meets the requirement, that it does what is really needed. Of course better communication should make it more likely that it meets what the customer thinks is the requirement. Then the formal specification may not correctly represent some external reality, something that is stated in the requirement but is simply in error in detail in the specification.

Perhaps the most misleading feature of the current state of Formal Methods is that what is formally specified is usually only a piece of the system. Maybe the specification has been checked, but has the compiler, the operating system, all the hardware – and so on? How much of the T800 transputer was actually verified – the logic of the multiplier, but how much else? How much of the Viper processor was actually checked? How much of CICS is being formally specified?

# The Current State

**Use**   The following list gives some indication of the most widely acknowledged users of formal methods in the UK.

| | |
|---|---|
| BAe | Aircraft Control; CORE/Z merging |
| BT | Secure Communications |
| CEGB | Power Station Control |
| Ferranti | Command Systems, Power Station Control |
| CESG | Security Modelling Work |
| GEC | Forest; Applications to Avionics |
| IBM | CICS Transaction Processing System |
| Inmos | T800 Transputer Circuit |
| Logica | Formaliser Method, Secure Projects Viper II |
| Plessey | Underwater Systems Control |
| Praxis | Toolkit Development |
| RSRE | Viper, etc |
| STC | Telecomms multiplexor management and control, RAISE, Office Systems |

| | |
|---|---|
| Bell Labs | |
| Bull | Secure Systems Development |
| Tektronix | Oscilloscope Development |

Figure 1: Some Users of Formal Methods

No doubt the list is far from complete. Outside the defence field, most of these entries represent pretty experimental work, with the honourable exception of the IBM work on CICS, which will be described in a subsequent paper. No doubt there are other, perhaps many other, examples of small scale work in the UK. But it is doubtful if they are much more than pilot or experimental in nature and scale. This table ignores the strong work in the Universities, Oxford, Cambridge, Kent, Manchester, and of course others. A more complete list of users is being compiled by the PRG; the current list contains the names of some 20 industrial companies in the UK[1].

Looking at the overseas picture it is noticeable that there seems to be even less work in the USA, with a few well known examples such as Tektronix and Bell Labs where the name of Subrabmangam appears from time to time. Much of the academic work on higher order logic applications seems to be more related to automatic logical

---

[1]A revised list of Z Users appears in this Proceedings (editor).

proof of theorems rather than Formal Methods. On the Continent it is known that Bull are taking Formal Methods seriously. In Germany there is work in institutes like that for Datenteknich at Darmstadt and the University of Kiel. And the Dutch seem to be very active in universities like that at Nijmegen.

There seems to be little doubt that this is a field where the work in the UK still leads the world, especially the academic work, though I think industry is also ahead of their international competitors. It is worth pausing to note that this academic work has passed directly and relatively easily into the hands of our industry. It should be remembered as an example of academic work which few, if any industrialists would have asked for 10 or less years ago, but looks set to be of enormous economic importance to our IT industry and IT users alike.

That there is a great growth of interest in Formal Methods in the UK is shown by the rise in numbers attending this conference, 120 this year against 80 last year, and 45 in 1987.

**Management Reluctance**  It must be admitted that there seems to be a real reluctance in industry to invest in any significant scale in Formal Methods work. It is, of course, partly a matter of typical British reluctance to invest, typical conservatism. But there is the added complication of the inaccessibility of higher order logic, with its frightening cabalistic symbols. After all, how many people in industry even know what they mean? In the current state of the art, Formal Methods are not easy to use. No doubt the logic is easy enough once one has studied it, but knowing how to construct an abstract model requires real understanding and experience. Though work is going on it is still early days for "methods" like those that are commonly used for software engineering, such as Yourdon or SSADM, to emerge. And though some tools are now available, (Forsite from Racal, Genesis from IST, Formaliser from Logica), they are still pretty much at the experimental stage. There are some training courses beginning to emerge, notably here in Oxford, and at Edinburgh, Glasgow, Leicester Universities, and Cranfield IT Institute and in various polytechnic computing science courses. In industry, Praxis and Logica are giving short courses, but as someone said, "Would one send someone for two weeks to learn physics?". Maybe the parallel is not appropriate, but there is no doubt that this remains a field where there is no alternative to building up experience.

# Where do we go from here?

From the above it is really pretty obvious what needs to be done. Clearly we need continuing concentration in the Universities and Polytechnics on the development of the subject, and on its teaching. We need more and better books and training material (rumour has it that Jim Woodcock from PRG has another book called "Using Z" on the stocks; and Ben Potter of STC and his co-workers have a "Plain Man's Guide" nearing completion). We need more of that crucial, but currently rather neglected academic activity, "scholarship" applied to the subject. Scholarship, in this context, is the art of condensing, simplifying, codifying as a subject; producing good literature, good training material and courses. It is one of the fields of academic endeavour that gets neglected when the UGC or UFC establishes numerical criteria for evaluation of departmental worth, yet it is a crucial activity for the community at large.

We must get more experience through more use of Formal Methods carried out in industry, even if, for some time to come, this will tend to be rather experimental in nature. That means more trained people, and that means University and Polytechnic courses. Incidentally there seems some evidence that Polytechnics have been rather readier than Universities to put Formal Methods into their syllabuses. It is interesting to speculate on why this might be. Could it be that they are rather nearer to the very real, if rather sordid, needs of software systems developers in the real world where quality matters? In my experience, as a subject becomes widely taught, so it, magically, becomes easier to learn, understand and practise. It is very interesting to speculate on whether we are going to see a time when any chartered software engineer will know how to use Formal Methods, or whether firms are going to keep a few back room experts – rather as telecommunications firms used to keep a few mathematicians (for some reason they were always Poles or Hungarians), who understood erlangs and queueing theory and exotic matters like that in order to carry out their network loading analysis. I tend to the view that, by the turn of the century, every computer science graduate will be able to practise, indeed will have to be able to practise, Formal Methods.

This country has a great, and in my opinion deserved, reputation for its software. Certainly many of the great innovations in software have stemmed from the UK. Due to our academic community we hold a leading position in the world in the Formal Methods field. We must ensure that we take advantage of that lead by gaining the reputation for being the people who know how to make software of real quality. That demands the widespread use of Formal Methods.

# Type Inference in Z

J. M. Spivey & B.A. Sufrin
Oxford University Computing Laboratory
Programming Research Group
11 Keble Road, Oxford OX1 3QD, UK

## Abstract
Generic definitions provide an important part of the power of the Z notation, allowing the standard toolkit of mathematical notation to be built up from a very small set of primitives, and permitting application—oriented theories to be constructed with an appropriate degree of abstraction and generality. Although there is a notation for supplying explicitly the actual generic parameters when a generic constant is used, it greatly improves the readability of a Z document if the actual parameters are left to be inferred from the context, especially since every symbol from the basic mathematical toolkit would otherwise need explicit generic type parameters. In this paper we present and justify a method by which a type—checking program can carry out this inference of implicit generic parameters and check that the context determines them unambiguously. In the appendix we show the text of a type—checker for Z written in standard ML.

## 0. Types in Z
Z is a notation based on set theory, and in the mathematical sublanguage of Z some sets are considered to be *types*. Such sets are formed in one of three ways:

1. A type may be a *given set*, in which case it is a sort of global parameter of a Z theory and no *a—priori* assumptions are made about any internal structure which it may have. Any assumptions about the internal structure of a given set are made explicitly in the theory. Given types $t_1, ... t_n$ are introduced at the start of a theory by writing $[t_1, ... t_n]$.

2. The *n—fold product* of the types $t_1, ... t_n$, written $t_1 \times t_2 \times ... \times t_n$ is a type.

3. The set of all subsets of the elements which populate a type $t$, written $\mathbb{P}\, t$ is a type.

**Remark**

The only other way of forming a type in the mathematical sublanguage is the *data type* definition which permits the introduction of disjoint union and recursively specified types. For example:

$$L ::= nil \mid cons \ll E \times L \gg$$

Every occurrence of this form of definition can be systematically eliminated from a Z theory by introducing an additional given type and explicit assumptions about the constructors of the datatype [*Spivey 88*]. For the example above this means introducing the extra given type [L], and adding the following assumptions to the theory

$$
\begin{array}{|l l l}
\hline
nil & : & L \\
cons & : & E \times L \rightarrowtail L \\
\hline
\multicolumn{3}{|l}{\{nil\} \cap ran \ cons = \emptyset} \\
\end{array}
$$

We shall not discuss the data type notation any further.

$\square$

There are no distinct function or relation types in Z. Both relations and functions are identified with their graphs. Thus the set $S_1 \leftrightarrow S_2$ of all relations between elements of the sets $S_1$ and $S_2$ is identified with $\mathbb{P}(S_1 \times S_2)$, and when $R \in S_1 \leftrightarrow S_2$ we define $xRy \hat{=} (x,y) \in R$. The set of (partial) functions $S_1 \nrightarrow S_2$ from $S_1$ to $S_2$ is identified with $\{R: S_1 \leftrightarrow S_2 \mid \forall x: S_1; \ y,z: S_2 \bullet xRy \wedge xRz \Rightarrow y=z\}$, and the total functions $S_1 \rightarrow S_2$ are identified with $\{f: S_1 \nrightarrow S_2 \mid dom \ f = S_1\}$.

For the purposes of our exposition it will be convenient to assume that the set $\mathbb{Z}$ of integers has been given (and is therefore a type), and that we have defined the usual arithmetic functions and relations on it. We shall also assume that $\mathbb{N} \hat{=} \{n: \mathbb{Z} \mid n \geq 0\}$, so that $\mathbb{N} \subseteq \mathbb{Z}$.

## 1. Generic Definition and Instantiation

Generic definition allows us to define families of functions whose behaviour is the same for objects of different types. For example the following signature and axiom defines the family of functions $first$ so that $first(a,b)=a$, whatever the types of $a$, and $b$.

$$
\begin{array}{|l}
\hline
[X,Y] \\
\hline
first: X \times Y \rightarrow X \\
\hline
\forall \ x:X; \ y:Y \bullet \\
\quad first(x, y)=x \\
\hline
\end{array}
$$

The two *formal generic parameters* are $X$ and $Y$; the definition of *first* is the same whatever we take $X$ and $Y$ to be.

Different members of the family of *first* functions are written *first*[Z,Z], *first*[CH,Z], *first*[Z,N] and so on. The first of these is the function which selects the first of a pair of integers, the second is the function which selects the first of a pair consisting of a character and an integer. The third is like the first, except that it is defined only on pairs with a non−negative second component. Applying both to the pair (*3*, −*4*) we find that *first*[Z,Z](*3*,−*4*) has value 3, but *first*[Z,N](*3*, −*4*) is undefined. Such niceties are usually of no importance, however, and when this is the case we are content to leave the parameters implicit — writing *first*(*3*, −*4*) to mean *first*[Z,Z](3, −4).

The generic parameters are both taken to be Z because that is the type of both *3* and −*4*. The reason for this is that *first*[$X$,$Y$](*3*, −*4*) would be defined and have the same value for *any* sets $X$, $Y$ satisfying *3*∈$X$ and −*4*∈$Y$, and the *largest* such sets coincide with the *types* of *3* and −*4*.

**Remark:** The above rationale for the choice of implicit parameters is not appropriate unless the parameterised object depends *monotonically* on its generic parameters. For example, the family *comp* defined below has the property that *comp*[{*0*}] and *comp*[{*0,1*}] are incomparable: the value of the former is {{}↦{0},{0}↦{}}, and that of the latter is {{}↦{0,1},{0}↦{1}, {1}↦{0},{0,1}↦{}}.

$$
\begin{array}{|l}
\hline
[X] \\
comp : \mathbb{P}X \to \mathbb{P}X \\
\hline
\forall\ S{:}\mathbb{P}X \bullet\ comp\ S = X \backslash S \\
\hline
\end{array}
$$

So the choice of generic parameter [$X$] affects the value of *comp*($S$). The rationale for making the automatic choice be a *type* (in this case it would be the base type of $S$) is that such a choice is consistent with that made in the monotonic cases.

□

Constants may also be defined generically, as in the following definition of the empty set sign ∅.

$$
\begin{array}{|l}
\hline
[X] \\
\emptyset : \mathbb{P}X \\
\hline
\emptyset = \{x{:}X \mid false\} \\
\hline
\end{array}
$$

We can write equations such as $\{3,4,5\}=\emptyset$ (which is false) and predicates such as $\emptyset\subseteq\{3,4,5\}$ (which is true), and leave the generic parameter implicit again. We can reason as follows when considering the equation: if the generic parameter is $\alpha$, then the type of $\emptyset[\alpha]$ is $\mathbb{P}\alpha$. But the type of $\{3,4,5\}$ is $\mathbb{P}\mathbb{Z}$, and $\mathbb{P}\alpha$ and $\mathbb{P}\mathbb{Z}$ must be the same type because they are the types of the values on each side of an equation. So $\alpha$ is $\mathbb{Z}$, and the equation is short for $\{3,4,5\}=\emptyset[\mathbb{Z}]$.

The infix relation symbol $\subseteq$ also has a generic definition:

$$
\begin{array}{|l}
\hline
\quad [X] \\
\hline
\_\subseteq\_ \; : \; \mathbb{P}X \leftrightarrow \mathbb{P}X \\
\hline
\forall \; S,T{:}\mathbb{P}X \; \bullet \\
\quad S\subseteq T \Leftrightarrow \forall x{:}S \; \bullet \; x \in T \\
\hline
\end{array}
$$

The predicate $\emptyset\subseteq\{3,4,5\}$ is short for $(\emptyset, \{3,4,5\}) \in (\_\subseteq\_)$ and our reasoning is as follows: writing placeholders $\alpha$ and $\beta$ for the implicit parameters, we have

$$(\emptyset[\alpha], \{3,4,5\}) \in (\_\subseteq\_)[\beta].$$

Now $\emptyset[\alpha]$ has type $\mathbb{P}\alpha$ and $\{3,4,5\}$ has type $\mathbb{P}\mathbb{Z}$, so the pair on the left has type $\mathbb{P}\alpha \times \mathbb{P}\mathbb{Z}$. The term $(\_\subseteq\_)[\beta]$ has type $\mathbb{P}(\mathbb{P}\beta \times \mathbb{P}\beta)$, since that is the type of a relation between $\mathbb{P}\beta$ and $\mathbb{P}\beta$. For the membership predicate to be correctly typed, $\mathbb{P}(\mathbb{P}\beta \times \mathbb{P}\beta)$ must be the same as $\mathbb{P}(\mathbb{P}\alpha \times \mathbb{P}\mathbb{Z})$, since $(\mathbb{P}\alpha \times \mathbb{P}\mathbb{Z})$ is the type of the term on the left. We conclude that $\alpha=\beta=\mathbb{Z}$, so that our original predicate is short for

$$(\emptyset[\mathbb{Z}], \{3,4,5\}) \in (\_\subseteq\_)[\mathbb{Z}].$$

Such reasoning may seem laborious, but it is easily implemented using the techniques pioneered by Milner [*Milner 78*] for functional programs. In this approach, types are regarded as first—order terms in the "type variables" $\alpha$, $\beta$, ..., and unification is used whenever types must match: across equality and membership signs, between functions and their arguments, and so on. In section 3 we present the outline of a type checking algorithm based on this idea.

There is, however, an extra check which must be made in a type checker for Z but which is not needed in a type checker for a polymorphic programming language such as ML. It is the check that implicit parameters are determined *unambiguously* by the context. This check is necessary because a generic definition in Z describes not a *single* polymorphic object (as in the typed $\lambda$—calculus), but a *family* of "monomorphic" objects indexed by the parameters, and the way in which the members of this family depend on the parameters can be subtle.

To see that consistently—typed terms can suffer from ambiguity about implicit parameters consider the term $first(3,\emptyset)$. Making the implicit parameters explicit gives us $first[\alpha,\beta](3, \emptyset[\gamma])$, (for some $\gamma$) and for consistency we must have $\alpha{=}\mathbf{Z}$ and $\beta{=}\mathbb{P}\gamma$. So the term means $first[\mathbf{Z},\mathbb{P}\gamma](3, \emptyset[\gamma])$, and its type is $\mathbf{Z}$. That is all the information available, and because $\gamma$ does not appear in the type of the term, no more information could be deduced from the wider context in which it appears: the term is therefore ambiguous. In this example the ambiguity is harmless enough: whatever type we substitute for $\gamma$, the value of the term is the same, namely 3.

For an example where the ambiguity is positively harmful we need a generic definition which depends a little more subtly on its generic parameters. Let us say that a natural number $n$ *covers* a set $X$ if there is a function from the interval *1..n* whose range is $X$. Define $cover[X]$ to be the set of numbers which cover $X$:

$$
\begin{array}{|l}
\hline
\;[X] \\
\hline
\quad cover: \mathbb{P}\mathbb{N} \\
\hline
\quad cover = \{\ n{:}\mathbb{N} \mid (\exists\ f{:}1..n{\rightarrow}X \cdot ran\ f{=}\ X)\ \} \\
\hline
\end{array}
$$

So if $X$ is a finite set with $N(\geq 1)$ elements, then $cover[X] = \{N,\ N{+}1,\ ..\ \}$, and if $X$ is infinite then $cover[X]{=}\emptyset$. If $X$ is empty, then $cover[X]{=}\{0\}$ (think about it!). The point is that the equation $cover{=}\emptyset$ is ambiguous about the implicit parameter of $cover$ in a harmful way: if the type parameter is finite, the equation is false; if it is infinite, the equation is true. Hence the need to check that implicit parameters are determined unambiguously.

## 2. Well—typing rules

The rules by which types are assigned to terms can be described as a formal system of inference rules. In this system, sentences have the form

$$\rho \vdash E \; \Im \; t$$

where $\rho$ is a *type environment*, $E$ is a term, and $t$ is a type. The details of what a type environment is need not concern us here, except that $\rho$ determines the types assigned to the free variables of $E$. The whole sentence may be read "in environment $\rho$, term $E$ is assigned type $t$".

The derivation rules of the inference system allow such type—assignments to be derived from others. For example, the rule for ordered pairs is:

$$\frac{\rho \vdash E_2 \ \vdots \ t_2 \qquad\qquad \rho \vdash E_1 \ \vdots \ t_1}{\rho \vdash (E_1,\ E_2) \ \vdots \ (t_1 \times t_2)} \qquad\qquad pair$$

This rule allows us to derive the type of an ordered pair $(E_1,\ E_2)$ from the types of $E_1$ and $E_2$ : the pair is well–typed if the terms $E_1$ and $E_2$ are well–typed, and the type of the pair is the Cartesian product of their two types.

More complex antecedents allow restrictions to be placed on the types of subterms. For example, the rule for Cartesian product terms:

$$\frac{\rho \vdash E_2 \ \vdots \ \mathbb{P}t_2 \qquad\qquad \rho \vdash E_1 \ \vdots \ \mathbb{P}t_1}{\rho \vdash E_1 \times E_2 \ \vdots \ \mathbb{P}(t_1 \times t_2)} \qquad\qquad product$$

For a term $E_1 \times E_2$ to be well–typed, the terms $E_1$ and $E_2$ must denote sets, *i.e.* their types must match the patterns $\mathbb{P}t_1$ and $\mathbb{P}t_2$. The type of $E_1 \times E_2$ is then $\mathbb{P}(t_1 \times t_2)$. [In standard Z these two rules are generalised to allow $n$–tuples and products of $n$ factors].

The rule which covers function application is

$$\frac{\rho \vdash E_2 \ \vdots \ t_1 \qquad\qquad \rho \vdash E_1 \ \vdots \ \mathbb{P}(t_1 \times t_2)}{\rho \vdash E_1 \ E_2 \ \vdots \ t_2} \qquad\qquad apply$$

For the application $E_1\ E_2$ to be well–typed, $E_1$ must have a type matching the pattern $\mathbb{P}(t_1 \times t_2)$, since that is the type of a function from $t_1$ to $t_2$. If the function $E_1$ has type $\mathbb{P}(t_1 \times t_2)$, then the argument $E_2$ must have type $t_1$ and the type of the result —that is, of the whole term — is $t_2$.

Since terms constructed with infix operators are just syntactic sugar for applications, this rule also covers them. For example the term $3+4$ is just sugar for $(\_+\_)(3,4)$ — the application of the function $\_+\_$ to the tuple $(3,4)$. Pragmatically a Z type checker may check such sugared terms separately so that better error messages may be produced.

The axioms of our inference system are the assertions which give the types of identifiers in an environment. For the sake of uniformity we show the *axiom scheme* describing these as a rule with no antecedents:

$$\frac{}{\rho \vdash x \ \vdots \ t} \ (\rho\ x = t) \qquad\qquad ident$$

The "side condition" on this rule is that environment ρ gives identifier $x$ type $t$. By adding antecedents to this rule we can give a rule for generic constants with explicit parameters:

$$\rho \vdash E_1 : \mathbb{P}t_1$$

$$\cdot$$
$$\cdot$$
$$\cdot$$

$$\frac{\rho \vdash E_n : \mathbb{P}t_n}{\rho \vdash x[E_1, \ldots E_n] : t[t_1/X_1, \ldots t_n/X_n]} \quad (\rho\ x = [X_1, \ldots X_n] \star t) \qquad explicit$$

This time the side condition states that ρ gives generic constant $x$ with type parameters $[X_1, \ldots X_n]$ the type $t$. Here the notation $t[t_1/X_1, \ldots t_n/X_n]$ denotes the result of substituting $t_1, \ldots t_n$ simultaneously for $X_1, \ldots X_n$ respectively in $t$.

Finally, the rule schema which deals with implicit instantiation is

$$\frac{\exists[t_1, \ldots t_n]}{\rho \vdash x : t[t_1/X_1, \ldots t_n/X_n]} \quad (\rho\ x = [X_1, \ldots X_n] \star t) \qquad implicit$$

The side condition requires, as before, that ρ gives generic constant $x$ with type parameters $[X_1, \ldots X_n]$ the type $t$, and permits $t_1, \ldots t_n$ to be *any types well−formed with respect to* ρ (we express this condition by the suggestive, though not formally defined, notation $\exists[t_1, \ldots t_n]$).

How can this inference system be used to check types in environment ρ? In the case of the equation $E_1 = E_2$ the two sides, $E_1$ and $E_2$ must have the same type, so there should be a unique type $t$ such that both well−typing assertions $\rho \vdash E_1 : t$ and $\rho \vdash E_2 : t$ are derivable in the inference system. Any implicit parameters must uniquely determined, and we can make sure of this by checking that there are *unique derivation trees* for the assertions $\rho \vdash E_1 : t$ and $\rho \vdash E_2 : t$.

**Remark:** We can formalise the idea just outlined by adding a new kind of sentence to our formal system. The sentence

$$\rho \vdash P \sqrt{}$$

may be read "in type environment ρ, the predicate $P$ is well−typed". In our extended formal system, the equality rule is written formally as

$$\frac{\rho \vdash E_1 \, \text{\scriptsize ?} \, t \qquad\qquad \rho \vdash E_2 \, \text{\scriptsize ?} \, t}{\rho \vdash E_1 = E_2 \, \checkmark} \qquad\qquad\qquad equality$$

Treatment of membership predicates $E_1 \in E_2$ is similar, except that there should be a unique type $t$ such that $\rho\vdash E_1\text{\scriptsize ?}t$ and $\rho\vdash E_2\text{\scriptsize ?}\mathbb{P}t$ are uniquely derivable. The appropriate rule is

$$\frac{\rho\vdash E_1 \, \text{\scriptsize ?} \, t \qquad\qquad \rho \vdash E_2 \, \text{\scriptsize ?} \, \mathbb{P}t}{\rho \vdash E_1 \in E_2 \, \checkmark} \qquad\qquad\qquad membership$$

Since predicates such as $3<4$ are just sugar for membership predicates such as $(3,4)\in(\_<\_)$, this rule for membership also covers them, although again it may be pragmatically better to treat them separately for the purposes of error reporting.

□

Apart from the rule *implicit*, the derivation of a well−typing assertion for a phrase in environment $\rho$ is entirely determined by the structure of the phrase, because there is one rule for each of the ways of constructing terms or predicates. So different derivation trees correspond exactly to different choices of implicit parameters. By "choosing" the unique common type $t$ *before* deriving the well−typing assertions, we can allow for the propagation of type information through the structure of the phrases involved.

In fact the "choice" we make is to invent a symbol to stand for the type $t$, and we apply the well−typing rules "backward" — recording, and finally solving, the constraints on $t$ which would be necessary for the well−typing assertions to hold.

For example, consider the predicate $\{3\}=\emptyset$, where both sides can be assigned the type $\mathbb{P}Z$ in just one way. A well−typing derivation tree for it must be of the form

$$\frac{\begin{array}{cc} \overset{D_1}{\diagdown \diagup} & \overset{D_2}{\diagdown \diagup} \\ \rho \vdash \{3\} \, \text{\scriptsize ?} \, t & \rho \vdash \emptyset \, \text{\scriptsize ?} \, t \end{array}}{\rho \vdash \{3\}=\emptyset \, \checkmark} \qquad\qquad equality$$

for some type $t$. In order to discover the derivation tree we will work backwards from the root. First let us try to find $D_1$. The only rule whose consequent is in the form $\{3\} \mathbin{s} t$ is the set extension rule

$$\frac{\rho \vdash\ E_1 \mathbin{s} t \quad \dots \quad \rho \vdash\ E_n \mathbin{s} t}{\rho \vdash\ \{E_1, \dots\ E_n\} \mathbin{s} \mathbb{P}\ t} \qquad \textit{extension}$$

So (taking it as an axiom that $\rho \vdash\ 3 \mathbin{s} \mathbf{Z}$) $D_1$ must be

$$\frac{\rho \vdash\ 3 \mathbin{s} \mathbf{Z}}{\rho \vdash\ \{3\} \mathbin{s} \mathbb{P}\ \mathbf{Z}} \qquad \textit{extension}$$

Thus the type $t$ *must be* $\mathbb{P}\ \mathbf{Z}$. This information about $t$ propagates into derivation $D_2$, which must therefore be rooted at the sentence

$$\rho \vdash\ \emptyset \mathbin{s} \mathbb{P}\ \mathbf{Z}$$

which is derived from the *implicit* rule

$$\frac{}{\rho \vdash\ \emptyset \mathbin{s} \mathbb{P}\ X[\mathbf{Z}/X]} \overset{\exists\ [\mathbf{Z}]}{\underset{\rho}{}} \emptyset = [X] \star \mathbb{P}\ X \qquad \textit{implicit}$$

The inference system introduced here has shown how to make formal the notion "$E$ has type $t$", and allowed us to be precise about the requirement that implicit parameters be uniquely determined. We have not given the rules for every kind of term, nor shown how the scope rules of Z can be incorporated, but the details are covered in [*Spivey 88*], and in [*Sufrin(ed) 86*] We now turn to the implementation of the inference system using type variables.

## 3. Type Variables
The inference system for well–typing which we have presented reduces the problem of type–checking to that of searching for derivations of certain well–typing assertions. But the task of finding *all* derivations of a sentence in an inference system is at best laborious and at worst uncomputable; we must look for a decision procedure.

Let us introduce an alphabet of *type variables* which we write $\alpha$, $\beta$, $\gamma$, ... . These are distinct from the "basic types" or "given set names" from which genuine Z types are constructed, they are also different from the identifiers used as *type parameters* by which generic definitions are parametrised. We do not say what these type variables mean, but instead will use them as tokens in a formal game. Let the inference system of section 2 be extended to allow these type variables to appear in types. They may appear in the type substituted for formal parameters in the *implicit* rule, and are propagated by other rules so that terms of any kind may be assigned types which contain these variables.

The utility of type variables depends on two properties of this new inference system — both of them proved by induction over the structure of derivations in the system. These properties are:

1. If $D$ is any derivation containing one or more type variables, then we can obtain another derivation by uniformly substituting types for some of the type variables in $D$.

2. For each environment $\rho$ and term $E$ for which at least one typing is derivable, there is a type $t$ and a most general derivation $D$ of $\rho \vdash E \colon t$ such that all other derivations of well–typing assertions for $E$ in $\rho$ are instances of $D$ under substitution of types for type variables.

As an example of a step in the proof of (2) we consider function application $E_1\ E_2$. Appealing to the induction hypotheses, let $D_1$ and $D_2$ be most general derivations respectively ending in $\rho \vdash E_1 \colon t_1$ and $\rho \vdash E_2 \colon t_2$. We may assume, with no loss of generality, that the type variables appearing in $D_1$ and $D_2$ are distinct. For the application to be well–typed, the types $t_1$ and $\mathbb{P}(t_2 \times \alpha)$ must have a common instance (here $\alpha$ is a type variable not appearing in either $D_1$ or $D_2$). Now let $\sigma$ be a most general unifier of $t_1$ and $\mathbb{P}(t_2 \times \alpha)$, and construct the derivation

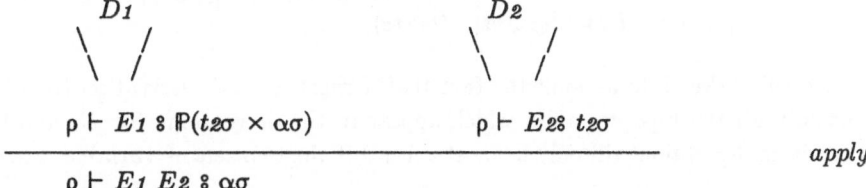

$$\frac{\rho \vdash E_1 \colon \mathbb{P}(t_2\sigma \times \alpha\sigma) \qquad\qquad \rho \vdash E_2 \colon t_2\sigma}{\rho \vdash E_1\ E_2 \colon \alpha\sigma} \quad apply$$

Plainly any derivation of a typing of $E_1\ E_2$ in $\rho$ must be an instance of this one.

**Remark:** In this context, a *unifier* of two type terms $t_1$ and $t_2$ is a mapping $\sigma$ from type variables to type terms such that $t_1\sigma = t_2\sigma$. Here and henceforth we use the notation $t\sigma$ to denote the process of making the substitution specified by $\sigma$ in the type $t$. A *most general unifier* of two type terms is a unifier from which all their unifiers may be derived by further substitution. ☐

These properties mean that we can replace the problem of finding *all* derivations of well−typings of $E$ in $\rho$ with that of finding a *most general* derivation, and as the argument above indicates, a most general derivation can be found by a process of unification. The implicit parameters in a term are uniquely determined if there is exactly one derivation of its well−typing, and that is so exactly if its most general derivation contains no type variables.

To check an equation $E_1{=}E_2$ in $\rho$, we find most general derivations $D_1$ and $D_2$ ending in $\rho{\vdash}E_1{\text{\^{}}}t_1$ and $\rho{\vdash}E_2{\text{\^{}}}t_2$ respectively. If $t_1$ and $t_2$ cannot be unified, then there is a type mismatch; otherwise let $\sigma$ be their most general unifier. If the instances $D_1\sigma$ and $D_2\sigma$ of the two derivations contain any type variables, then the equation is ambiguous; otherwise it is well−typed. In this method it is not necessary to keep explicit representations of the two derivations $D_1$ and $D_2$ but only the information about the types and type variables they contain. We can obtain an efficient algorithm by just keeping track of the types and type variables, and we present this algorithm below as a new inference system, in which sentences have the form

$$\rho \vdash E \; \text{\^{}} \; [\alpha_1, \dots \alpha_n] \cdot t$$

The intention is that this sentence will be a theorem of the new system if there is a most general derivation of $\rho \vdash E{\text{\^{}}}t$ in the old system which contains *exactly* the type variables $\alpha_1, \dots \alpha_n$.

First we present the rule for ordered pairs:

$$\frac{\begin{array}{l} \rho \vdash E_1 \; \text{\^{}} \; [v_1] \cdot t_1 \\ \rho \vdash E_2 \; \text{\^{}} \; [v_2] \cdot t_2 \end{array}}{\rho \vdash (E_1, E_2) \; \text{\^{}} \; [v_1 \cup v_2] \cdot (t_1 {\times} t_2)} (disjoint \; \{v_1, v_2\}) \qquad pair$$

This rule takes into account the fact that a most general derivation for $(E_1, E_2)$ will contain all the type variables which appear in the derivations for $E_1$ and for $E_2$. The resulting derivation will only be most general if the two sets of variables are disjoint.

The rule for Cartesian products is

$$\frac{\begin{array}{l} \rho \vdash E_1 \; \text{\^{}} \; [v_1] \cdot t_1 \\ \rho \vdash E_2 \; \text{\^{}} \; [v_2] \cdot t_2 \\ \sigma_1 = mgu(t_1, \mathbb{P}\alpha) \\ \sigma_2 = mgu(t_2, \mathbb{P}\beta) \end{array}}{\rho \vdash E_1 {\times} E_2 \; \text{\^{}} \; [(v_1 \cup v_2 \cup \{\alpha, \beta\})\sigma_1\sigma_2] \cdot \mathbb{P}(\alpha\sigma_1 {\times} \beta\sigma_2)} (disjoint \; \{v_1, v_2, \{\alpha, \beta\}\})$$

To find a well–typing of $E_1 \times E_2$ using this rule we have to find most general well–typings of the terms $E_1$ and $E_2$, and match their types against the patterns $\mathbb{P}\alpha$ and $\mathbb{P}\beta$ by unification ($\alpha$ and $\beta$ must be fresh type variables). The type of the product can then be constructed from the types which match $\alpha$ and $\beta$. The variables which occur in the derivation are all those used so far, less any which are instantiated as a result of unification. Here and henceforth we use the notation $V\sigma$ to denote the set of variables in the types which are the image of the elements of the set of variables $V$ under the substitution $\sigma$.

As a third example here is the rule for application:

$$
\frac{\begin{array}{l} \rho \vdash E_1 \,\text{\reflectbox{\textsc{s}}}\, [v_1] \bullet t_1 \\ \rho \vdash E_2 \,\text{\reflectbox{\textsc{s}}}\, [v_2] \bullet t_2 \\ \sigma = mgu(t_1, \mathbb{P}(t_2 \times \alpha)) \end{array}}{\rho \vdash E_1\,E_2 \,\text{\reflectbox{\textsc{s}}}\, [(v_1 \cup v_2 \cup \{\alpha\})\sigma] \bullet \alpha\sigma} (disjoint\ \{v_1, v_2, \{\alpha\}\}) \qquad apply
$$

Once again, $\alpha$ must be a fresh type variable.

The rules in this inference system can be transcribed directly into a programming language to give the core of a type–checker for Z, and the authors have both implemented complete Z type–checkers in this way. One is written in $ML$, the other is written in $C$: both are associated with systems which support the development of documents containing formal material in Z. In the appendix we present an annotated and self–contained implementation of a simplified variant of the ML system [*Sufrin 87*]. Other work in this area is reported in [*Reed&Sinclair 89*], which presents the outline of an algorithm in Z itself.

## Summary
Generic definitions are the means by which Z combines the power of algebraic notations to build an extensive mathematical toolkit on a small foundation with the convenience of model–based specification languages like the VDM metalanguage. In this paper we have shown how the facility of Z for inferring implicit generic parameters can be effectively implemented in a type checking program.

**References**

Milner, A.J.R.G (1978) A Theory of Type Polymorphism in Programming Languages. *Journal of Computer and System Science, 17, 348–357.*

Spivey, J.M. (1988) Understanding Z: a Specification Language and its Formal Semantics. *Cambridge Tracts in Theoretical Computer Science, 3.*

Sufrin, B.A. (ed) (1986) The Z Handbook. Programming Research Group.

Sufrin, B.A. (1987) The Zebra Typechecker. Programming Research Group.

Reed, J.N. and Sinclair, J.E. (1989) An algorithm for type checking Z. Programming Research Group, 1987.

### Appendix: A typechecker for Z

The typechecker presented herein is a simplified form of the one used in the *Zebra* and *Hippo* systems developed by the second author. The main simplifications have been

- Eliminating the treatment of schemas
- Eliminating datatype declarations
- Eliminating overloading
- Drastic curtailment of the description of error—recovery
- Simplification of the representation of identifiers
- Simplification of the representation of the top—level type environment

Our presentation will be more or less top—down: this is not the order in which the ML compiler requires the definitions to be made, but is the order most convenient for exposition.

### 1. Abstract Syntax

| | | | | |
|---|---|---|---|---|
| **type** | $NUM = string$ **and** $ID = string$ | | | |
| **datatype** $T$ | $=$ | | | (* *terms* *) |
| | $Null$ | | | |
| | $\mid$ $Id$ | **of** | $ID$ | |
| | $\mid$ $Num$ | **of** | $NUM$ | |
| | $\mid$ $Instance$ | **of** | $ID \times T\ list$ | |
| | $\mid$ $Apply$ | **of** | $T \times T$ | |
| | $\mid$ $Lambda$ | **of** | $D\ list \times P \times T$ | |
| | $\mid$ $Mu$ | **of** | $D\ list \times P \times T$ | |
| | $\mid$ $Comprehension$ | **of** | $D\ list \times P \times T$ | |
| | $\mid$ $Extension$ | **of** | $T\ list$ | |
| | $\mid$ $Prod$ | **of** | $T\ list$ | |
| | $\mid$ $Tuple$ | **of** | $T\ list$ | |
| | $\mid$ $Seq$ | **of** | $T\ list$ | |
| | $\mid$ $Pow$ | **of** | $T$ | |
| **and** $P$ $=$ | $Member$ | **of** | $T \times T$ | (* *predicates* *) |
| | $\mid$ $Equal$ | **of** | $T \times T$ | |
| | $\mid$ $Conj$ | **of** | $P \times P$ | |
| | $\mid$ $Disj$ | **of** | $P \times P$ | |
| | $\mid$ $Imp$ | **of** | $P \times P$ | |
| | $\mid$ $Iff$ | **of** | $P \times P$ | |
| | $\mid$ $Neg$ | **of** | $P$ | |
| | $\mid$ $True$ | | | |
| | $ForAll$ | **of** | $D\ list \times P \times P$ | |
| | $\mid$ $Exists$ | **of** | $D\ list \times P \times P$ | |
| | $\mid$ $Exists_1$ | **of** | $D\ list \times P \times P$ | |
| **and** $Para =$ | $GivenDef$ | **of** | $ID\ list$ | (* *definitions* *) |
| | $\mid$ $GenericDef$ | **of** | $ID\ list \times Def$ | |
| **and** $Def =$ | $TermAbbr$ | **of** | $T \times T$ | |
| | $\mid$ $AxiomDef$ | **of** | $D\ list \times P$ | |
| **withtype** | | | | |
| $D$ | $=$ | $T \times T$ | | (* *declarations* *) |

## 2. Type Expressions

If $x$ is a generically—defined constant with parameters $[X_1, \ldots X_n]$, then it is bound to $GenericType([X_1, \ldots X_n], T)$ in the top—level environment: in this case each occurence of one of the $X_i$ in the type $T$ will be represented as $ParamType\ X_i$. Generic quantification in types is always "shallow" — no $GenericType$ will ever appear *within* another type.

Our choice of representation of type variables reflects the fact that we never *re—use* a type variable once it has participated in the checking of a definition. Each type variable $\alpha$ is represented by a *reference* to a type constraint: this is initially *unconstrained*, but if an attempt to unify two type expressions results in the discovery that the variable $\alpha$ and the type $t$ ought to be the same, then a constraint with value *unconstrained* will be set to *like t*. The substitutions discussed in the derivation of the algorithm will be implemented here by direct assignment to the type variables.

| **datatype** *Type =* | *PowerType* | **of** | *Type* |
|---|---|---|---|
| | | *ProductType* | **of** | *Type list* |
| | | *GivenType* | **of** | *I D* |
| | | *ParamType* | **of** | *I D* |
| | | *TypeVar* | **of** | *Constraint ref* |
| | | *GenericType* | **of** | *I D list* $\times$ *Type* |
| **and** *Constraint=* | *like* | **of** | *Type* |
| | | *unconstrained* | | |

## 3. Unification

The unifiers referred to in the body of the paper are represented (implicitly) in our typechecker by the values of the currently—being—used type variables. When two type expressions are unified, the implicit constraints on type variables are recorded by assigning to them. Thus the *structure* of type expressions being unified is not copied: instead, links are made between the type variables they contain.

For example: the unification of the type expressions $\mathbb{P}\ \alpha$ and $\mathbb{P}\ \mathbb{P}\ \beta$ proceeds "operationally" as follows:

$$
\begin{array}{lll}
Unify & (\mathbb{P}\alpha)\ (\mathbb{P}\mathbb{P}\beta) & \Leftrightarrow \\
Unify & \alpha \quad \mathbb{P}\beta & \Leftrightarrow \\
(\alpha := like(\mathbb{P}\beta);\ true)
\end{array}
$$

In making the assignment to $\alpha$ we are effectively performing the *substitution* into $(\mathbb{P}\alpha)$ before the unifier has been constructed — thereby eliminating $\alpha$ from that type expressions *and all others in which it appears*. Subsequent traversal of the expression which started as $\mathbb{P}\alpha$ should yield $\mathbb{P}\mathbb{P}\beta$, so that later unification of $\mathbb{P}\alpha$ with (say), the type expression $\mathbb{P}\mathbb{P}Z$ will proceed as

$$
\begin{array}{lll}
Unify & (\mathbb{P}(like(\mathbb{P}\beta))) & (\mathbb{P}\mathbb{P}Z) & \Leftrightarrow \\
Unify & (like(\mathbb{P}\beta) & (\mathbb{P}Z) & \Leftrightarrow \\
Unify & (\mathbb{P}\beta) & (\mathbb{P}Z) & \Leftrightarrow \\
Unify & (\beta) & (Z) & \Leftrightarrow \\
(\beta := like\ Z;\ true)
\end{array}
$$

The effective elimination of instantiated variables is performed by the function *Class*, which follows (and, incidentally, shortens) chains of constraints until it finds either an uninstantiated variable or a proper type.

```
fun  Class T =
case T of  TypeVar(ref unconstrained)       •   T
       |    TypeVar(c as ref (like T'))        •   let val t' = Class T' in c:=like t'; t' end
       |    _                                  •   T


fun  Unify(S: Type, T: Type) : bool =
let   val  S = Class S and T = Class T in
      case  (S, T) of  (GivenType i,       GivenType j)    • i=j
                   |    (ParamType i,       ParamType j)    • i=j
                   |    (PowerType S,       PowerType T)    • Unify(S, T)
                   |    (_,                 TypeVar _)      • Unify(T, S)
                   |    (ProductType Ss,    ProductType Ts) •
                        length Ss=length Ts ∧ ∀ Unify (Ss ||| Ts)
                   |    (TypeVar constraint, _)             •
                        if Occurs S T then IsTypeVar T else (constraint := like T; true)
                   |    (_,                 _)              • false
end
```

The *Occurs* check is used to prevent the construction of constraints which yield *cyclic* types: this reflects the fact that there is no type $t$ which satisfies $t=\mathbb{P}t$ or $t=(t\times s)$ or $t=(s\times t)$.

```
and  Occurs (S as TypeVar s) T =
     case Class T   of   TypeVar t      •   s=t
                   |      PowerType T    •   Occurs S T
                   |      ProductType Ts •   ∃ (Occurs S) Ts
                   |      _              •   false
and  IsTypeVar(TypeVar _)    = true
 |   IsTypeVar _             = false;
```

## 4.  Top Level

The checker processes Z documents paragraph by paragraph (by calling *TopLevel*). Each paragraph represents a group of one or more definitions, and as each group is processed its well−typedness with respect to the current top−level type environment is checked. The new type bindings it yields are added to the top level environment providing they are well− formed and their derivation is unambiguous. The former check is performed within *Paragraph*; the latter check is performed by *NoTypeVariables*.

A type environment is represented by a finite mapping from identifiers to types.

```
type ENV               =    (ID, Type) mapping
val  NumberType :Type  =    GivenType "nat";
val  InitialEnv : ENV  =    "nat" ↦ PowerType(NumberType);
val  GlobalEnv : ENV ref =  ref InitialEnv;


fun  TopLevel (para: Para) =
let   val  defs = (ResetTypeVariables(); Paragraph (!GlobalEnv) para)
in   if   NoTypeVariables()   then GlobalEnv := !GlobalEnv ⊕ mapping defs
      else  Err "type ambiguity in definition %." [PARA para] ∅
end
```

The function *Paragraph* yields the list of bindings made by a definition. If the definition introduces given types $X_1, \ldots X_n$, then the bindings which result are: $X_i \mapsto \mathbb{P} \, X_i$. If the definition is *generic*, with parameters $[X_1, \ldots X_n]$, then the definition "proper" is evaluated in the global environment extended by the bindings $X_i \mapsto PowerType(ParamType \, X_i)$. Evaluation yields a list of $(ID, \, Type)$ pairs, whose freedom from uninstantiated type variables is checked. If free from uninstantiated type variables, the types involved are "pruned", by replacing each type variable by its definition (*PruneType: Type→Type* does this). The primitive operators $\|\|$ (zip), $\star$ (map), $\oplus$ (override), and $*\!\mapsto\!*$ (makemapping) are defined in sections 11 and 12.

```
and   Paragraph (ρ : ENV) (para : Para) : (ID×Type) list =
case para of
      GivenDef ids              •        ids ||| ((PowerType ∘ GivenType) ⋆ ids)
|     GenericDef(params, def) •
      let   val  ρ′ = ρ ⊕ (params *↦* ((PowerType ∘ ParamType) ⋆ params))  in
            Generalise params  (Define ρ′ params def)
      end


and   Generalise (params: ID list) (defs: (ID×Type) list) : (ID×Type) list =
let   fun  Gen(i, Ty) =
           if   VarFree Ty then
                if params = [] then (i, Ty) else (i, GenericType(params, PruneType Ty))
           else  Err "Nongeneric type for % : %" [ID i, TY Ty] ∅;
in
      Gen ⋆ defs
end
```

*Define* is the top–level workhorse: it deals both with axiomatic definitions and with abbreviations. Abbreviations such as $[X,Y] \, id \, p_1 \ldots p_n \triangleq expression$ are treated as if they were function definitions.

```
and   Define (ρ: ENV)  (generics: ID list) (def: Def) : (ID×Type) list  =
case def of
      AxiomDef(ds, p)
      let   val (ρ′, decs) = Signature ρ ds in
            Predicate ρ′ p;
            decs
      end
|     TermAbbr(l, r) •
      case FreeVars generics l of
            []      •       Err "Nothing to define in %" [DEF def] ρ
|           frees •
      let   val  ρ′ = ρ ⊕ (frees *↦* (FreshTypeVar ⋆ frees))
            val  Tyl  = TermType ρ′ l
            val  Tyr  = TermType ρ′ r
            val  id   = Operator l
      in    if   Unify(Tyl, Tyr)
            then [(id, Class(TypeI n ρ′ id))]
            else Err "Bad abb'n %.\nLhs: %\nRhs: %\n" [DEF def, TY Tyl, TY Tyr] ρ
      end
```

```
and   FreeVars exclude t =
let   val rec F =
      λ     Id i          • if i∈exclude then [] else [i]
      |     Apply(l,r)    • F l ⌢ F r
      |     Tuple ts      • ⌢/(F ∗ ts)
      |     _             • Err "Ill−formed declaration/abb'n lhs %" [TRM t] ∅
in    F t
end


and   Operator  term =
let   val rec O =
      λ     (Id i)        • i
      |     (Apply(l,_))  • O l
      |     _             • Err "Ill−formed abb'n lhs %" [TRM term] ∅
in    O term
end
```

## 5. Checking Terms

The following function yields the type of an identifier in the environment.

```
fun   TypeIn (ρ:ENV) (i: ID) : Type option =
case ρ at i of
      SOME t   •    t
|     NONE     •    Err "Variable % not defined. " [ID i] ρ;
```

Rules involving sentences of the form

$$\rho \vdash term ⦂ Type$$

are implemented by the function *TermType*, which does so by trying to establish the type of *term* in the environment $\rho$ — creating new type variables in situations where the type is not known precisely, and using unification to impose constraints on type variables when it is appropriate to do so.

```
fun   TermType (ρ: ENV)  (term: T) :Type  = case term of
```

If an identifier $x$ has type $[X_1, ... X_n] \star T$, then whenever it is *used* without being explicitly instantiated, we substitute fresh type variables for the type parameters $X_1,...X_n$ in $T$. The details of this are handled by *ImplicitType*: $Type{\rightarrow}Type$.

```
      Id i                    ImplicitType(TypeIn ρ i)
```

If an identifier $x$ of type $[X_1, \dots X_n] \star T$ is *explicitly* instantiated with terms $[E_1, \dots E_n]$ then we use $UnPower\ \rho \star Ts$ to find types $t_1, \dots t_n$ such that $\rho \vdash E_i \mathord{:} Pt_i$ $(i{=}1..n)$ and substitute these $t_i$ for the $X_i$ within $T$.

```
|   Instance(i, Ts)  •
    (caseTypeIn ρ i of
        GenericType(ids, Ty)•
        if    length ids ≠ length Ts then
              Err "% params required (%)" [NUM(length ids), TRM term] ρ
        else  Substitute ids (UnPower ρ ⋆ Ts) Ty
|       Ty •  Err "% is not generic (%)" [ID i, TRM term] ρ
)
```

The *apply* rule is implemented by generating a new type variable, $RESULTt$, to denote the type of the result. Successful unification will result on additional constraints being made on $RESULTt$ and perhaps the type variables within $ARGt$, and $FNt$.

```
|   Apply(E₁, E₂)      •
    let   val   RESULTt = FreshTypeVar()
          val   ARGt    = TermType ρ E₂
          val   SHAPEt  = RelationType[ARG, RESULT]
          val   FNt     = TermType ρ E₁
    in    if    Unify(FNt, SHAPEt) then RESULTt
          else  Err "in (%). Operator: %; operand: %" [TRM term, TY FNt, TY ARGt] ρ
    end
```

Terms within which declarations are made require more or less standard processing of the declarations. The function $Declare\colon (\rho{:}ENV) \rightarrow (ds\colon D\ list) \rightarrow (\rho'\colon ENV, t{:}Type)$ yields the environment $\rho'$ which is the extension of $\rho$ by the declarations made in the list $ds$. It also yields the "characteristic type", $t$, determined by those declarations.

```
|   Mu(ds, p, t)•
    let   val   (ρ', Ty) = Declare ρ ds
    in    Predicate ρ' p;
          case t of Null • Ty | _ • TermType ρ' t
    end

|   Lambda(ds, p, t)•
    let   val   (ρ', Ty) = Declare ρ ds
    in    Predicate ρ' p;
          RelationType[Ty, TermType ρ' t]
    end

|   Comprehension(ds, p, t)•
    let   val   (ρ', Ty) = Declare ρ ds
    in    Predicate ρ' p;
          case t of Null • PowerType Ty | _ • PowerType(TermType ρ' t)
    end
```

The remaining cases are completely straightforward.

| | | | |
|---|---|---|---|
| \| | *Pow* | *t* | • | *PowerType(TermType ρ t)* |
| \| | *Prod* | *ts* | • | *RelationType(UnPower ρ ⋆ ts)* |
| \| | *Tuple* | *ts* | • | *TupleType(TermType ρ ⋆ ts)* |
| \| | *Seq* | *ts* | • | *RelationType[NumberType, TheUniqueType term ρ ts]* |
| \| | *Extension ts* | | • | *PowerType(TheUniqueType term ρ ts)* |
| \| | *Num _* | | • | *NumberType* |
| \| | *Null* | | • | *TupleType []* |

Type extensions and sequences involve terms which must all be of the same type.

**and** *TheUniqueType term ρ terms =*
**let**    **val**   *types = TermType ρ ⋆ terms*
       **val**   *Ty*   *= FreshTypeVar()*
**in**     **if**   ∀ (λ *ty* • *Unify(ty, Ty)) types* **then** *Ty*
       **else**   *Err "Element types differ in %." [TRM term] ρ*
**end**

In forming the type of a tuple we must not generate a one–tuple type.

**and** *TupleType [T]*     =     *T*
 \|    *TupleType Ts*     =     *ProductType Ts;*

We frequently need to construct types of the form $\mathbb{P}(T_1 \times ... T_n)$

**and** *RelationType Ts*     =     *PowerType(ProductType Ts);*

## 6. Checking Predicates

Rules of the form $\rho \vdash P \surd$ are implemented by the following function. Type constraints are propagated by the *Member* and *Equal* cases.

```
and  Predicate (ρ: ENV)  (pred: P) : bool =
case pred of
      Conj pair  • PredPair ρ pair
   |  Disj pair  • PredPair ρ pair
   |  Imp  pair  • PredPair ρ pair
   |  Iff  pair  • PredPair ρ pair
   |  Neg  p     • Predicate ρ p
   |  ForAll  q  • Quant ρ q
   |  Exists  q  • Quant ρ q
   |  Exists₁ q  • Quant ρ q
   |  True       • true
   |  Member(E₁, E₂)    •
      let   val  Ty₁   = TermType ρ E₁
            val  Ty₂   = TermType ρ E₂
      in    if   Unify(PowerType Ty₁, Ty₂)
            then true
            else Err "in predicate %.\nLhs: %\nRhs: %" [PR pred, TY Ty₁, TY Ty₂] ρ
      end
   |  Equal(E₁, E₂)    •
      let   val  Ty₁   = TermType ρ E₁
            val  Ty₂   = TermType ρ E₂
      in    if   Unify(Ty₁, Ty₂)
            then true
            else Err "in predicate %.\nLhs: %\nRhs: %" [PR pred, TY Ty₁, TY Ty₂] ρ
      end

and  Quant ρ (ds, p, p') =
let   val  (ρ', _) = Declare ρ ds in
      PredPair ρ' (p, p')
end

and PredPair ρ (p₁, p₂) = Predicate ρ p₁ ∧ Predicate ρ p₂
```

## 7. Checking Declarations

The function *Declare*: $(\rho{:}ENV) \to (ds{:}\ D\ list) \to (ENV \times Type)$ yields the environment $\rho'$ which is the extension of $\rho$ by the declarations made in the list *ds*. It also yields the "characteristic type", $t$, determined by those declarations. Its workhorse is *UnfoldDeclarations*, which yields the list of $(ID,Type)$ bindings generated by the declarations.

```
and   Declare (ρ: ENV) (ds : D list) : ENV × Type =
let   val bindings = UnfoldDeclarations ρ ds  in
      (ρ⊕mapping bindings, TupleType(#2 ⋆ bindings))
end


and   UnfoldDeclarations ρ ds =
let   fun  Dec(l, term)      = DecType(l, Class(UnPower ρ term))
      and  DecType(l, Ty) =
      case (l, Ty) of
           (Id i, t)                          •        [(i, t)]
      |    (Tuple ls, Ty as ProductType Ts)   •
                     if    length ls = length Ts then ⌢/(DecType ⋆ (ls ⫴ Ts))
                     else  Err "Bad declaration %:%" [TRM l, TY Ty] ρ
      |    (l, Ty)   •        Err "Bad declaration %:%" [TRM l, TY Ty] ρ
in
      ⌢/(Dec ⋆ ds)
end
```

The function *UnPower* is used in situations where it is *required* that *term* be of type $\mathbb{P}Ty$ for some type $Ty$. It invents type variables only when strictly necessary.

```
and   UnPower (ρ:ENV) (term:T) : Type   =
case Class(TermType ρ term) of
      PowerType Ty  • Ty
|     Ty                •
      let   val  PT = FreshTypeVar() in
            if    Unify(PowerType PT, Ty) then PT
            else  Err "% has type % (should be P(...))" [TRM term, TY Ty] ρ
      end


and   Signature ρ ds =
let   val  bindings = UnfoldDeclarations ρ ds  in
      (ρ⊕mapping bindings, bindings)
end
```

## 8. Type Variables

We need to keep track of the type variables used for each definition

> **val** *TypeVarsUsed*    = *ref(nil: Constraint ref list)*
> **fun** *ResetTypeVariables()* = *TypeVarsUsed* := [];
>
> **fun** *FreshTypeVar _ : Type =*
> **let**   **val** *constraint = ref unconstrained* **in**
>       *TypeVarsUsed := constraint ⦂ !TypeVarsUsed;*
>       *TypeVar constraint*
> **end;**

When we are about to install the type bindings derived from a definition into the top—level
environment we make sure that each of the type variables used during its derivation is con—
strained to a *specific* type.

> **fun** *NoTypeVariables() : bool =*
>       ∀ (λ *ref unconstrained • false | _ • true*) (*Class ⋆ !TypeVarsUsed*);

In performing the generalisation step which is required to implement generic definitions, we
need to check that the type of the defininiens is free of nonspecific type variables.

> **fun** *VarFree Ty =*
> **case** *Ty* **of**
>       *PowerType Ty*                • *VarFree Ty*
>    |  *ProductType Tys*             • ∀ *VarFree Tys*
>    |  *TypeVar(ref unconstrained)*  • *false*
>    |  *TypeVar(ref(like Ty))*       • *VarFree Ty*
>    |  _                             • *true*

## 9. Substitution

Substitution is used for three purposes:

- To implement the *explicit* rule: *Substitute* substitutes actual generic parameters for formals.

- To implement the *implicit* rule: *ImplicitType* substitutes a fresh type variable for each of the parameters in a generically quantified type.

- When the type of a well–generically–typed identifier is installed in the top–level environment all its type constraints will be specific. The function *PruneType* makes the null substitution in such a type, and this has the effect of replacing type variables by their values. Whilst not strictly necessary this can save a great deal of space in the top level environment.

```
structure Substitution :
sig     eqtype      ID
        type        Type
        type (α, β) Mapping
        exception BadSubst
        val         Substitute      :   ID list → Type list → Type → Type
        val         ImplicitType    :   Type → Type
        val         PruneType       :   Type → Type
end =
struct
        open        Mappings Types
        exception BadSubst

        fun  Subst map t =
        case t of
              GivenType _       • t
        |     ParamType i       • (case map at i of SOME t • t | NONE • t)
        |     PowerType T       • PowerType(Subst map T)
        |     ProductType Ts •  ProductType(Subst map * Ts)
        |     TypeVar _         • (case Class t of TypeVar _ • raise BadSubst | t • Subst map t)
        |     _                 • raise BadSubst

        fun  Substitute ids types t = Subst (ids *↦* types) t

        fun  ImplicitType t     =
        case t of
              GenericType(ids, t)    • Substitute ids (FreshTypeVar * ids) t
        |     _                      • t

        fun  PruneType Ty = Subst ∅ Ty
end;
```

## 10. Error Reports

The following is a universal type whose existence simplifies the construction of error reports.

```
datatype  object         =
          ID       of    ID
     |    NUM      of    int
     |    ENV      of    ENV
     |    TRM      of    T
     |    TY       of    Type
     |    DEF      of    Def
     |    PARA     of    Para
     |    PR       of    P;
```

Error handling is utterly minimal here: in our production typecheckers we are very much more sophisticated.

```
exception
     Error

val   ErrorEnv : ENV ref = ref ∅

fun   Err format objects errorenv =
      (writef writeobject format objects;
      ErrorEnv := errorenv;
      raise Error)
```

## 11. Lists

The following signature describes the classical mapping, zipping, predicate test and membership operations on lists.

```
signature list = sig
     infixr   6   ⋆
     infix    4   |||
     infix    3   ∈
     val ⋆:       (α → β) ⋆ α list → β list                              (* map *)
     val |||:     α list × β list → (α × β) list     exception Zip       (* zip   *)
     val ∃:       (α → bool) → α list → bool
     val ∀ :      (α → bool) → α list → bool
     val ⌢/:      α list list → α list                                   (* dist append *)
     val ⌢:       α list × α list → α list                               (* append *)
     val ∈:       'α ⋆ 'α list → bool
laws
     f ⋆ [x₁, ... xₘ]            = [f x₁, ... f xₘ]
     [x₁, ... xₙ] ||| [y₁, ... yₘ] = if  m=n then [(x₁,y₁), ... (xₙ, yₙ)] else raise Zip
     ∃ P xs                     = P◁xs ≠ []
     ∀ P xs                     = (¬∘P)◁xs = []
     [x₁, ... xₙ] ⌢ [y₁, ... yₘ] = [x₁, ... xₙ, y₁, ... yₘ]
     ⌢/ []                      = []
     ⌢/ (xs⦂xss)                = xs ⌢ ⌢/xss
end;
```

## 12. Finite Mappings

The environments used in the inference system are implemented as finite mappings represented as lists of (*id*, *type*) pairs, as are the substitutions which are required to implement the *implicit* rule.

**abstraction** *Mappings*:
**sig**    **type** $(\alpha, \beta)$ *Mapping*
      **infixr**    *9*    *at*
      **infixr**    *8*    $\mapsto$
      **infixr**    *7*    $\oplus$
      **infixr**    *3*    $*\mapsto*$
      **val**  $\emptyset$    :    $(\alpha, \beta)$ *Mapping*
      **val**  $\mapsto$    :    $'\alpha \times \beta \longrightarrow ('\alpha, \beta)$ *Mapping*
      **val**  $\oplus$    :    $(\alpha, \beta)$ *Mapping* $\times (\alpha, \beta)$ *Mapping* $\longrightarrow (\alpha, \beta)$ *Mapping*
      **val**  *at*    :    $('\alpha, \beta)$ *Mapping* $\times '\alpha \longrightarrow \beta$ *option*
      **val**  $*\mapsto*$  :    $'\alpha$ *list* $\times \beta$ *list* $\longrightarrow ('\alpha, \beta)$ *Mapping*
      **val**  *mapping*:  $('\alpha \times \beta)$ *list* $\longrightarrow ('\alpha, \beta)$ *Mapping*
**laws**
      $\emptyset$ *at* $x$                     $= NONE$
      $(x \mapsto y)$ *at* $x$            $= SOME\ y$
      $(m \oplus n)$ *at* $x$            $=$ **case** $n$ *at* $x$ **of** $SOME\ y \cdot y\ |\ NONE \cdot\ m$ *at* $x$
      $[x_1, ... x_n] *\mapsto* [y_1, ... y_n] = x_n \mapsto y_n \oplus ... \oplus x_1 \mapsto y_1$
      *mapping* $[]$                $= \emptyset$
      *mapping* $((x,y) \& l)$     $= l \oplus (x \mapsto y)$
**end** =
**struct**
      **type** $(\alpha, \beta)$ *Mapping* $= (\alpha \times \beta)$ *list*
      **infixr**    *9*    *at*
      **infixr**    *8*    $\mapsto$
      **infixr**    *7*    $\oplus$
      **infixr**    *3*    $*\mapsto*$
      **val**  $\emptyset$        $= []$
      **fun**  $a \mapsto b$    $= [(a,b)]$
      **fun**  $m \oplus n$      $= n \frown m$
      **fun**  *map at* $a$ =
      **let**   **fun**  $F\ [] = NONE\ |\ F\ ((x,y) \& map) =$ **if** $x=a$ **then** $SOME\ y$ **else** $F\ map$ **in**
           $F\ map$
      **end**
      **fun**  $As *\mapsto* Bs = mapping(As\ |||\ Bs)$
      **and**  *mapping* $l = l$
**end**;

---

# Minimisation in Formal Specification and Design

A.M. Gravell

Department of Electronics and Computer Science

University of Southampton

## Abstract

Minimisation is a useful technique both in specification and in design. In specification it can lead to shorter and more elegant definitions. These will communicate more clearly the intent of the specifier. In design, minimisation can be used to eliminate non-determinism, for instance after a data refinement step. Minimisation is a general technique for removing non-determinism, and can be applied during a constructive refinement. It records the quantity the designer is optimising, which will help later developers to understand the decisions which were taken during design. These points are supported by some simple examples. The Z notation is used in the examples, and it is suggested that the notation would be improved if minimisation could be expressed more concisely. Following the principle of separation of concerns, a suitable notation for minimisation is one which encourages separate definitions of the set of possible solutions and the function (or relation) which will be used to select the minimal solution or solutions.

## 1 Introduction

Many problems in computing involve minimising some quantity. In design we typically wish to minimise the number of instructions executed, or the amount of storage required. In the specification of an interactive system we will probably be concerned to minimise the amount of user input required to achieve a given result.

Often these concerns are not explicitly stated, whereas the message of this paper is to suggest that a clearer specification or design would result if they were.

Historically, minimisation was used to introduce partial functions into recursive function theory [Kleene 36]. In recent times, a number of important algorithms for solving minimisation problems have helped to solve problems in economics, transportation and scheduling. The techniques are collectively known as mathematical programming, though in this context "programming" actually means optimisation.

Minimisation in formal specification and design is a separate though related topic. In formal specification and design, minimisation is used as an aid to communication. In many cases, the minimisation can be simplified or solved before the programming stage. Only where this is not possible would the program designer need to apply the techniques of mathematical programming. An example of this is mentioned later.

A particularly elegant use of minimisation occurs in Carroll Morgan's Telephone Network, where the technique permits a highly implicit or non-operational specification [Morgan 86]. The benefits of implicit specifications are described, for example, by Ian Hayes [Hayes 89]. An important concern is to leave the designer sufficient freedom to develop an efficient system. This is achieved by giving the designer a non-deterministic specification. The non-determinism can then be resolved by selecting the most efficient implementation of the specification. Once the measure of efficiency has been defined, minimising the specification with respect to this measure is one way of constructing the most efficient implementation. This shows how minimisation can arise in formal design.

In this paper, some examples of minimisation will be explored arising both in specification and in design. The examples are covered first, followed by some comments on notation, and finally the conclusions are summarised.

For the benefit of readers unfamiliar with the notation a glossary, including a definition of minimisation, and a discussion of its role in refinement, can be found in appendix A.

## 2  Minimisation in Specification

### 2.1  Resource Allocation and Text Formatting

A common specification asks for a task to be performed subject to minimal use of resources.

A trivial example, but one which will be familiar to many computer users, is the problem of formatting text into paragraphs, which is a facility provided by simple word processors, as well as more sophisticated desktop publishing and typesetting programs. This problem has been studied extensively, for example by Bertrand Meyer, Richard Bird and Donald Knuth [Meyer 85, Bird 86, Knuth 81]. The concensus seems to be that the best way to specify this problem is to require the output of the formatting process to contain the same sequence of words as the input, subject to minimising some cost function of the output.

The simplest approach, chosen by Meyer, is to require a minimal number of lines to be output. This strategy clearly saves paper! Bird shows that this specification is still non-deterministic since there may be several ways of breaking the text into the minimal number of lines. He investigates the effect of applying further cost functions, such as charging for white space at different rates in different places. These functions are shown to lead to different deterministic algorithms which also vary in their efficiency.

The most sophisticated specification is that of Knuth, whose TEX program produces layout which compares favourably with that of type set by hand. "The breakpoints are chosen so that the paragraph is mathematically optimal, i.e., best possible, in the sense that it has no more 'demerits' than you could obtain by any other sequence of breakpoints". The quantity being optimised is a function of many variables, such as the number of hyphenations required, and the size of the interword gaps. The minimisation cannot be solved as part of the design process, but is implemented using dynamic programming [Bellman 57].

## 2.2  Resource Re-allocation

Closely associated with resource allocation is resource re-allocation. Here we are considering systems in a particular configuration as a result of certain input constraints. If the constraints change a new configuration must be sought. Often, for logistical reasons, the best new configuration is in some sense closest to the previous configuration. In other words, the re-allocation should minimise change.

As a concrete example of a resource re-allocation problem, consider the following specification of a (fictitious) multiprocessor system, which defines the allocation of programs to the available machines.

$[PROG, MC]$

$$
\begin{array}{|l}
\hline
\_MultiProcessor_____ \\
\quad Programs : \mathbf{P}\ PROG \\
\quad Alloc : PROG \nrightarrow MC \\
\hline
\quad \mathrm{dom}\ Alloc \subseteq Programs \\
\hline
\end{array}
$$

The situation described is one where a number of programs are active, some of which are allocated to each machine, which presumably time-slices between them.

In a real situation, the operating system would probably impose some constraints on the allocation, thus defining the valid states of the multiprocessor system.

$$
\begin{array}{|l}
\hline
\_ValidMP_____ \\
\quad MultiProcessor \\
\hline
\quad \forall\, m : MC \bullet \#Alloc^{-1}(\!|m|\!) \leq 8 \\
\quad \#Programs \leq (8 * \#MC) \Rightarrow \mathrm{dom}\ Alloc = Programs \\
\quad \forall\, m1, m2 : MC \bullet \#Alloc^{-1}(\!|m1|\!) - 3 \leq \#Alloc^{-1}(\!|m2|\!) \\
\hline
\end{array}
$$

The policy described above ensures that no machine runs more than eight programs, that no program is idle if there is a machine available that can run it, and that there are no two machines whose loads differ by more than three.

When a new program becomes available to run, or when an active program terminates, the operating system must re-allocate programs in such a way as to minimise change, while ensuring that the new configuration still satisfies the policy constraints. With each such transition we can associate a cost.

$$
\begin{array}{l}
cost : ((PROG \nrightarrow MC) \times (PROG \nrightarrow MC)) \rightarrow \mathbb{N} \\
\forall\, Alloc, Alloc' : PROG \nrightarrow MC \bullet \\
\quad cost(Alloc, Alloc') = \#(Alloc - Alloc') + \#(Alloc' - Alloc)
\end{array}
$$

This cost function can also be expressed as follows.

$$
\begin{array}{l}
cost(Alloc, Alloc') = \\
\quad \#\{pm : PROG \times MC \mid pm \in Alloc \wedge pm \notin Alloc'\}+ \\
\quad \#\{pm : PROG \times MC \mid pm \in Alloc' \wedge pm \notin Alloc\}
\end{array}
$$

This charges one for each program added to, and one for each program removed from, each machine. Re-allocation then involves finding a minimal cost re-distribution of the new programs around the available processors.

$$
\begin{array}{|l}
\underline{\ ReAllocate}\phantom{xxxxxxxxxxxxxxxxxxxxxxxxxxxxxx} \\
ValidMP \\
ValidMP' \\
\hline
\forall\ ValidMP''\ \bullet\ Programs'' = Programs' \Rightarrow \\
\quad cost(Alloc, Alloc'') \geq cost(Alloc, Alloc') \\
\end{array}
$$

This schema can then be re-used, for instance, in the operation to add a new program.

$$
\begin{array}{|l}
\underline{\ AddProgram}\phantom{xxxxxxxxxxxxxxxxxxxxxxxxxxxxx} \\
p? : PROG \\
ValidMP \\
ValidMP' \\
\hline
Programs' = Programs \cup \{new?\} \\
ReAllocate \\
\end{array}
$$

This example follows closely the style of Carroll Morgan's Telephone Network. And indeed a similar style can be adopted for any resource resource re-allocation problem. The problem of maintaining integrity of references can even be viewed in this light. This problem arises in programming languages with dynamically allocated data, and also in databases where information is stored in multiple tables. The function of tidying up the system after deletions can be specified by defining the new system to be the one in which the deleted data is not present, there are no dangling references, and which, subject to the first two properties, is as close as possible to the original state.

The benefit of minimisation in these examples is that it leads to an elegant and compact specification of the function required. In the multiprocessor system, a more direct or operational specification of re-allocation would inevitably have to consider different cases such as when a processor is already loaded to the maximum, or when two processors have workloads differing by more than three. The specification would then be longer, and thus harder to understand. It would also duplicate many of the conditions already expressed in the *ValidMP* schema, so that it would be harder to maintain. In contrast, the specification given has separated different requirement issues into different schemas. A change to the requirements, such as a different allocation policy, or a non-uniform processor topology (in which it costs more to relocate a program to a more distant processor), could therefore be incorporated more easily and more reliably.

Thus, where it is appropriate, minimisation leads to specifications of a particular style, which is short, easy to understand, and to maintain.

# 3 Minimisation in Design

This example of minimisation in design arises in the data refinement of a simple data type. To represent a bounded set (one which has at most $M$ elements for some number $M$), an array provides an easy (if not particularly efficient) implementation. The refinement can be documented using Z as follows.

## 3.1 The Abstract Data Type

$[Element]$
$M : \mathbb{N}$

```
┌─ BS ────────────────────────────────────────
│ s : ℙ Element
├──────────────────────────────────────────────
│ #s ≤ M
└──────────────────────────────────────────────
```

The insert operation can be defined as follows.

```
┌─ Insert ─────────────────────────────────────
│ BS
│ BS'
│ e? : Element
├──────────────────────────────────────────────
│ e? ∉ s
│ s' = {e?} ∪ s
└──────────────────────────────────────────────
```

Other operations, including initialisation, would also be provided. For reasons of space, they are omitted here.

## 3.2 The Concrete Data Type

This consists of an array and a high water mark which indexes into the array. No elements are duplicated in the active part of the array.

```
┌─ BS1 ────────────────────────────────────────
│ ar : 1 .. M → Element
│ hi : 0 .. M
├──────────────────────────────────────────────
│ ∀ x, y : 1 .. hi • x ≠ y ⇒ ar(x) ≠ ar(y)
└──────────────────────────────────────────────
```

The concrete state is related to the abstract state as follows.

```
┌─ Retrieve ───────────────────────────────────
│ BS
│ BS1
├──────────────────────────────────────────────
│ s = ar⦇1 .. hi⦈
└──────────────────────────────────────────────
```

A standard development would go on now to specify the concrete initialisation and other operations, proving each of them correct, using the proof obligations as explained for example in [Spivey 89]. More recently constructive techniques for data refinement are described in [Hoare 87, Josephs 88, Morgan 88]. Applying these techniques in this case involves using the retrieval relation as a substitution. We can then derive the following, most general, concrete insert operation.

```
┌─ Insert1 ──────────────────────────────────
│ BS1
│ BS1'
│ e? : Element
├───────────────────────────────────────────
│ e? ∉ ar(|1 .. hi|)
│ ar'(|1 .. hi'|) = {e?} ∪ ar(|1 .. hi|)
└───────────────────────────────────────────
```

This definition is highly non-deterministic, and needs to be strengthened by extra predicates before it is implemented. This is where minimisation has a role to play in the development. We can simply define how we measure the cost of any particular implementation of any array operation, and choose the implementation with the least cost.

## 3.3 Minimising the Cost of Array Operations

A suitable cost function charges one for each cell of the array that is changed. This can be expressed as follows.

$$\#\{n : 1 .. M \mid ar'(n) \neq ar(n)\}$$

or equivalently

$$\#(ar' - ar)$$

(Notice that this cost function is only a lower bound for the number of write accesses to the array. In particular, there will be occasions when the same value is to be rewritten into some cell of the array, and it will not be worth checking if this is so before writing the value.)

The cheapest concrete insert operation with respect to this cost function is then as follows.

```
┌─ Insert2 ──────────────────────────────────
│ Insert1
├───────────────────────────────────────────
│ ∀ BS1'' • Insert1[BS1''/BS1'] ⇒ #(ar'' − ar) ≥ #(ar' − ar)
└───────────────────────────────────────────
```

This can be simplified to give the following definition. This is shown in appendix B.

```
┌─ Insert2 ──────────────────────────────────
│ BS
│ BS'
│ e? : Element
├───────────────────────────────────────────
│ e? ∉ ar(|1 .. hi|)
│ hi' = hi + 1
│ (ar' = ar ⊕ {hi' ↦ e?}) ∨
│ (∃ n : 1 .. hi • ar(n) = ar(hi') ∧ ar' = ar ⊕ {n ↦ e?})
└───────────────────────────────────────────
```

This can clearly be refined to give the expected definition.

```
┌─ Insert3 ──────────────────────────────────────
│ BS
│ BS'
│ e? : Element
├────────────────────────────────────────────────
│ e? ∉ ar⟨1 .. hi⟩
│ hi' = hi + 1
│ ar' = ar ⊕ {hi' ↦ e?}
└────────────────────────────────────────────────
```

The same techniques can be applied to the specifications of the other operations, such as lookup and delete. For example, suppose the abstract delete operation is specified as follows.

```
┌─ Delete ───────────────────────────────────────
│ BS
│ BS'
│ e? : Element
├────────────────────────────────────────────────
│ e? ∈ s
│ s' = s − {e?}
└────────────────────────────────────────────────
```

We can derive the most general concrete delete operation.

```
┌─ Delete1 ──────────────────────────────────────
│ BS1
│ BS1'
│ e? : Element
├────────────────────────────────────────────────
│ e? ∈ ar⟨1 .. hi⟩
│ ar'⟨1 .. hi'⟩ = ar⟨1 .. hi⟩ − {e?}
└────────────────────────────────────────────────
```

Minimising this and simplifying (see appendix B), gives the following.

```
┌─ Delete2 ──────────────────────────────────────
│ BS1
│ BS1'
│ e? : Element
├────────────────────────────────────────────────
│ hi' = hi − 1
│ ∃ n : 1 .. hi • ar(n) = e? ∧ ar' = ar ⊕ {n ↦ ar(hi)}
└────────────────────────────────────────────────
```

This operation alters at most one element in the array. Another solution, perhaps more obvious, but not minimal, and hence less efficient, deletes the element by shifting all following elements down, and adding the new element at the end.

So, in this example, minimisation has supported a constructive style of refinement, and has helped to find an efficient design.

# 4   Notation for Minimisation

In the examples given, no special notation for minimisation has been used. This is because there is none defined in standard Z. A good notation for minimisation would have the following benefits for the reader. First, it would make explicit the cost function (or ordering relation) which was being minimised. Second, it would avoid the need for the rather clumsy quantification used in the schemas *ReAllocate* and *Insert2*.

Z is an extensible language, and, for instance, the notion of minimisation presented in appendix A can be expressed using the standard language extension mechanisms, which allow generic functions and relations to be defined. However, the usual style of Z specifications uses schemas to define operations. In keeping with this style, one would want to define the cost (or ordering relation) using a schema, and would want to go on to give a schema expression for the minimised operation. This would lead to a style of definition looking somewhat like

$$Op2 == Op1 \text{ schemaMin } Cost$$

There is however no schema expression for minimisation pre-defined in Z. Nor is it possible to define one as there is no mechanism for introducing new schema expressions. These seem to be unfortunate omissions, which should perhaps be rectified in later versions of the Z notation.

## 5 Summary and Conclusions

The aim of this paper has been to show that minimisation is a technique with a number of applications in both specification and design. Minimisation makes explicit the notion of cost. This helps the reader to understand more clearly the concerns of the specifier and designer. It leads to concise, well-structured, specifications which are easier to maintain. In addition, minimisation supports a more constructive approach to refinement, where less of the design is pulled like a rabbit from a hat (a process which is charmingly illustrated by Bernhard Möller [Möller 89]), but is derived by mathematical manipulation, and hence known to be correct. The derived design is known to be as efficient as possible (with respect to a stated notion of efficiency).

A secondary aim of this paper has been to show that applying minimisation in Z is rather cumbersome, as there is no special syntax to support it. Further, although Z is an extensible language, it is not possible to define new operators that apply to schemas.

I hope therefore that authors of formal specifications and designs will consider where minimisation might be applied in their work. And I hope that the designers of the Z notation will consider including in future versions some notation for minimisation, or, more generally, the ability to define schema operators.

# References

[Bellman 57]     R. Bellman. *Dynamic Programming*. Princeton University Press. 1957.

[Bird 86]     R. S. Bird. *Transformational Programming and the Paragraph Problem*. Science of Computer Programming no 6. Pages 159-189. 1986.

[Dijkstra 89]     E. W. Dijkstra. *A Computing Scientist's Approach to a Once-Deep Theorem of Sylvester's*. In Constructive Methods in Computing Science. Ed. Manfred Broy. Springer Verlag Series F vol 55. 1989.

[van Gasteren 88] A. J. M. van Gasteren. *On the Shape of Mathematical Arguments*. PhD Thesis. Eindhoven University. 1988.

[Hayes 89]     I. J. Hayes and C. B. Jones. *Specifications are not (necessarily) executable*. Private communication. 1989.

[Hoare 87]     C. A. R. Hoare, J. He, and J. Sanders. *Prespecification in Data Refinement*. Information Processing Letters vol 25 no 2 pages 71-76. 1987.

[Josephs 88]     M. B. Josephs. *The Data Refinement Calculator for Z Specifications*. Information Processing Letters vol 27 no 1 pages 29-33. Feb 1988.

[Kleene 36]     S. C. Kleene. *General Recursive Functions of Natural Numbers*. Mathematische Annalen Band 112, Heft 5. 1936 pp 727-742. Reprinted in The Undecidable. Ed. Martin Davis. Pages 236-253. Raven Press. 1965.

[Knuth 81]     D. E. Knuth. *Breaking Paragraphs into Lines*. Software Practice and Experience vol 11 pages 1119-1184. 1981.

[Meyer 85]     B. Meyer. *On Formalism in Specifications*. IEEE Software vol 2 no 1 pages 159-176. 1985.

[Möller 89]     B. Möller. Illustrations in Constructive Methods in Computing Science. Ed. Manfred Broy. Springer Verlag Series F vol 55. 1989.

[Morgan 86]     C. Morgan. *Telephone Network*. In Specification Case Studies. Ed. I. J. Hayes. Pages 73-87. Prentice Hall. 1986.

[Morgan 88]     C. Morgan. *On the Refinement Calculus*. Programming Research Group Monograph 70. 1988.

[Spivey 89]     J. M. Spivey. *The Z Notation: a Reference Manual*. Prentice Hall. 1989.

# A    Notation and Definitions

## A.1    Glossary of Notation

| | | | |
|---|---|---|---|
| $lo \mathbin{..} hi$ | == | $\{n : \mathsf{Z} \mid lo \le n \le hi\}$ | interval |
| $f(\!\|s\!\|)$ | == | $\{e : s \bullet f(e)\}$ | relational application |
| $s \lhd f$ | == | $\{p : f \mid first(p) \in s\}$ | domain restrict |
| $s1 - s2$ | == | $\{x : s1 \mid x \notin s2\}$ | set difference |
| $f1 \oplus f2$ | == | $(f1 - (\operatorname{dom} f2) \lhd f1) \cup f2$ | relational override |

## A.2    Definitions of minimisation

The function min is defined in Mike Spivey's Z reference manual [Spivey 89] to return the smallest of a non-empty set of numbers. The definition is essentially the following one.

$$min : \mathsf{P}\,\mathsf{Z} \to \mathsf{Z}$$
$$\forall S : \mathsf{P}\,\mathsf{Z};\ m : \mathsf{Z} \bullet min(S) = m \Leftrightarrow$$
$$m \in S \wedge \forall n : S \bullet m \le n$$

A similar minimum function can be defined on any set with a total ordering. In fact, the ordering need not be total, though in such cases there may no longer be a unique minimum. The function *minimise* must therefore return the set of minimal values. The most general definition is thus

$$[X]$$
$$minimise : ((\mathsf{P}\,X) \times (X \leftrightarrow X)) \to \mathsf{P}\,X$$
$$\forall S : \mathsf{P}\,X;\ R : X \leftrightarrow X \bullet$$
$$minimise(S, R) = \{x : S \mid \forall y : S \bullet xRy\}$$

A similar definition, which coincides with the first if $R$ is a total order, would form the set $\{x : S \mid \not\exists y : S \bullet yRx\}$. I prefer here to use the definition with no negation.

Maximisation is clearly related to minimisation, and can be defined as minimisation over the dual ordering (in which all the arrows are reversed).

The relation $R$ will typically be a (total or partial) ordering, though this is not required. It will also often be the case that the relation $R$ is defined by means of a cost function which assigns a number [1] to each element of the type $X$. In such a case the definition of $R$ would be as follows.

$$cost : X \to \mathsf{N}$$
$$R : X \leftrightarrow X$$
$$\forall x, y : X \bullet xRy \Leftrightarrow cost(x) \le cost(y)$$

Such an $R$ is reflexive and transitive, but not always antisymmetric (it may be the case that $xRy$ and $yRx$ but $x \ne y$ for two values $x$ and $y$). This is because the cost function might not be injective. The relation $R$ would then be a pre-order.

Minimising any set $S$ can, by appropriate choice of $R$, give any subset $S2$ of $S$.

---

[1] Natural numbers make a good choice for costs since any non-empty set of naturals has a minimum element. This would not the case if costs were real numbers, or even positive reals, say.

$$\forall S2 : \mathbb{P}\, S;\ R : X \leftrightarrow X \bullet$$
$$(xRy \Leftrightarrow x \in S2 \wedge y \in S) \Rightarrow$$
$$minimise(S, R) = S2$$

A non-deterministic operation may be defined by a relation which relates a source state preceding the operation to each of the possible target states that may be reached as a result of the operation. The operation may be refined by reducing the non-determinism.

[State]
$Op, Op2 : State \leftrightarrow State$
dom $Op2 =$ dom $Op$
$Op2 \subseteq Op$

The second operation refines in first in the (limited) sense that any state in the domain of the first operation is mapped to a smaller (but non-empty) set of possible target states by the second operation, and there are no new source states in the domain of the refined operation.

Since the second operation is a subset of the first it follows, using the above remark, that the refinement can, in general, be expressed as a minimisation. Note that, in such a case, the relation $R$ is between pairs of states; in other words, $R$ indicates that one transition from state to state is preferable to another.

It is often convenient to express refinements using cost functions. To do so, a cost is associated with each possible transition from state to state. This is more general than simply associating costs with states. Such a cost can be used to give a (pre-)ordering on transitions.

$$cost : (State \times State) \rightarrow \mathbb{N}$$
$$R : (State \times State) \leftrightarrow (State \times State)$$
$$\forall s1, t1, s2, t2 : State \bullet$$
$$(s1, t1)R(s2, t2) \Leftrightarrow s1 = s2 \wedge$$
$$cost(s1, t1) \leq cost(s2, t2)$$

Once again, this relation can be used to define a refinement by minimisation. Perhaps more surprisingly, any refinement (arrived at by reducing non-determinism) can be defined by minimising over an appropriate cost function. A possible cost function would charge 0 for any transition allowed by the refined operation, and 1 otherwise.

## B   Proof of Minimisation

Herein lies the main difficulty of minimisation. It is usually not too difficult to order possible solutions, for example by providing a cost function. However to simplify an expression involving minimisation, or, equivalently, to find a proof of minimisation, is, in general, not easy.

Minimisation is closely related to induction. Just as an inductive proof comes in two parts (the base case, and the inductive step), so the definition of a minimum has two parts (the minimum of a set is in the set, and smaller than other members of the set). It is not surprising therefore that proofs of minimisation often involve induction. Inductive proofs depend on special knowledge of the inductive domain of the problem. In the case of the array representing a set, we are really interested in different permutations of the array. As is well known, all permutations can be generated as a sequence of swaps. This suggests also that the problem is related to sorting the array.

The discussion here is presented in a semi-formal way. An earlier draft of this paper included a more formal proof, but this was rather longer and did not add much to the main points of the paper. The correct balance between intuition and formality is hard to achieve, and useful advice is given by Edsger Dijkstra [Dijkstra 89] and Netty van Gasteren [van Gasteren 88].

It seems best to find a general characterisation of a minimal array. So let us take as given a starting state, and a target state which is minimal among those representing the same abstract set, with respect to our chosen cost function.

$$ar : 1 .. M \rightarrow Element; \ hi : 0 .. M \mid BS1$$
$$ar' : 1 .. M \rightarrow Element; \ hi' : 0 .. M \mid BS1'$$
$$\forall \, BS1'' \bullet ar''(\!(1 .. hi'')\!) = ar'(\!(1 .. hi')\!) \Rightarrow$$
$$\#(ar'' - ar) \geq \#(ar' - ar)$$

The first observation we can make is that the upper half of the minimal array is the same as the corresponding part of the original array.

$$\forall \, n : (hi' + 1) .. M \bullet ar'(n) = ar(n)$$

To see this, pick an arbitrary index n in the upper half of the minimal array. Consider overwriting the minimal array to give $ar' \oplus \{n \mapsto ar(n)\}$. This satisfies the data type invariant and represents the same abstract set. It must therefore cost no less than the minimal array. But, since it is closer to the original array, it can cost no more. Hence it must cost the same, from which we can see $ar'(n) = ar(n)$. This proves our first observation.

This means that the cost of the minimal array is determined solely by the values at the lower indices. By definition the cost is

$$\#(ar' - ar)$$
$$= \#\{n : 1 .. M \mid ar'(n) \neq ar(n)\}$$

from our first observation this is

$$= \#\{n : 1 .. hi' \mid ar'(n) \neq ar(n)\}$$

and, strengthening the predicate, this is

$$\geq \#\{n : 1 .. hi' \mid ar'(n) \notin ar(\!(1 .. hi')\!)\}$$

This gives us a lower bound on the minimal cost. In fact this bound is attained.

Consider all the values present in the lower half of both the minimal and the original array ($ar'(\!(1 .. hi')\!) \cap ar(\!(1 .. hi')\!)$). Call these the common values. With each such value we can associate the least index at which it occurs in the original array. In fact this association is a bijection. From the data type invariant, there is also a bijection between values and indices in the lower half of the minimal array. Combining the two bijections gives a bijection between the indices of the common values in the minimal array and their least indices in the original array. This bijection can be extended to give a permutation of the indices in the interval $1 .. hi'$. We can use this permutation to rearrange the minimal array so that all the common values are located at their least index in the original array. This rearranged array also satisfies the data type invariant, and represents the same abstract set. It coincides with the original array precisely at the common values. The minimal array must cost no more than the rearranged array, so

$$\#(ar' - ar)$$
$$\leq hi' - \#(ar'(\!|1 .. hi'|\!) \cap ar(\!|1 .. hi'|\!))$$

and by set theory, this is

$$= \#\{n : 1 .. hi' \mid ar'(n) \notin ar(\!|1 .. hi'|\!)\}$$

Combining the last two results tells us

$$\#(ar' - ar)$$
$$= \#\{n : 1 .. hi' \mid ar'(n) \notin ar(\!|1 .. hi'|\!)\}$$

which, re-arranging using set theory, is

$$= \#(ar'(\!|1 .. hi'|\!) - ar(\!|1 .. hi'|\!))$$

Thus the minimal cost depends not only on the new abstract set to be represented, but also on the values present in the lower half of the original array. This general result can be used to simplify the minimised operations.

In the case of insert the new state is determined by the input element.

$$e? : Element$$
$$e? \notin ar(\!|1 .. hi|\!)$$
$$ar'(\!|1 .. hi'|\!) = \{e?\} \cup ar(\!|1 .. hi|\!)$$

Because the union is disjoint, and elements are not repeated, the size of the new abstract set can be determined.

$$hi' = hi + 1$$

The minimal cost can then be seen.

$$\#(ar' - ar) = \#(\{e?\} - \{ar(hi')\})$$

Thus at most one change to the array is permitted. It is simplest to put the new element at the new high water mark, though there are in fact three possible cases.

$$(e? = ar(hi') \wedge ar' = ar) \vee$$
$$(ar' = ar \oplus \{hi' \mapsto e?\}) \vee$$
$$(\exists n : 1 .. hi \bullet ar(n) = ar(hi') \wedge ar' = ar \oplus \{n \mapsto e?\})$$

The first two cases combine to give the simplified definition used earlier.

$$(ar' = ar \oplus \{hi' \mapsto e?\}) \vee$$
$$(\exists n : 1 .. hi \bullet ar(n) = ar(hi') \wedge ar' = ar \oplus \{n \mapsto e?\})$$

The other case applies in a situation where, for historical reasons, an active element also happens to be present at the next available index. For example, consider the following sequence of operations:

```
Empty;
Insert 1;
Insert 2;
Insert 3;
Delete 3;
Delete 2;
Insert 3;
```

After these operations, 3 would be present at indices 2 and 3 in the array.

```
1   3   3   ...
    ^
```

If the next action were to insert 4, it would be feasible to choose to overwrite the first occurrence of 3 to give

```
1   4   3   ...
    ^
```

rather than the obvious

```
1   3   4   ...
        ^
```

Either possibility gives rise to minimal changes to the array. In practice however it is simpler to put the new value at the new high water mark in all cases.

In the case of delete, reasoning as for insert shows that the new high water mark is

$$hi' = hi - 1$$

and the minimal cost is

$$\#(\{ar(hi)\} - \{e?\})$$

There are two possible cases in general

$$(e? = ar(hi) \wedge ar' = ar) \vee$$
$$(\exists\, n : 1 .. hi' \bullet ar(n) = e? \wedge ar' = ar \oplus \{n \mapsto ar(hi)\})$$

These two cases can fortunately be combined to give the result used earlier.

$$(\exists\, n : 1 .. hi \bullet ar(n) = e? \wedge ar' = ar \oplus \{n \mapsto ar(hi)\})$$

# From Programs to Z Specifications

K. Lano, P.T. Breuer
Programming Research Group,
Oxford University Computing Laboratory

## Abstract

Universal techniques for transforming code from a typical procedural language to Z-like specifications will be discussed first; the latter make good starting points for the *post hoc validation* of programs which lack formal documentation. We prove properties of *classes* of programs, before we move on to discuss the further set of techniques we use to prove properties of individual programs. In the foundational work, we provide a concise algebraic language and axioms based on the simple mathematical theory of monads, and show that it is sufficiently expressive. We then give practical validation techniques which extend these transformations and provide several examples of such heuristically driven program validations.

## Introduction

Techniques for *reverse-engineering* software (that is, transforming procedural code into mathematical representations) have been developed using knowledge-based methods [14],[2]. These attempt to recognise possible design intentions in source code, and typically require a great deal of human interaction.

In place of these we present a method with its roots in software verification which relies on formal reasoning on low-level code instead of pattern recognition. This can function completely automatically and algorithmically in simple cases and uses heuristics in more complicated situations. If all else fails, guidance will have to be given by the operator.

In essence, we have found that the attempt to apply theorem-proving techniques within an environment where the theorem to be proved is not completely defined at the outset results in the gradual refinement of the theorem, from an initial wild guess about an unannotated program, to a final statement which is in complete agreement with what the proof mechanisms say about the final program plus annotations. The resulting system serves as a useful aid in the comprehension of raw code, and also transforms it into a concise mathematical representation which can support further development work. This clearly supports the software maintenance task since a large proportion of the effort put into maintenance is simply the initial code comprehension.

### REDO

REDO (Restructuring, Maintenance, Validation and Documentation of Software Systems), is an ESPRIT II project, which started in 1989, and is concerned with 'rejuvenating' existing applications into more maintainable forms by improving documentation, by restructuring code, and by validating the code against original intentions. The work reported on in this paper has been conducted under the auspices of this project. *Validation* here means comparing the implementation against the design or requirements specification, preferably by formal methods (verification). Typically the applications will be large, poorly documented, and written in COBOL or FORTRAN. A central feature of the project is the use of a high-level Intermediate Language, called UNIFORM [3], into which the source languages will be compiled, so eliminating implementation dependencies, and the project tools will then work on the representation of the application in this language. UNIFORM also has the advantage of being a completely formally specified language.

The intermediate language is considerably simpler than either COBOL or FORTRAN, and is close to PASCAL in its structural concepts. It is also intended as an interface with more formal specifications, and allows logical analysis and transformations into specifications to be performed. Reverse-engineering and *re-engineering* (using the derived specifications to create new implementations), were prominent in the original descriptions of the project.

## Contents

There are four sections to this paper, plus a technical appendix.

1. The first section provides the background theory for the work within the framework of categories and monads. This will be used to provide a well structured high-level approach to code representation. *No knowledge of category theory is required to understand this section.*

2. The second section gives a structural proof that all commands in the procedural language can be expressed in terms of guarded assignments, and hence in Z. A monadic treatment of the same proposition is also included.

3. The third section describes the practical techniques used to transform programs into specifications

4. Section four gives examples of reverse-engineering using these techniques.

The appendix gives further properties of the monad operations and related predicate transformers.

# 1 Definitions and Theory

In this section we set out some notation and definitions. Both these come in two parts; standard and non-standard. We use the standard notation of set theory and Z, together with the equivalences forced by the axiom structure. On top of this we introduce the notation of monad theory, explained in terms of a Z semantics for our particular application. We deal with most of the theory in the appendix, but the idea is an important part of our approach, and so we do not shirk putting at least some of it upfront.

# Notation

We write $\Omega$ for the set of truth values - usually, but not necessarily, $\{True, False\}$. For a predicate $\theta$ with a set of accessible free variables $\vec{v}$ we write $\vec{v} : \theta$. Note that there may be yet more free variables than these in $\theta$. We generally decorate symbols with an arrow above to indicate that they are a tuple (a vector), and otherwise the arrow signifies nothing. It is intended as a helpful reminder.

We not only use $X \rightarrow Y$ as the notation for the space of functions from $X$ to $Y$, but also the more classical mathematical notation $Y^X$, particularly when we consider the space of relations between $X$ and $Y$, which we write as $\Omega^{X \times Y}$ - strictly, this set is merely *isomorphic*, being more exactly the set of predicates on the cartesian product $X \times Y$, but the notation serves to remind us of the functional nature of the predicate representation, at least, which since we make use of this representation, is a good idea.

# Convention

$\psi'$ denotes the predicate $\psi$ with each free occurrence of a declared variable $v$ replaced by $v'$ - this is a convention which we will make use of repeatedly, literally; if $\psi$ contains variables already written with a prime, then they obtain an extra prime in $\psi'$.

# Program Semantics – the Weakest Precondition Transform

The weakest precondition semantics for a code $C$ gives a view of the program as a transformation from predicates which refer to its final state $\vec{v}'$, into predicates which refer to its initial state $\vec{v}$. The transformer is denoted by the function $wp(C, -)$, and given a predicate $\psi'$ (the prime is deliberate) referring to its states $\vec{v}'$, it produces the predicate $wp(C, \psi)$ (no prime), referring only to its initial state. $wp(C, \psi)$ is the *weakest precondition* which will force $\psi'$ to be true after the code $C$ has executed.

**Definition:** A predicate $\theta \in \Omega^{\vec{v} \times \vec{v}}$ in the variables $\vec{v}$ of the program, and $\vec{v}'$ of the poststate, *expresses the semantics* of a command $C$ if, in terms of the well-known *weakest precondition* transformer semantics, $wp(C, -)$ for the code [4]:

$$wp(C, \psi) \equiv \forall \vec{v}' \bullet (\theta \Rightarrow \psi')$$

for all $\psi$ in the set of predicates with the free variables $\vec{v}$.

We are associating the code $C$ with a predicate $\theta$, asserting a relation between initial states $\vec{v}$ and final states $\vec{v}'$. The definition above says that the relation is the one that would give rise to the known weakest precondition transformer for the code. Of course, we define the weakest precondition transformer for *predicates* in a way which gives the same result:

**Definition:**

$$wp(\vec{v} : \theta, \psi) = \forall \vec{v}' \bullet (\theta \Rightarrow \psi')$$

This is the *partial correctness* interpretation [6],

*every post-state that results from an execution of θ satisfies ψ*

and it is concerned only with the behaviour of the code in the cases when execution completes successfully. The *complete correctness* transformer *wpc* will be treated in the appendix. Note that the map from predicate to transformer is 1-1, so that we can be sure that the definition of the relation representing a code as the one which is compatible with the weakest precondition transformation must succeed uniquely.

The partial correctness interpretation is appropriate for the procedural language we are concerned with, since this allows concurrent execution and correct but non-terminating programs. The references will supply the basic explanations, if it is required.

## The Representation of Code with Results

Although the predicate θ above represents the code *C* in the predicate space $\Omega^{\vec{v} \times \vec{v}}$, and this is sufficient for the representation of codes which evoke pure side-effects, it is not sufficient to represent codes which also return a value. Therefore we shall be concerned with a generalisation which represents it in the *parameterised predicate* space $R \to \Omega^{\vec{v} \times \vec{v}}$, which is able to represent these kinds of code. Here *R* is the type of an ephemeral *result value* which the code may produce. Certainly, *expressions* need such a type. The map *constantly* θ will be the standard representation of a code without an intrinsic result value. The result value is never represented amongst the program state-variables, and in consequence is not persistent.

If $\phi$ represents code *C* as a parameterised predicate, then $\phi_r$ represents code *C* as a predicate $\theta = \phi_r$ 'in the circumstances in which it produces result *r*'. This seems backwards, but it is convenient.

## The Anti-Weakest Precondition Operator $\overline{wp}$

It turns out that we can combine parametrised predicates conveniently according to the semantics of the $\overline{wp}$ operator. This predicate-transformer is given by the expression

$$\overline{wp}(C, R) = \neg\ wp(C, \neg\ R)$$

which expands to

$$\overline{wp}(C, R) = \exists\ \vec{v}' \bullet \phi\ r \wedge R'$$

for result value *r* and initial and final state variables $\vec{v}$, $\vec{v}'$. In the situation where the predicate *R* itself expresses the idea of a relation, just as $\phi_r$ does, then $\overline{wp}(C, R)$ is the *relational composition* $\phi_r$ o *R'* of $\phi_r$ and *R'*. We adopt this idea in developing combining forms for predicates.

## The *Switch* Operator

The most general combining form that we shall use is the operator which takes code *C* (which may deliver results $x \in X$) and *switches* on the result *x* to a set of distinct *cases*. Each case is another piece of code $D_x$, which may deliver its own result $y \in Y_x$. Note that there are a range of types $\{Y_x\}$ for *y*. We represent the union type of these types as $\sum_{x \in X} Y_x$.

If $C$ is represented by the map $\phi : X \to \Omega^{\vec{v} \times \vec{v}}$, and the family of codes $\{D_x\}_{x \in X}$ is represented by the family $\zeta : X \to \sum_{x \in X} Y_x \to \Omega^{\vec{v} \times \vec{v}}$. Then the code

$$switch(C)\{$$
$$cases \ x \ in \ D_x$$
$$\}$$

is represented by the '$*$' map

$$\zeta * \phi : \sum_{x \in X} Y_x \to \Omega^{\vec{v} \times \vec{v}}$$

which for result value $y$ gives the predicate

$$\exists \vec{v}' \bullet \exists x \bullet \phi \, x \, \wedge (\zeta \, x \, y)'$$

in initial and final state variables $\vec{v}$, $\vec{v}''$ respectively ($(\zeta \, x \, y)'$, by the convention announced at the beginning of this section, denotes the value $\zeta \, x \, y \, (\vec{v}', \vec{v}'')$ ).

## The *Return* Operator

A much easier combining form is the *return* operator – it combines nothing at all. $Return(x)$ just represents the code which returns the value of $x$, without any side-effects. This implies, of course, that $x$ is a simple expression, involving only constants and pure functions and operators (eg. $2+2$). It is represented by the map $\eta_x : X \to \Omega^{\vec{v} \times \vec{v}}$ given by

$$\eta_x \ = \ x' \mapsto (x = x') \wedge (\vec{v} = \vec{v}')$$

for a trial result value $x'$. This predicate just asserts that the result value *is* $x$ and the underlying state does not change.

## Monads

The operators $*$ (*switch*) and $\eta$ (*return*) above are the two operators in a *monad of logical interpretations* for programs. A monad $M$ is a set of types $\{M_X\}_{X \in type}$ with two operators $* : (X \to M_Y) \to M_X \to M_Y$ and $\eta : X \to M_X$. We take the monad types to be

$$M_X = X \to \Omega^{\vec{v} \times \vec{v}}$$

There are three laws which connect these operators:

$$c * (b * a) \ = \ (x \mapsto c * b \, x) * a$$
$$a * \eta \, x \quad = \ a \, x$$
$$\eta * b \qquad = \ b$$

It may be verified that the $*$ operator satisfies the first monad law (a generalisation of the lambda-calculus law relating to the associativity of functional composition). For each $x \in X$, $\eta \, x$ represents the code *return* $x$, as detailed above. This code has no side effect. This denotation satisfies the remaining two monad laws (these laws are generalisations of the properties of the identity function).

## Subroutines

It may be necessary on occasion to change the monad. This will happen when we consider a block of code with local variables. These are invisible outside of the block and the state-space of the whole program will be smaller than the state-space of the block. In this case the monad associated with the block may be designated $N_X = X \to \Omega^{(\vec{U} \times \vec{V}) \times (\vec{U} \times \vec{V})}$, while that of the program is $M_X = X \to \Omega^{\vec{V} \times \vec{V}}$. There is a map, $hide_{\vec{u}} : N_X \to M_X$ which transforms the block semantics back into program semantics; it invents extra local variables $\vec{u}$ and then removes them again:

$$hide_{\vec{u}} \ \phi \ x = \exists \ \vec{u} \bullet \exists \ \vec{u}' \bullet \phi \ x$$

More information about this map is given in the appendix.

## Abelian Monads

It is the case that the predicate space $\Omega^{\vec{V} \times \vec{V}}$ is an *abelian* category. Predicates $\theta_1$, $\theta_2$ may be composed as $\theta_1 \wedge \theta'_2$, and they may also be *added* as $\theta_1 \vee \theta_2$ (no prime on $\theta_2$). This represents non-deterministic choice. The zero for this 'addition' is the *False* predicate (no choices). The inter-distributivity of the logical operators makes 'addition' respect composition in the category.

It follows that the monad $M$ derived from the category is also abelian. It contains an operator, $+ : M_X \to M_X \to M_X$ and a polymorphic zero, $0 : M_X$ defined by

$$(\phi_1 + \phi_2) \ x = \phi_1 \ x \ \vee \ \phi_2 \ x$$

$$0 \ x = \textit{False}$$

satisfying the *linearity* conditions:

$$
\begin{aligned}
f * (a + b) &= f * a + f * b \\
(x \mapsto f \ x + g \ x) * a &= f * a + g * a \\
f * 0 &= 0 \\
(x \mapsto 0) * a &= 0
\end{aligned}
$$

It may be verified that these equalities hold identically for the given denotations of $+$, $0$ and $*$.

## Fixed Points

It is proved in the appendix that this abelian monad possesses a fixed point operator. That is to say; we can write down recursion equations for programs, and so long as they are couched in terms of the four abelian monad operators (and the *hiding* function), there will be a solution in the monad. Since the members of the monad correspond to (non-deterministic) programs with result, there will be a real program corresponding to the solution.

## Why Monads?

The motivation for using this structure for the representation of code is to reduce the number of program constructs to a minimum: four. This allows us to produce far simpler proofs of properties of classes of programs, since one only has to prove that the property is preserved by these constructs. Amongst the properties that we may readily prove by this means, for example, are that programs are representable as guarded commands, that programs are monotonic, that gotos can be eliminated, and so forth.

Moreover, our investigations have actually been *guided* by the understanding given to us by the monad structure. In particular, the meaning of recursion equations for programs has been made clear to us through the fixed-point interpretation in the monad. It is our opinion that the monad algebra clarifies the otherwise murky calculus which appears when pure logic is mixed with the idea of variables representing changes of state in an executing program. Although one can say things with predicates and primed variables which do not correspond to any procedural program, one cannot construct a monad expression which does not represent such a program (possibly with non-deterministic aspects). Given that all programs may be emulated using only certain basic programming constructs we can show that the predicates representing programs fall within the class of predicates representing monad expressions. Of course, along the way, one has shown that predicates suffice, and this is what the next section proves. But one can show many more delicate properties still of classes of programs and predicates, using the monad algebra. Although it is not reported on here, one can show that monad expressions have a unique *normal form*, so that it is possible to compare two programs by means of their expansion into monadic operations.

# 2   Z is Sufficient

Below we give a proof that all constructs of the procedural language with message-passing are expressible in Z, that is, by single predicates in pre and post-state variables, without need for miracles. Let *CMD* denote the syntactic class of programs in our subset of the UNIFORM language, essentially PASCAL-S extended by communication primitives. A syntax description is given in the appendix.

We have defined the semantics of the language in terms of the predicate transformer function $wp$ [4], so that $wp(C, P)$ for a predicate $P$ and command $C \in CMD$ makes sense. Let $\vec{v}$ be the list of all program variables.

## Lemma 1
Each $c \in CMD$ can be expressed as a guarded multiple assignment of the form

$$G \;\rightarrow\; \vec{v} := \vec{e}$$

where $G$ is the condition under which the program can complete execution.

**Proof:**  By induction on the structure of commands:

**Atomic Commands.**  Simple and concurrent assignments themselves can be described as such assignments; the guard $G$ being the condition that each expression on the right hand side is well-defined and that each expression on the left hand side denotes a permissible variable.

**Conditionals.** If $c_1$ and $c_2$ can be expressed in this way, then
IF $e$ THEN $c_1$ ELSE $c_2$ END IF can be expressed as

$$(e \wedge G_1) \vee (\neg\, e \wedge G_2) \;\rightarrow\; \vec{v} := cond(e, \vec{g}, \vec{f})$$

where
$G_1 \;\rightarrow\; \vec{v} := \vec{g}$ expresses $c_1$, $\quad G_2 \;\rightarrow\; \vec{v} := \vec{f}$ expresses $c_2$. $cond(e, x, y)$ is the
conditional expression, with value $x$ if $e$ holds, value $y$ otherwise.

**Sequential Composition.** If $c_1$ is expressed by $G_1 \rightarrow \vec{v} := \vec{e}$ and $\quad c_2$ is
expressed by $\quad G_2 \rightarrow \vec{v} := \vec{f}$ then $c_1$; $c_2$ is expressed by

$$G_1 \wedge G_2[\vec{e}/\vec{v}] \;\rightarrow\; \vec{v} := \vec{g}$$

where

$$g_j = f_j[\vec{e}/\vec{v}]$$

for each $j \in 1 \,..\, n$.

**Unbounded Loops.** For loops, assuming that the effect of the code $C$ in a loop
DO WHILE $E$ : $C$ END DO can be expressed as $\quad G \rightarrow \vec{v} := \vec{e}$ then we can express
the values of the variables $\vec{v}$ after $k$ iterations as a function of the initial values of
these variables and the number of iterations: Define

$$\vec{v}^{(k)} = e^k(\vec{v})$$

the $k$-*fold* application of the functions $e$. We denote the formula

$$\vec{v}' = \vec{v}^{(k)}$$

by $Eqns(k)$. Then the loop is expressed by an assignment

$$GS \rightarrow \vec{v} := \vec{v}^{(\nu)}$$

where

$$\nu = \mu\, k : \mathsf{N} \bullet (Eqns(k) \wedge \neg\, E')$$

and the guard

$$GS \;=\; \exists\, k \in \mathsf{N} \bullet (\, Eqns(k) \wedge \neg\, E' \wedge \forall l \in \mathsf{N} \bullet (\, l \leq k \wedge Eqns(l) \Rightarrow G'\,)\,)$$

states that the guard $G$ is valid in each iteration, and that the loop terminates.

**Bounded Loops.** A similar analysis serves for bounded iteration loops except
that we can explicitly give the number of iterations: DO VARYING i FROM $e_1$ TO $e_2$
BY $e_3$ : $C$ executes $\lfloor (e_2 - e_1)/e_3 \rfloor + 1$ times. Here $\lfloor x \rfloor$ for a real number $x$ denotes
the greatest integer less than or equal to $x$.

**Message Passing.** Message-passing commands SEND $x$ TO $ms$ and
RECEIVE $x$ FROM $ms$ are expressible as combinations of assignments to queue histories and of local blocks.

**Procedure Call.**   Parameter passing into procedures is by call-by-value and call-by-value/result, so that these also simplify to concurrent assignments.

**Local Variables.**   The introduction of new local variables or formal parameters can be treated as follows: if we have a block:

$$\textbf{var } \vec{l} : \vec{t} \quad Code$$

with the scope of the local variables extending to the end of the named code, then we consider predicates $R$ in the variables global to this section, and we assume that all the new local variables have distinct names from the global variables. The weakest precondition of this local block is then

$$\forall \vec{l} : \vec{t} \bullet wp(Code,\ R)$$

But by induction the *Code* can be expressed as a guarded assignment

$$G \rightarrow \vec{x} := \vec{e}$$

where $\vec{x}$ includes the local and global variables. The final values of the local variables can be ignored as no predicate $R$ mentions them. The initial values can be replaced by new terms

$$f_j(\vec{v}) \quad \text{for} \quad l_j$$

which depend only on the global variables, with the stipulations that the formula $f_j(\vec{v}) \in t_j$   for each $j$ is added to the guard:

$$G[\vec{f}/\vec{l}] \curlywedge f(\vec{v}) \in \vec{t} \ \rightarrow \ \vec{v} := \vec{g}$$

where $g_i = e_i[\vec{f}/\vec{l}]$.   □

**Proposition 1:**   For $c \in CMD$, there is a predicate $\theta$ in the variables $\vec{v}, \vec{v}'$ such that

$$\forall R \bullet (wp(c, R) \ \equiv \ \forall \vec{v}' \bullet (\theta \Rightarrow R'))$$

**Proof:**   From Lemma 1. The predicate $\theta$ is $G \wedge (\vec{v}' = \vec{e})$.   □

## Alternative Proof of the Proposition

There is a proof of Proposition 1 using the monad operators. We can show that we can build up the commands using $\eta$, $*$ and $0$, plus some atomic primitives (we do not need non-deterministic choice here) within the monad. we show by induction that all the commands have result type ( ) – the empty tuple type, and this is enough to supply the result, because then the representing parameterised predicate for a program is from ( ), which is to say that it is not parameterised at all! This is just what the proposition asserts.

We clearly need primitives which can read the global variables non-destructively, and update them destructively. We also need a '*nop*' instruction. These can be supplied as follows:

| | | | |
|---|---|---|---|
| *read* | $: M_{\vec{v}}$ | *read* $\vec{x}$ | $= (\vec{v} = \vec{v}' = \vec{x})$ |
| *write* | $: \vec{V} \rightarrow M_{(\ )}$ | *write* $\vec{x}$ ( ) | $= (\vec{v}' = \vec{x})$ |
| *nop* | $: M_{(\ )}$ | *nop* ( ) | $= (\vec{v} = \vec{v}')$ |

**Assignments.**  $\vec{v} := \vec{e}$ can be represented as *write* operators of the form

$$(\vec{v} \mapsto write \ \vec{e}) \ * \ read$$

This has the type $M_{(\ )}$, as required.

**Conditionals.**  IF $e$ THEN $\phi_1$ ELSE $\phi_2$ can be rendered

$$(\vec{v} \mapsto cond(e, \phi_1, \phi_2)) \ * \ read$$

and this has the same type as $\phi_1$ and $\phi_2$ (by induction, $M_{(\ )}$).

**Sequences.**  $\phi_1$; $\phi_2$ is represented as

$$constantly \ \phi_2 \ * \ \phi_1$$

and this has the same type as $\phi_2$; by induction, $M_{(\ )}$.

**Unbounded Loops.**  These are the least fixed-point solutions of the recursion equation

$$\text{WHILE } e \text{ DO } \phi \ = \ \text{IF } e \text{ THEN } (\phi; \text{ WHILE } e \text{ DO } \phi) \text{ ELSE NOP}$$

- that is the predicate $\phi_\omega$ which asserts that the loop terminates after some finite number of steps. We do not have to adjoin the possibility $\phi_\infty$ that it never terminates because this contributes nothing to the relation between initial and final states. $\phi_\omega$ has the same type as *nop*, that is, $M_{(\ )}$.

**Bounded Loops.**  These can of course be represented as (guarded) unbounded loops.

**Local Variables.**  These can be handled using the $hide_{\vec{u}}$ map. var $\vec{u} : \vec{U} \ \phi$ takes $\phi$ in $N_{(\ )} = \Omega^{(\vec{U} \times \vec{V}) \times (\vec{U} \times \vec{V})}$ and transforms it to $hide_{\vec{u}} \ \phi$ in $M_{(\ )} = \Omega^{\vec{V} \times \vec{V}}$.  $\square$

# 3   Transforming Programs into Specifications

The above proposition shows that some mathematical description can be generated automatically for any program, however these descriptions need not be very helpful. The present section treats ways of deriving useful and concise descriptions from code, with the automatic method being used if these cannot be applied.

## Mathematical Expression of Types

The type structures included in the UNIFORM language encompass the usual array and record structures as used in PASCAL (although without recursive data types), and additionally include file structures able to support the file operations used in COBOL, such as accessing a record in a file by referring to a value of a key field of a record. All of these data structures can be represented mathematically as functions or tuples of functions and data, and it is these representations that are then used in proving properties of programs. As an example, the type of multi-dimensional arrays on type *texp*:

> *fle* CONTAINS $N$ OCCURRENCES OF *texp* SELECTABLE BY
> INDEX WHICH CONSISTS OF $< e_{11}, e_{12} >$ BY $\ldots < e_{n1}, e_{n2} >$

is represented by a mathematical type of 4-tuples $(x, first(x), order(x), bound(x))$, in which $x$ carries the basic information; it is a total function of the mathematical type *fle*, represented in Z as:

$$fle == (e_{11} \ldots e_{12} \times \ldots \times e_{n1} \ldots e_{n2}) \rightarrow texp$$

and $bound(x)$ is a predicate which states that $x$ represents a valid instance of the corresponding UNIFORM type:

$$bound(x) = (0 \leq \#x \leq N)$$

$order(x)$ is an ordering relation on the domain $(e_{11} \ldots e_{12} \times \ldots \times e_{n1} \ldots e_{n2})$ of $x$, derived by restriction from the lexicographic product ordering of the built-in orderings on the index sets, and $first(x)$ is the image in file $x$ of the least index $(i_1, \ldots, i_n)$ under $order(x)$:

$$first(x) = x(i_1, \ldots, i_n)$$

In this way, the UNIFORM data type is represented as an *abstract data type*: a mathematical type *fle* and a finite set of operators $\{first, order, bound\}$ on the elements of the type.

## The Expression of Commands

Each command of the language can be represented as a Z schema of form

$$
\begin{array}{|l|}
\hline
C \\
\hline
\begin{array}{rcl}
w_1, w_1' &:& t_1; \\
\ldots & & \\
w_m, w_m' &:& t_m
\end{array} \\
\hline
\theta \\
\hline
\end{array}
$$

listing the variables of the current state, together with a predicate expressing the effect of the command. In practice we determine the predicate for each procedure declaration and process class declaration from the declarations of the program, and form schemas representing the meaning of each call or instance of these modules. Below we give a method for determining the predicates for each command in the language.

**Basic Commands.** Simple assignments and conditionals can be translated into specifications directly, without analysis of the meaning of the code; a concurrent assignment

$$\vec{v} \, \vec{s} := \vec{e}$$

becomes simply

$$v_1' = rep(v_1, s_1, e_1) \quad \wedge \ldots \wedge \quad v_n' = rep(v_n, s_n, e_n)$$

Where $rep(x, i, a)$ (here with $x = v_k$ and $i = s_k$, $a = e_k$) yields the expression produced by replacing the contents of the given variable $x$ $i$ by $a$, where $x$ is an identifier, $i$ is a selector expression (a nested sequence of array/file references or record field selections), and $a$ is an expression. This is defined by recursion on the structure of the selector. That is, an assignment to a component of a complex variable is represented logically as an update of the whole structure as a single object.

If the commands $C1$, $C2$ are transformable into specifications $C_1$, $C_2$, then a conditional

    IF $E$ THEN $C1$ ELSE $C2$ END IF

becomes

$$(E \Rightarrow C_1) \wedge (\neg E \Rightarrow C_2)$$

Similarly

$$\exists \vec{v}'' \bullet C_1[\vec{v}''/\vec{v}'] \wedge C_2[\vec{v}''/\vec{v}]$$

expresses $C1$ ; $C2$.

**Loops.** The difficulty, as with validation, comes in determining the effect of loops, particularly unbounded loops, DO WHILE or DO UNTIL constructs. The method described in lemma 1 for explicitly calculating the effect of a loop as a *μ-recursive* function is always possible, but may not be of practical use in condensing the code into a mathematical expression. For example in the case of the algorithm for obtaining the *gcd* of $a, b$ by successive subtraction:

```
x := a; y := b;
DO  WHILE NOT(x = y):
        IF x < y THEN y := y - x ELSE x := x - y END IF
END DO
```

We would, applying the default reasoning, assume that the invariant is some new arbitrary relation $r_L$ of the program variables, with properties:

$$r_L(a, b, a, b)$$

and

$$x \neq y \wedge r_L(a, b, x, y) \Rightarrow \begin{cases} r_L(a, b, x, y - x) & x < y \\ r_L(a, b, x - y, y) & x \geq y \end{cases}$$

The relation $r_L$ here is stronger than the simple condition $gcd(x, y) = gcd(a, b)$ which is all that is needed to derive the effect of the loop, it is almost as opaque as the code as a description of the algorithm.

We are seeking a concise and expressive description of what the loop achieves; an exhaustive description as a recursive function can be as obscure as the original code, although potentially useful as input to a theorem-prover.

Instead, the method adopted was to seek specifications that are *refined by* the code, rather than being equivalent to it: We try to determine a predicate $\theta$ for which the half

$$(\forall R \bullet (\forall \vec{v}' \bullet \theta \Rightarrow R') \Rightarrow wp(C, R))$$

holds. Various heuristics using the structure of the code and the form of required postconditions can be applied to 'guess' likely invariants *Inv* for the loop, and these are tested against the requirement that

$$\{Inv \wedge E\}\ C\ \{Inv\}$$

for a loop

```
DO WHILE E : C END DO
```

The meaning of the loop could then be given as a specification statement

$$\vec{v} : [Inv,\ Inv' \wedge \neg E']$$

in the style of [8]; with

$$wp(\vec{v} : [Inv,\ Inv' \wedge \neg E'],\ R)\ =\ Inv \wedge (\forall \vec{v}' \bullet Inv' \wedge \neg E' \Rightarrow R')$$

which implies $wp(\texttt{DO WHILE E} \cdot : \texttt{C END DO},\ R)$.

## Heuristics

The following heuristics are adapted from those given by Gries in [9] in connection with the derivation of programs from a given postcondition. They can also be used to generate invariants for an existing loop command, and have been used in the automatic documentation and verification of PASCAL programs.

The postconditions in practice would come from original documentation or source code comments, translated together with the code and formalised as far as possible.

Let the command $L$ be a loop DO WHILE $E$ : *cmd* END DO, and the required postcondition be $R$. Then candidates for invariants can be constructed by:

1. **Deleting a conjunct:** If $R$ has the form of a conjunction $C_1 \wedge \ldots \wedge C_n$, then any of the predicates $P$ formed by deleting one or more of the conjuncts of $R$ are candidate invariants. The first choices for deletion are those conjuncts $C_j$ which have

    $$\neg E \Rightarrow C_j$$

    valid under the global or local invariants of the program.

2. **Replacing a constant by a variable:** The loop expression $e$ is examined for equations or inequations of the form $v\ \theta\ exp$, with $\theta \in \{\leq, \geq, <, >, =, \neq\}$ and $v$ a variable. In $R$, $exp$ is then replaced by suitable expressions involving $v$, and appropriate bounds for $v$ are conjoined to the resulting predicate to yield a candidate invariant.

3. **Enlarging the range of a variable:** This strategy makes no use of $e$, instead subexpressions of $R$ that are equations $v = exp$ with $v$ a variable, are replaced in $R$ by the weaker inequalities
$l \leq v \wedge v \leq u$, where $l$ and $u$ are appropriate bounds for $v$, derived from $e$. Only equations not occurring inside a negation or antecedent of an implication in $R$ are considered.

Modifications of these strategies can also be applied to derive appropriate invariant candidates for bounded iteration loops. For example, $R[i - E3/E2]$ is a suitable candidate invariant for a loop and postcondition

DO VARYING i FROM $E1$ TO $E2$ BY $E3$ WHILE $E$ : $cmd$ END DO$\{R\}$

if $E2$ is a variable.

## If All Else Fails
If all the above heuristics fail, we denote the effect of the loop by some (new) arbitrary relation $r_L(\vec{v})$ of the program variables, and give an implicit definition of the loop effect by asserting that the properties

$$(1) \quad \forall \vec{v} \bullet \left( r_L(\vec{v}) \Rightarrow \left\{ \begin{matrix} R & \neg E \\ wp(C, r_L(\vec{v})) & E \end{matrix} \right\} \right)$$

hold of $r_L$ (where $R$ is the desired postcondition, which may also involve relations representing other loops). Additional (initial) conditions on $r_L$ emerge as proof obligations generated by tracing back through the program, having assumed $r_L(\vec{v})$ as the precondition of the loop. The least (in the usual denotational semantics sense of least defined) solution of these requirements provides us with the strongest definition of the effect of the loop ($r_L$ as given by this solution will imply the $r'_L$ obtained from any other solution). This solution is given by taking equivalence instead of $\Rightarrow$ in (1).

Another alternative is simply to leave the loop as a loop, after having derived a schema in the variables $\vec{v}, \vec{v}'$ representing the code of the loop:

```
 ┌─ C ───────────────────────────────────────────
 │  v₁, v₁′   :   t₁;
 │  ...
 │  vₙ, vₙ′   :   tₙ
 │──────────────────────────────────────────────
 │  θ
 └───────────────────────────────────────────────
```

And then to define another schema as the iteration of this [7] in a recognised extension to Z:

$L \cong$ while $E$ do $C$

## Concurrency and Message-Passing
The form of concurrency adopted in the UNIFORM language is message-passing with both blocking and non-blocking semantics; processes can execute in parallel, communicating only via message streams (queues), and without reference to a

global clock. UNIFORM is thus an asynchronous co-operation, synchronous communication language (like CSP), and also an asynchronous co-operation, asynchronous communication language (like Chill, or data flow networks). Only the asynchronous aspect (unbounded message queues being used for communication) will be considered below. Looking at message-passing commands from a global (sequential) viewpoint, we can define

$$wp(\texttt{RECEIVE } x \texttt{ FROM } b, \ P) = (b \neq \langle \ \rangle \Rightarrow P[tail(b)/b \quad head(b)/x])$$

That is, if $b$ denotes an unbounded queue, if $b$ is empty when an attempt to execute this command is made, then no execution takes place, and only those initial states in which the command is not blocked in this way are of interest. This is again a 'guarded assignment' and can be expressed by the predicate

$$(b \neq \langle \ \rangle) \ \wedge \ (b' = tail(b)) \ \wedge \ (x' = head(b))$$

A SEND command can always be executed, and amounts simply to an assignment:

$$wp(\texttt{SEND } x \texttt{ TO } b, \ P) = P[b \frown \langle x \rangle / b]$$

But these definitions assume that no interruption by another process can occur during the execution of the process containing these commands. If another process could update the queue at indeterminate intervals during this execution they would not be correct. Instead we have to separate the local and global views of the queues. The message-passing concept of process communication used in UNIFORM is almost identical to that used in the system GYPSY [12] of software specification and development. Proof methods based on buffer histories (the total sequence of messages sent or received from a particular queue by a given process) are used, and interactions between processes and their environment are restricted to message-passing. An interesting additional feature of the GYPSY methods is to treat *suspensions* (blocking of a process on an attempted read or write to a queue) as another form of exit, and to prove properties of the form:

$$\{ \ \textbf{prove} \ : \ (b = \langle \ \rangle) \Rightarrow P \ \}$$

asserting that whenever the process is suspended on a read from queue $b$, the assertion $P$ holds true. Given certain restrictions on the connection of processes, we can then denote each process class as a schema, which operates to transform histories of input queues into histories of output queues; these transformations not necessarily being functional or deterministic. Viewing RECEIVE and SEND commands as transformations on buffer histories (represented by new variables $b_{in,p}$ for the total sequence of messages received along $b$ by process instance $p$, and $b_{out,p}$ for the total sequence of messages output along $b$ by $p$), we can define

$$wp(\texttt{SEND } x \texttt{ TO } b, \ R) \quad = \quad R[b_{out,p} \frown \langle x \rangle \ / \ b_{out,p}]$$

$$wp(\texttt{RECEIVE } x \texttt{ FROM } b, \ R) \quad = \quad \forall \nu \bullet R[\nu/x \quad b_{in,p} \frown \langle \nu \rangle \ / \ b_{in,p}]$$

representing the fact that the value of the next item to be received from the queue is unknown. This command can be expressed by the predicate

$$\exists \nu \bullet (x' = \nu \quad \wedge \quad b'_{in,p} = b_{in,p} \frown \langle \nu \rangle)$$

where $\nu$ is a variable new to the program. Notice that we have no knowledge of *when* the attempt to receive a message will block; as we have no knowledge of the global state of the message queue from within a particular process – unless the queue is in both the SEND and RECEIVE lists of the process. As each queue $b$ can be used by at most two processes, say $p$ sending to $b$ and $q$ receiving from $b$, we can however assert that

$$b_{out,p} = b_{in,q} \frown b$$

(The actual contents of the queue $b$ is the remainder – tail – of the total sequence of messages sent to $b$ after the total sequence of messages received from $b$ has been removed) is a global invariant of the program. To determine the effect of a process $p$, we place blockage specifications

$$\{\textbf{prove}: \ (b = \langle \rangle) \ \Rightarrow \ \phi(\vec{ins}, \vec{outs})\}$$

immediately prior to each RECEIVE $x$ FROM $b$ command in the process body, and, if the process can terminate, at the end of the code of the process. The predicate $\phi$ stands for the yet to be determined effect of the process. We then work back from these requirements to deduce what properties are needed for this predicate $\phi$, and in this way we are often able to determine it completely from the proof obligations generated by the code. The process can then be represented as a schema

```
┌─ pinst ──────────────────────────────────
│  A?;  B!;  C;
│  locals
├───────────────────────────────────────────
│  p(\vec{a}?, \vec{b}!, \vec{c})
└───────────────────────────────────────────
```

The outputs of the process (the total output histories of the output message queues) are denoted by $\vec{b}!$, and may be expressed as a function of the total input histories, denoted by $\vec{a}?$ and parameters, denoted by $\vec{c}$. The schemas containing declarations of these parameters and their types are denoted by $B!$, $A?$, and $C$ respectively.

The properties of predicate $\phi$ are given by separate assertions

$$\theta_1(\phi) \ \wedge \ \ldots \ \wedge \ \theta_m(\phi)$$

corresponding to the proof obligations on this predicate needed to prove the code correct.

## Combining the Effect of Several Processes

In a more general framework processes could be represented as specifications ('communication assertions') of the form $\vec{b} : [\ \Theta(\vec{a}?, \vec{c}), \ \Phi(\vec{a}?, \vec{b}!, \vec{c})\ ]$ where we decorate variables that are input streams to a process by the postfix '?', and variables that are output streams by the postfix '!'. $\Theta$ is a predicate on input streams and input (value) parameters only, $\Phi$ a predicate on outputs and inputs. Given such assertions, the behavior of a group of processes concurrently active can be described by means of the composition operations $\gg_{\vec{b}}$, defined on communication assertions by:

$$\vec{b} : [\ \theta(\vec{a}?, \vec{c}), \ \phi(\vec{a}?, \vec{b}!, \vec{c})\ ] \ \gg_{\vec{b}} \ \vec{e} : [\ \varphi(\vec{b}?, \vec{d}), \ \psi(\vec{b}?, \vec{e}!, \vec{d})\ ]$$

$$\equiv$$

$$\vec{e} : [\ \theta(\vec{a}?, \vec{c}) \wedge \forall \vec{b} \bullet (\phi(\vec{a}?, \vec{b}, \vec{c}) \ \Rightarrow \ \varphi(\vec{b}, \vec{d})), \ \exists \vec{b} \bullet (\phi(\vec{a}?, \vec{b}, \vec{c}) \wedge \psi(\vec{b}, \vec{e}!, \vec{d}))\ ]$$

When both of the preconditions are *true*, this simplifies to

$$\vec{e} : [\; true, \; \exists \vec{b} \bullet (\phi(\vec{a?}, \vec{b}, \vec{c}) \wedge \psi(\vec{b}, \vec{e!}, \vec{d})) \;]$$

Then if the process instances $id1(\vec{c}, \vec{a}, \vec{b})$ and $id2(\vec{d}, \vec{b}, \vec{e})$ respectively satisfy

$$\vec{b} : [\; \theta(\vec{a?}, \vec{c}), \quad \phi(\vec{a?}, \vec{b!}, \vec{c}) \;]$$

$$\vec{e} : [\; \varphi(\vec{b?}, \vec{d}), \quad \psi(\vec{b?}, \vec{e!}, \vec{d}) \;]$$

then the concurrent execution of the two instances, $id1$ supplying input to $id2$ via the channels $\vec{b}$, satisfies the above composition of the two assertions.

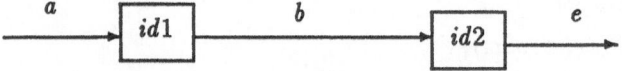

It is assumed in the above that the lists $\vec{a}, \vec{b}, \vec{c}$ are mutually disjoint.

This composition generalises to define the meaning of networks of processes in which the communication paths do not form circuits; for instance the composition

$$sorter(a?, b!) \gg_b (sorter(c?, d!) \gg_d merger(b?, d?, e!))$$

defines the same process as

$$sorter(c?, d!) \gg_d (sorter(a?, b!) \gg_b merger(b?, d?, e!))$$

This technique allows us to determine the meaning of any collection of processes connected together in a directed acyclic network.

If processes form a circuit of communications then, if they are all functional, the meaning of the combination of the processes can be determined by using fixed points; as in the analysis of Kahn networks [5], or the semantics of LUCID. For instance, in the simple case of feedback from the output of one process into one of its inputs via another process:

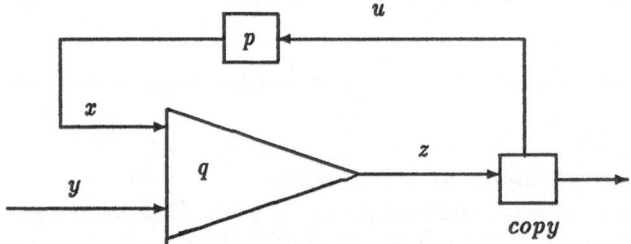

Where $q$ transforms inputs $x$ and $y$ into $z$, which is copied onto two streams, one of which is the final output, and the other returns to the input of $q$ after transformation via $p$. This arrangement can be expressed by a recursive equation:

$$z = q(x, y) \quad where \quad x = p(q(x, y))$$

Functional networks can always be reduced to a sequence of equations possibly involving mutual recursion. In UNIFORM, since each queue can have at most one process writing to it, and at most one reading from it, we must put in explicit *copy* processes if we wish two processes to read from a single queue, and (deterministic) merge processes to combine two streams into one.

## Procedure Calls and Process Instances

If we have derived the effect of the code of a procedure declaration

```
PROCEDURE   p(IN:x_1, ..., x_n; OUT:y_1, ..., y_m; INOUT:z_1, ..., z_k);
    OWNS    locals;
    BEGIN
        ... code ...
    END
```

as a schema

$$
\begin{array}{|l}
\hline
p \\
\hline
X;\ Y';\ \Delta Z; \\
locals \\
\hline
\theta \\
\hline
\end{array}
$$

where $X$ stands for the schema with signature consisting of the translation of the declaration of the formal value parameters $x_1, \ldots, x_n$, and so forth; then a call $p(\vec{a}, \vec{b}, \vec{c})$ of the procedure can be represented as the composition

$$pcall \ \widehat{=} \ pentry \ \overset{\circ}{,} \ (p \setminus locals) \ \overset{\circ}{,} \ pexit$$

where

$$
\begin{array}{|l}
\hline
pentry \\
\hline
X';\quad Z'; \\
A;\quad C \\
\hline
x_1' = a_1 \ \wedge \ \ldots \ \wedge \ x_n' = a_n \\
z_1' = c_1 \ \wedge \ \ldots \ \wedge \ z_k' = c_k \\
\hline
\end{array}
$$

and

$$
\begin{array}{|l}
\hline
pexit \\
\hline
Y;\quad Z; \\
C'';\quad B' \\
\hline
b_1' = y_1 \ \wedge \ \ldots \ \wedge \ b_m' = y_m \\
c_1' = z_1 \ \wedge \ \ldots \ \wedge \ c_k' = z_k \\
\hline
\end{array}
$$

So that overall the call is a schema on inputs $\vec{a}, \vec{c}$ and outputs $\vec{b'}, \vec{c'}$.

Similarly, we could represent a process declaration

```
PROCESS   ptype
    RECEIVES  a_1:t_1; ... a_n:t_n;
    SENDS     b_1:s_1; ... b_m:s_m;
    USES      c_1:r_1; ... c_k:r_k;
    OWNS      locals
    BEGIN
        ... code ...
    END
```

as a schema

┌─ *ptype* ─────────────────────────────────────────
│  $a_1?$ : seq $t_1$;   ...   $a_n?$ : seq $t_n$;
│  $b_1!$ : seq $s_1$;   ...   $b_m!$ : seq $s_m$;
│  $C$; *locals*
├───────────────────────────────────────────────────
│  $\theta[\vec{a?}/\vec{a_{in,p}}\;\;\vec{b!}/\vec{b_{out,p}}]$
└───────────────────────────────────────────────────

where $\theta$ expresses the effect of the code of the process on the histories of the formal input and output queues, together with the initialisations

$$a_{1,in,p} \;:=\; \langle\;\rangle;\; \ldots\; a_{n,in,p} \;:=\; \langle\;\rangle;$$
$$b_{1,out,p} \;:=\; \langle\;\rangle;\; \ldots\; b_{m,out,p} \;:=\; \langle\;\rangle$$

stating that initially the histories are empty. Then a call of the process, generating an instance *pinst* of the process:

```
GENERATE  pinst
    EXECUTING  ptype
    RECEIVING  x_1, ..., x_n
    SENDING    y_1, ..., y_m
    USING      z_1, ..., z_k
```

has a definition

$$pinst \;\triangleq\; pentry\,;\, (ptype \setminus locals)[\vec{x?}/\vec{a?}\;\;\vec{y!}/\vec{b!}]$$

where

┌─ *Pentry* ────────────────────────────────────────
│  $C'$; $Z$
├───────────────────────────────────────────────────
│  $c_1' = z_1 \;\;\wedge \ldots \wedge\;\; c_k' = z_k$
└───────────────────────────────────────────────────

So that the overall schema has inputs $\vec{x?}$, $\vec{z}$ and outputs $\vec{y!}$.

# 4 Examples

The following is a derivation of the effect of a simple process, illustrating the method: Given

```
PROCESS  inc
    RECEIVES  fs2:integer
    SENDS     fs1:integer
    BEGIN
        x  := 1;
        DO   WHILE   true:
             SEND    x+1 TO fs1;
             RECEIVE x FROM fs2
        END  DO
```

```
END
BEGIN
    GENERATE     incp
    EXECUTING    inc
    RECEIVING    ms2
    SENDING      ms1
END
```

as a program, we determine the meaning of the process class as a relation between the input history $fs2_{in}$ and output history $fs1_{out}$: we call this (unknown) relation $inc(fs2_{in}, fs1_{out})$ and at every exit point of the process code we require this relation to hold:

```
PROCESS  inc
    RECEIVES  fs2:integer
    SENDS     fs1:integer
    BEGIN
        x := 1;
        DO   WHILE   true:
             SEND    x+1 TO fs1;
             {PROVE: fs2 = ⟨ ⟩  ⇒  inc(fs2_in, fs1_out) }
             RECEIVE x FROM fs2
        END  DO
    END
```

This requires us to prove that $inc(fs2_{in}, fs1_{out}{}^\frown \langle x + 1 \rangle)$ is an invariant of the loop, ie: that

$$inc(fs2_{in}, fs1_{out}{}^\frown \langle x + 1 \rangle) \; \Rightarrow \forall \nu_1 : Z \bullet inc(fs2_{in}{}^\frown \langle \nu_1 \rangle, \; fs1_{out}{}^\frown \langle x + 1, \nu_1 + 1 \rangle)$$

Assuming this as a *property* of *inc*, we can then take the supposed invariant as a precondition of the loop, and thus obtain the precondition:

$$inc(\langle \; \rangle, \; \langle 2 \rangle)$$

at the beginning of the process code. Together these tell us what the process does, ie: it increments each element of the input sequence by 1:

$$fs1_{out} = \langle 2 \rangle \frown increment(fs2_{in})$$

Much more complex examples can be treated in the same systematic way; for this example we could include an additional process

```
PROCESS  dec
    RECEIVES  fs1:integer
    SENDS     fs2:integer
    BEGIN
        y:=1;
        DO   WHILE   true:
             SEND    y-1 TO fs2;
             RECEIVE y FROM fs1
        END DO
    END
```

And a call of

```
GENERATE   decp
    EXECUTING  dec
    RECEIVING  ms1
    SENDING    ms2
```

in the main program body, for this second process we can establish that

$$fs2_{out} = \langle 0 \rangle \frown decrement(fs1_{in})$$

ie: that the output is the input sequence with every element decreased by 1. We can in fact also deduce that – in the actual program execution – $\#ms1 + \#ms2 \le 2$ which is perhaps non-obvious. To prove this we note that

$$\#ms1_{out} \le \#ms2_{in} + 1$$

is an invariant of the process instance *incp*, and that

$$\#ms2_{out} \le \#ms1_{in} + 1$$

is an invariant of the process instance *decp*. We also know that

$$ms1_{out} = ms1_{in} \frown ms1,$$
$$ms2_{out} = ms2_{in} \frown ms2$$

hold globally. Hence

$$
\begin{aligned}
\#ms1_{out} &\le \#ms2_{in} + 1 \\
&\le \#ms2_{out} - \#ms2 + 1 \\
&\le \#ms1_{in} - \#ms2 + 2 \\
&\le \#ms1_{out} - (\#ms1 + \#ms2) + 2
\end{aligned}
$$

which gives us the result.

# Conclusion

We have shown how a systematic conversion of procedural code into a higher level mathematical representation can be achieved, using the language of category theory and monads to provide a precise basis for the correctness of this transformation.

An application would be to provide automated support for program comprehension and the generation of technical documentation from software systems as part of maintenance. In addition once a formal representation of the software has been obtained properties and theorems about the programs can be more easily derived using this representation than at the lower, code, level.

# Appendix

## Further Properties of Predicate Transformers

The definition of *wp* is in contrast to the definition of *total correctness* preconditions for predicates $\theta$, used in [8] and [6]:

**Definition:**

$$wpc(\vec{v} : \theta, \; R) \;=\; (\exists \, \vec{v}' \bullet \theta) \land \forall \, \vec{v}' \bullet (\theta \Rightarrow R')$$

which requires that the specification can execute.

In fact these two are inter-definable [1]:

$$wp(\vec{v} : \theta, \; R) = \neg \; wpc(\vec{v} : \theta, \; true) \lor wpc(\vec{v} : \theta, \; R)$$

since $\neg \; wpc(\vec{v} : \theta, \; true)$ is the set of states in which $\vec{v} : \theta$ cannot execute, and

$$wpc(\vec{v} : \theta, \; R) = \neg \; wp(\vec{v} : \theta, false) \land wp(\vec{v} : \theta, \; R)$$

since $\neg \; wp(\vec{v} : \theta, false)$ is the set of states in which $\vec{v} : \theta$ can execute.

The partial correctness definition of predicate transformers we have used here is *monotone* and *conjunctive*, it fails to be strict or continuous:

**Proposition 2:**

$$\forall \, R_1, R_2 \bullet ((R_1 \Rightarrow R_2) \Rightarrow (wp(\vec{v} : \theta, R_1) \Rightarrow wp(\vec{v} : \theta, R_2)) \;)$$
$$\forall \, R_1, R_2 \bullet (wp(\vec{v} : \theta, R_1 \land R_2) \; \Leftrightarrow \; wp(\vec{v} : \theta, R_1) \land wp(\vec{v} : \theta, R_2) \;)$$

**Proof:** Clear. □

In contrast the definition

$$\overline{wp}(\vec{v} : \theta, \; R) \;=\; (\exists \, \vec{v}' \bullet \theta \land R')$$

of the *anti-weakest precondition* is strict and continuous but not conjunctive. The conjunction $\overline{wp}(S, R) \land wp(S, R)$ yields $wpc(S, R)$.

## Hiding of Local Variables in the Monad of Predicates

The monad associated with a block of code containing local variables $\vec{u}$ may be designated $N_X = X \to \Omega^{(\vec{u} \times \vec{v}) \times (\vec{u} \times \vec{v})}$, while that of the program is $M_X = X \to \Omega^{\vec{v} \times \vec{v}}$. There is a map, $hide_{\vec{u}} : N_X \to M_X$ which transforms the block semantics back into program semantics:

$$hide_{\vec{u}} \; \phi \; x = \exists \, \vec{u} \bullet \exists \, \vec{u}' \bullet \phi \; x$$

*Linear* monad maps $h$ satisfy

$$h \, (a \, + \, b) = h \; a \, + \, h \; b$$

$$h \; 0 = 0$$

and the map $hide_{\vec{u}}$ is linear.

# Least Fixed Points in the Monad of Predicates

It is also true that the underlying category $\Omega^{\mathring{\mathcal{V}} \times \mathring{\mathcal{V}}}$ (which contains only totally defined predicates) is *ordered* by the logical ordering on $\Omega$. This ordering is inherited by the monad $M_X$ pointwise, so that

$$(\phi_1 \leq \phi_2) \equiv \forall x \in X \bullet (\phi_1 \, x \leq \phi_2 \, x)$$

for $\phi_1, \phi_2 \in M_X$. *Switch* preserves the ordering, in the sense that

$$(a \leq b) \Rightarrow (f \, * \, a \, \leq \, f \, * \, b)$$

$$\forall x \in X \bullet (f \, x \leq g \, x) \Rightarrow (f \, * \, a \, \leq \, g \, * \, a)$$

Of course, this follows from $(a \leq b) \equiv (a + b = b)$ and the fact that *switch* preserves $+$. It is true that $h = hide_{\mathring{\mathcal{q}}}$ preserves order, i.e.

$$(a \leq b) \Rightarrow (h \, a \leq h \, b)$$

The underlying category has all $\omega$-limits; countable disjunctions and conjunctions. This implies that such limits also exist in the monad $M_X$. Any sequence $a_0 \leq a_1 \leq a_2 \leq \ldots$ in $M_X$ has a least upper bound $\sum_{n \in nat} a_n$, and, symmetrically, any sequence in the other direction has a greatest lower bound. It happens that the *switch* operator is *continuous* with respect to arbitrary (increasing) limits. That is:

$$f \, * \, \sum_i a_i = \sum_i (f \, * \, a_i)$$

$$(x \mapsto \sum_i f_i \, x) \, * \, a = \sum_i (f_i \, * \, a)$$

and so is the monad $+$ and $0$, of course:

$$\sum_I 0 = 0, \qquad \text{if } I \neq \emptyset$$

$$a + \sum_i b_i = \sum_i (a + b_i)$$

Even the map $hide_{\mathring{\mathcal{q}}}$ preserves limits of this kind. This implies that we can solve *recursion equations* of the form

$$a = e(a)$$

in the monad $M_X$, where $e(-)$ is made up of monad operators. The solution is:

$$a = \sum_{n \in N} e^n(0)$$

(general theory assures us that there is a solution to the recursion equation even when the operators involved are merely monotone, and not continuous, it just is not necessarily the solution given above).

## BNF Syntax of UNIFORM

For simplicity only the syntax of commands will be presented here, in an abbreviated form.

| | | |
|---|---|---|
| *statements* | ::= | *statement* |
| | | *statement* ";" *statements* |
| *statement* | ::= | *assignment* |
| | \| | *multi_assign* |
| | \| | *conditional* |
| | \| | *iteration* |
| | \| | *generate* |
| | \| | *message* |
| | \| | *procedure_call* |

these classes being defined by:

| | | | | |
|---|---|---|---|---|
| *assignment* | ::= | *variable* " := " *expression* | | |
| *multi_assign* | ::= | "[" *variable internal expression* "]" | | |
| *internal* | ::= | "] := [" | | |
| | \| | "," *variable internal expression* "," | | |
| *message* | ::= | "SEND" *expression* | "TO" | *FormalBufferName* |
| | \| | "RECEIVE" *variable* | "FROM" | *FormalBufferName* |
| *generate* | ::= | "GENERATE" | *ProcessName* | |
| | | "EXECUTING" | *ClassName* | |
| | | [ "USING" | *parameters* | ] |
| | | [ "SENDING" "TO" | *parameters* | ] |
| | | [ "RECEIVING" "FROM" | *parameters* | ] |
| | | [ "ACCESSING" | *foreign_variables* | ] |
| | | [ "RETURNING" | *foreign_variables* | ] |
| *parameters* | ::= | *parameter* { "," *parameter* }* | | |
| *conditional* | ::= | "IF" | *expression* | |
| | | "THEN" | *statements* | |
| | | [ "ELSE" | *statements* ] | |
| | | "END" "IF" | | |
| *iteration* | ::= | "DO" [ *do_control* ] " : " | | |
| | | *statements* | | |
| | | "END" "DO" | | |
| *do_control* | ::= | *varying* \| *while* \| *until* | | |
| *varying* | ::= | "VARYING" *Variable* | { *bounds* [*step*] \| *range* } | |
| *range* | ::= | "IN" *Setname* | | |
| *bounds* | ::= | "FROM" *expression* | "TO" *expression* | |
| *step* | ::= | "BY" *expression* | | |
| *while* | ::= | "WHILE" *expression* | | |
| *until* | ::= | "UNTIL" *expression* | | |

# References

[1] Dijkstra E. W. *A Discipline Of Programming* Prentice Hall 1968.

[2] Ward M. *From Assembler To Z* Durham University 1989.

[3] UNIFORM: A Language Geared to System Description and Transformation, REDO (ESPRIT 2 Project P2487) document TN-NIL-1002.

[4] An Axiomatic Semantics for UNIFORM. REDO Document TN-PRG-1011

[5] Kahn, G. *The Semantics of a Simple Language for Parallel Programming* Information Processing 74, North Holland Amsterdam pp.471 - 475 (1974).

[6] Josephs, M. *The Data Refinement Calculator for Z Specifications* Inf. Proc. Lett., Vol 27, No1, pp 29-33, 1988.

[7] Bowen J., Gimson R., Topp-Jorgensen S. *Specifying System Implementations in Z* Technical monograph PRG-63. 1988.

[8] Morgan C. et al. *On the Refinement Calculus.* PRG-70 Technical Monograph. 1988.

[9] Gries D. *The Science of Programming* Springer-Verlag 1981.

[10] Stark, E. W. *On The Relations Computable by a Class of Concurrent Automata* Dept. Of Computer Science, State University of New York. 1989.

[11] Morgan C.C. *Programming From Specifications* Prentice Hall International Series in Computer Science, Prentice Hall International 1990.

[12] Good D. *Mechanical Proofs About Computer Programs* Artificial Intelligence and Software Engineering, Eds Rich C., Walters C. Morgan Korfmann Ltd 1984.

[13] Milner, R. *Using Algebra for Concurrency: Some Approaches* Springer-Verlag LNCS 207 Analysis of Concurrent Systems.

[14] Dershowitz N. *Program Abstraction and Instanciation* ACM Transactions on Programming Languages and Systems, Vol 7, No. 3, July 1985, pp 446 - 477.

# Computer Aided Transformation of Z into Prolog

*A. J. J. Dick*
*Racal Research Ltd., Reading*

*P. J. Krause[†] and J. Cozens*
*Dept. of Mathematics, University of Surrey*

[†]Now at Biomedical Computing Dept., Imperial Cancer Research Fund

## ABSTRACT

A strategy for the rapid prototyping of Z specifications is described. The semantics of Z are captured in a library of Prolog rules based on a standard specification of the language constructs. Each Z schema is translated directly into a Prolog rule which is then transformed for efficiency. A classical generate-and-test form is used to mirror the structure of a schema; goals resulting from the schema variable declarations are used to generate candidate instantiations, and goals resulting from the schema predicate part are used to test the instantiations for required properties. The incompleteness of the Prolog search strategy limits the approach to the use of finite sets. Negation by failure places limitations on the kinds of transformation that can be applied. A set of tools is being developed to explore the potential of this approach for the animation of Z specifications. These tools include a Z-to-Prolog translator, a transformation aid, and an animator. Initial experiments with the transformation tool suggest that the approach can offer more than simple animation; execution of the Prolog can also be used to check logical consistency and non-determinism.

## ACKNOWLEDGEMENTS

This work is based on a project initiated by Ron Knott, University of Surrey, who developed the library of Prolog rules referred to in the paper. His continued technical support is gratefully acknowledged. We also thank David Pitt, Steve Schuman and Paddy Byers for useful discussions on the formal specification side of the work.

# 1. Introduction

Rapid prototyping is seen as important method of validating a specification against its informally perceived requirements. This is especially so when the specification language used is not easily understood by the non-specialist reader who, nevertheless, has a strong interest in the consequences of the specification.

By their very nature, specification languages tend to be non-algorithmic, which inhibits direct execution. Rapid prototyping, therefore, involves making an interpretation of the specification in some language that does lend itself to direct execution. Having invested in a formal specification, it is highly desirable that the process of interpretation should itself have a formal basis. Otherwise, the interpretation may not truly reflect the consequences of the specification. Equally, the process should be as automatic as possible, to minimise the possibility of human error.

This paper reports some preliminary work on the automated rapid prototyping of Z specifications by a direct translation into Prolog. It builds on the work initiated by [Knott/Krause'88a] as part of the Alvey FORSITE project (SE/065), whose approach is reviewed here. Taking the basic types sets, sequences and relations, their manipulative environment is modelled using a library of Prolog rules whose specification is taken from the notation in the Glossary of *Specification Case Studies* [Hayes'87]. Z schemas follow the format of a declaration of variables grouped with predicates constraining the values of those variables. This can be translated directly into Prolog as a generate and test cycle, with the declarations generating candidate values of variables and the predicates checking for correctness. This will, however, lead to grossly inefficient programs and some thought to filter promotion is almost always required before the programs will run in a "reasonable" time.

In the preliminary work the translation of the Z specification into Prolog was carried out "by hand", although following fixed rules. Correctness preserving transformations were then also carried out by hand to improve the efficiency of the resulting program. Work is well under way to develop a syntax-directed editor and a translation program to enable a formal specification to be input into the computer and automatically translated into Prolog. Work has also been carried out to semi-automate the transformational part of this rapid prototyping process [Dick/Krause'89]. Some further details of this work can be found in Section 6. It is intended that this be the first stage of a specification development environment written in Prolog with a NeWS user interface.

In what follows, no attempt is made to explain the Z notation in detail; readers may wish to refer to [Spivey'88, Spivey'89] for a detailed description. A knowledge of Prolog [Stirling/Shapiro'86] is also assumed of the reader, although some operational aspects of the language are briefly explained below.

# 2. Construction of Prolog Rules from Z Schemas

We give here a brief characterisation of the approach taken to translating a Z specification into Prolog rules. Further details can be found in [Knott/Krause'88]. We concentrate for the time being on schemas, leaving a discussion of other aspects of the Z notation, such as axiomatic definitions and language extensions, to Section 5.

## 2.1 Basic Types

Z is a strongly typed set-theoretic language. A Z schema describes a collection of named variables and the relationships that must hold between them. To model the Z type system in Prolog, two basic patterns are defined which characterise *sets* and *tuples*. This enables the declaration of Prolog representations for *relations*, *functions* and *sequences*. A library of Prolog rules then define the manipulative environment, these rules being derived from the notation in the Z Glossary found in [Hayes'87]. The rules in this library have been very carefully designed by Dr. R. D. Knott to adhere to certain principles which facilitate transformation of the Prolog at a later stage. In particular :-

- the Prolog "cut" is avoided, except in a couple of built-in rules, by using `setof` and `forall` constructs and guarding rules whereever possible
- the rules are written so that a wide variety of flow modes apply

The default Prolog representation for sets is taken, namely ordered lists using the standard lexicographical ordering. Many of the operations involving sets can then be implemented in Prolog using the built in predicate `setof`. For example, set intersection may be defined as:

```
intersect (Xs,Ys,Zs) :-
    setof (X, (member (X,Xs),member (X,Ys)), Zs).
```

Note in passing that this rule has a restricted modality; `Xs` and `Ys` must both be instantiated when the rule is called.

Ordered n-tuples are represented in the conventional way: an ordered n-tuple of $t_1, t_2, \dots t_n$ being represented by :

$$(t_1, t_2, \dots t_n)$$

Structures representing relations, functions and sequences may now be defined in an obvious way. For example, the ubiquitous biblical parent relation is given as the set of ordered pairs:

```
[ (abraham,isaac), (haran,lot), (haran,micah),
        (haran,yiscah) ]
```

## 2.2 Strategy

A Z schema consists of a declaration part and a predicate part which constrain the possible states described. This format can be mirrored in Prolog by the classic generate and test cycle. The declarations are translated into Prolog goals which can be used to generate candidate solutions, and the predicate part into goals used to check the solutions for correctness.

Thus a schema becomes a Prolog rule with an argument for each state variable declared in the schema declarations, and an argument for every given set used in the schema. Execution is achieved by calling the rule with the given sets instantiated with "representative elements" of the required type. The rule then generates an instantiation of the state variables which satisfies the schema predicates, using Prolog's depth first search strategy.

This approach leads to two immediate problems :

1. The inherent unfairness of the depth first search strategy may lead to incompleteness of the Prolog rule.

2. Many iterations of the generate and test cycle may be required before the correct solution is found.

By only considering finite sets, the first problem should not arise (but see Section 3 for some further comments on this). The second problem is one of efficiency, and may be addressed by promoting the test goals into the generator wherever possible. The ability to do this is limited by the modality of the rules in the library used in the translation. Many of the rules are incomplete when certain combinations of arguments are uninstantiated. These limitations are discussed in detail in Section 3.

This provides the basis for a strategy for generating Prolog programs from a Z specification. In summary:

1. The *given sets* are instantiated with "representative elements" of the required type.

2. A "first order" Prolog rule is defined with goals derived from the schema declarations acting as generators, goals derived from predicate parts as tests.

3. Filter promotion and other transformations are applied, *when possible*, to improve the efficiency of the Prolog rule.

## 2.3   An Example

As a simple example of the construction of a Prolog rule from a Z schema, consider the specification of a *File Update* given in *Specification Case Studies* [Hayes'87, p.43] :

$$
\begin{array}{|l}
\hline
\textit{File Update}\underline{\hspace{3cm}}\\
f, f' : Key \nrightarrow Record;\\
d? : Record;\\
u? : Key \nrightarrow Record\\
\hline
d? \subseteq dom(f) \land\\
d? \cap dom(u) = \{\} \land\\
f' = (d? \vartriangleleft f) \oplus u?\\
\hline
\end{array}
$$

Each record in the file is indexed by a key, so that the file is modelled as a partial function from keys to records. A transaction involves specifying a set of keys of records to be deleted from the file, and/or a partial function giving the keys to be updated together with their new records. A literal line-by-line translation of the schema using the Prolog library yields the following rule:

```
file_update(Keys,Records,F,Fp,Di,Ui) :-
    partial_fn(F,Keys,Records),
    partial_fn(Fp,Keys,Records),
    powerset(Keys,Pset), member(Di,Pset),
    partial_fn(Ui,Keys,Records),
    dom(F,Dom), has_subset(Di,Dom),
    domain(Ui,Dom1), intersect(Di,Dom1,[]),
    domain_sub(F,Di,Temp), overriding(Temp,Ui,Fp).
```

This rule will execute very inefficiently because instantiations of Fp are generated in the second goal, and not checked until the last goal. If the modality of the overriding goal is such that it can be used to instantiate Fp, then the order of the goals can be changed so that the overriding goal acts as the generator. Checking the modality of the overriding goal, we can be sure that, if the two parameters Temp and Ui are ground when the rule is called, a ground instantiation of Fp will result. Hence the second goal can be demoted to a position following the overriding goal, to give the revised rule:

```
file_update(Keys,Records,F,Fp,Di,Ui) :-
    partial_fn(F,Keys,Records),
    powerset(Keys,Pset), member(Di,Pset),
    partial_fn(Ui,Keys,Records),
    dom(F,Dom), has_subset(Di,Dom),
    domain(Ui,Dom1), intersect(Di,Dom1,[]),
    domain_sub(F,Di,Temp), overriding(Temp,Ui,Fp),
    partial_fn(Fp,Keys,Records).
```

We could further improve the efficiency of this rule by replacing the two goals

```
    powerset(Keys,Pset), member(Di,Pset),
```

with the equivalent goal has_subset(Di,Keys). This avoids the time consuming generation of a powerset.

The two given sets Keys and Records contain the primitive type information for the file update. Prior to calling the file_update rule, they must be instantiated with "all possible" elements of type Key and type Record respectively.

The following is a transcription of a file update operation using the Prolog rule defined above :

```
|?-Keys = [k1,k2,k3,k4,k5,k6],
|: Records = [r1,r2,r3,r4,r5,r6],
|: F = [(k1,r1),(k2,r2),(k3,r3),(k4,r4)],
|: Ui = [(k3,r5),(k5,r6)],
|: Di = [k2, k4],
|: file_update(Keys,Records,F,Fp,Di,Ui).

    Fp = [(k1, r1),(k3,r5),(k5,r6)]
```

A more thorough example of the rapid prototyping of a Z specification in Prolog can be found in the report *LIBRARY SYSTEM: An example of rapid prototyping of a Z specification in PROLOG.* [Knott/Krause'88b].

## 3.  Limitations

### 3.1  Finite Sets

Mention was made in the previous section that sets should be finite. This is because of the following problem which arises as a result of Prolog's depth first search strategy. Suppose we require a program that generates all the triples of natural numbers $(x, y, h)$ such that $x^2 + y^2 = h^2$. This may be specified in Z as

```
┌ Pythag Triads ────────────────────────────┐
│   x!,y!,h! : N                             │
│ ───────────────────────────────────────── │
│   (x*x) + (y*y) = (h*h)                    │
└────────────────────────────────────────────┘
```

If we define a Prolog rule posnum which generates the infinite set of natural numbers:

```
posnum(1).
posnum(N) :- posnum(N1), N is N1 + 1.
```

Then we may naively translate the Z specification into :

```
pythagtri(X,Y,H) :-
      posnum(X),posnum(Y),posnum(Z),
      0 is H*H - X*X - Y*Y.
```

Although the solution X=3, Y=4, H=5 is in the meaning of the program, Prolog's depth first search strategy will never find this, or any other solution. Having tried and failed with X=1, Y=1, H=1, on backtracking it will try the solution X=1, Y=1, H=2, then H=3,4,5... and so on without terminating.

Thus Prolog's depth first search rule may lead to the incompleteness of a Prolog program. For example, Prolog could never show that pythagtri(X,Y,H), X=3, Y=4, H=5 was a logical consequence of the above program. Yet given the query

```
!? - pythagtri(3,4,5).
```

it will verify that the given parameters do have the pythagorean property. One way of overcoming this problem in this case would be to define a Prolog rule to generate successive triples of natural numbers with an ordering based on diagonalisation. This is fairly easy to do in this case, but more work is needed to obtain a more general "safe" strategy for handling infinite sets.

For current purposes we limit ourselves to the use of finite given sets. However, it would be premature to say that the use of finite sets completely removes problems of incompleteness due to "unfairness" of a depth first search strategy. One may for example refer to the simple program in [Lloyd'84] :

```
p(a,b).
p(c,b).
p(x,z)  :- p(x,y),p(y,z).
p(x,y)  :- p(y,x).
```

The query p(a,c) will result in a stack overflow in Prolog. It is not immediately clear that one may not be able to write a Z schema that would produce the same behaviour when translated into Prolog.

## 3.2    Negation by Failure

The general translation strategy described above works because the Prolog goals arising from variable declarations never contain negation, and can therefore be guaranteed to instantiate the variables. The Prolog goals arising from predicates may contain negation, but this is no problem as long as all variables in the negated goals have been previously instantiated. Prolog's negation as failure cannot be used to instantiate a variable.

Where negation as failure becomes a real limitation is in the ability to transform Prolog rules for greater efficiency. To illustrate this, consider the following event for inserting a new identifier into a set of identifiers:

$$\boxed{\begin{array}{l} File\ Insert \\ \hline x : N; \\ X, X' : P\ N \\ \hline x \notin X; \\ X' = X \cup \{x\} ; \end{array}}$$

The derived Prolog rule

```
file_insert(_x,X,Xp,NAT)  :-
      member(_x,NAT),
      has_subset(X,NAT),
      has_subset(Xp,NAT),
      not member(_x,X),
      union(X,[_x],Xp).
```

will generate an as yet unused identifier and insert it into an updated file. An attempt to promote the goals has_subset(X,NAT) and not member(_x,X) results in a rule that will behave quite differently:

```
file_insert(_x,X,Xp,NAT)  :-
      has_subset(X,NAT),
      not member(_x,X),
      member(_x,NAT),
      has_subset(Xp,NAT),
      union(X,[_x],Xp).
```

With X instantiated as any non empty set of identifiers and _x uninstantiated, the call to `member(_x,X)` will succeed and hence the negated goal will fail. The promotion of these goals has caused a negated goal to be called before all its variables have been instantiated. This becomes particularly problematic with the use of universal quantification in a schema, if implemented in Prolog as :

```
for_all(Generator,Predicate) :-
        not(call(Generator), not call(Predicate)).
```

Promotion of such a `for_all` goal may lead to less obviously incorrect behaviour. If `Predicate` contains an uninstantiated output parameter, rather than fail, the `for_all` goal may succeed, but return a still uninstantiated variable, and hence provides no constraint on its value. A universally quantified predicate cannot be used to generate values for state variables.

## 4. Modal Analysis in Rule Transformation

To determine the correctness of various transformations, two types of modal information have to be known: the valid static modes of all the library and system defined Prolog rules, and the transformational mode under which the a rule is being transformed.

The latter of these relates to the mode in which a specification is to be animated. The nature of Prolog is such that one may often be able to use a rule to determine the "inputs" that result in a specified "output" as well as determining the "outputs" that result from a specified "input". This is mirrored in the animation of Z specifications by allowing the animator to explore the consequences of event schemas by deriving the pre-states that result in a particular post-state, and *vice versa*.

If it is known in advance the mode in which a rule will be executed (that is, which arguments will be instantiated on call), there may be transformations that can be performed that are not possible in more general cases. Indeed, several different efficient versions of a rule may be created depending on the mode of use.

For instance, in the last example of `file_insert`, the proposed transformation would be correct if the variable _x was instantiated on call.

## 5. Other Constructs in the Z Notation

So far we have only considered simple Z schemas. Axiomatic descriptions and generic schemas involve other considerations which have not been fully worked out. Nor have we considered more complex forms of schema referencing, and the schema combinators. This section sketches some ideas in this area.

### 5.1 Schema Referencing.

Consider the following schemas, in which *schemaB* is a *schemaA* event, and *schemaC* names two occurrences of *schemaA*:

```
┌ schemaA ─────────────────────────┐
│  a, b : N                         │
│                                   │
└───────────────────────────────────┘
```

```
 schemaB ─────────────────────────────┐
 ΔschemaA
 ─────────────────────────
 a > b ;
 a' < b'
 ──────────────────────────────────────┘
```

```
 schemaC ─────────────────────────────┐
 x, y : schemaA
 ─────────────────────────
 x.a = y.a
 ──────────────────────────────────────┘
```

The Prolog translation of *schemaA* is performed in the way previously discussed:

```
schemaA(Nat,_a,_b) :-
    member(_a,Nat),
    member(_b,Nat).
```

The references to *schemaA* in *schemaB*, one of them decorated, are mirrored in the Prolog by two calls to *schemaA* in the obvious way:

```
schemaB(Nat,_a,_b,_ap,_bp) :-
    schemaA(Nat,_a,_b),
    schemaA(Nat,_ap,_bp),
    _a > _b,
    _ap < _bp.
```

In the Prolog translation of schema C, the variables $x$ and $y$ may be treated as tuples as follows:

```
schemaC(Nat,_x,_y) :-
    schemaA(Nat,_xa,_xb),
    _x = (_xa,_xb),
    schemaA(Nat,_ya,_yb),
    _y = (_ya,_yb)
    _xa = _ya.
```

This treatment reflects the Z concept of an instance of a schema being a tuple consisting of instantiations of the components of the schema. Note that the numbers of arguments in *schemaB* and *schemaC* mirror the number of named state variables in each, plus the given set of naturals.

## 5.2 Axiomatic Descriptions

Axiomatic descriptions can be treated as per the following example:

$$square : N \rightarrow N$$

$$\forall n : N \bullet square(n) = n*n$$

These may be translated to:

```
square(Nat,_square) :-
     total_fn(Nat,Nat,_square),
     for_all(member(N,Nat),
          ( is_related(_square,N,Temp),
            Temp is N*N
          )).
```

Since axiomatic descriptions are often given using universal quantification, making such definitions efficient in the Prolog frequently presents a problem. In this case, all possible partial functions will be generated until the square function is found — extremely inefficient. A possible transformation is to take advantage of the knowledge that square is a function, and eliminate the for_all by treating it as follows:

```
square(N,NN) :-
     NN is N*N.
```

However, it is probably better, in general, to consider transformations of axiomatic definitions in the context of particular references.

Axiomatic descriptions can be referenced as, for instance, in the following schema:-

```
ASquare ────────────────────
  size, area : N
  ──────────────────
  area = square(size)
```

Using the Prolog library rule is_related(Rel,X,Y), which instantiates related X, Y pairs in the relation Rel, the *ASquare* schema may be translated into:-

```
asquare(Nat,_size,_area) :-
     member(_size,Nat),
     member(_area,Nat),
     square(Nat,Square),
     is_related(Square,_size,_area).
```

By unfolding the definition of square into the body of asquare, one can envisage a series of transformations leading to the following rule which does not have to generate the entire square function:

```
asquare(Nat,_size,_area) :-
    member(_size,Nat),
    member(_area,Nat),
    _area is _size*_size.
```

### 5.3    Generics

By making given sets used in Z schemas into arguments in Prolog rules, schema have, in a sense, already become generic in the translation — that is, parameterised by the basic sets used in the schema. Explicit generics are treated in just this fashion.

## 6.    Support Tools

A specification tool set is being developed at the University of Surrey to investigate the usefulness of animation in the process of specification. The tool set being developed consists of five main components as shown in the figure below. At present the stages which have been implemented are the editor, translator and transformation system. Some initial ideas have been tried for the animator tool set.

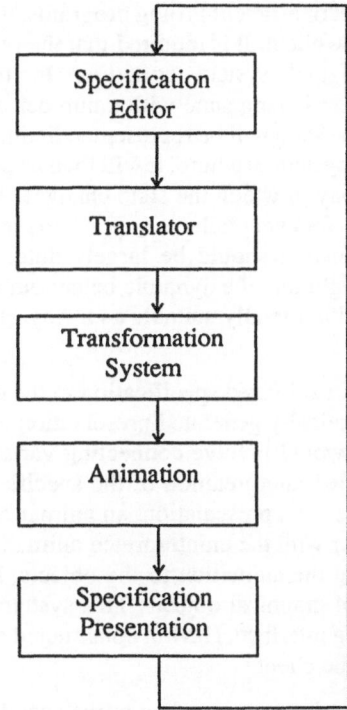

The editor has been developed using the SUN network extensible windowing system (NeWS). It lies somewhere between a syntax directed editor and a text editor. To the level of entering formulae the editor is syntax directed, with schemas being generated and the desired fields added to these schemas. The formulae are then entered into the fields as text. Having created/modified some schemas these may be checked selectively for syntactic correctness. Correct schema inclusion is built up, this is then used by the translator to generate the first version of the executable code.

An advantage of the editor is that it allows schemas to be viewed in any context, within a specification, as it is window based and there is no linear ordering of the schemas as in a text document. This facility allows selected parts of the specification to be viewed easily.

The translator is based on the work of [Krause/Knott'88a] and generates a Prolog program from the database created by the editor.

The transformation system is described in detail in [Dick/Krause'89]. It allows a variety of transformations to be selected by the user for application to Prolog rules. The transformations supported include unfolding, goal promotion/demotion, and removal of duplicate goals. It uses a set of inference rules that encode knowledge about the library of Prolog rules used in the translation process to reason about the goals in the rule. Modal analysis is carried out to ensure the correctness of the transformations performed. The execution of rules may be portrayed on the screen in a way that vividly portrays undesired inefficiency. The tool is itself written in Prolog, and a new graphics front end is being developed which allows easy case selection of schemas, rules and goals using a mouse.

Having obtained a set of efficient Prolog programs, the objective is now to present the system as specified to the client. It is required that the presentation (execution) of the programs reflects the original system structure. In the formalism being used, specifications model a system having state with a number of events over the state. As a first attempt at animation, the state will be represented listing its components, these being partitioned according to the system structure. It will then be possible to initiate events over this state and observe the way in which the state changes. A trace of the events may be recorded, along with reasons for event failures (*e.g.* when pre-condition not satisfied). The generation of such an animation should be largely automatic and should enable the designer to obtain some insight into the dynamic behaviour of the system specified. This presentation however is still not totally suitable as a way of presenting the specification to the client.

For presentation of an animated specification to the client, the designer should be able to start with the automatically generated presentation and enhance this with a more meaningful interface. This would involve connecting variables and events to graphical objects reflecting the intended interpretation of the specification. It is envisaged that to allow the designer to build such a presentation, an animation tool set will be developed. This will supply the designer with the uninterpreted animation, a set of graphical objects and the tools for connecting the animation to the objects. It should be possible for the designer to extend the set of graphical objects. This system would essentially be a high level graphical programming interface. Having constructed the interpreted animation this could then be presented to the client.

The client would now have an interface to the specification which can be used to assess whether the requirements have been met. On feedback from the client the designer can decide whether or not the underlying specification is correct. This will be dependent on the nature of the clients feedback, as some of the comments may simply require modifications to the presentation and not affect the underlying specification.

The development of a tool set for animating specifications is now being carried out in the SERC Animate project. This project started in November 1989 and involves the University of Surrey, Logica Cambridge Limited and Data Logic Limited.

# 7. Experiments

The main experiments that have been carried out have used

- the specification of Telephone Network from [HAYES'87].
- a lift system written in a language closely related to Z [Krause/ Knott'89].
- a specification of a vending machine.

Experiments on the Telephone Network demonstrated the value of rapid prototyping, in that it revealed what we believe to be unintended properties of the specification. The system is specified so that all outstanding requests for a telephone connection are satisfied subject to the constraint that no 'phone may be engaged in more than one connection at a time. If a call is made to an already connected 'phone, that call is queued as an outstanding request until the first caller hangs up. Then the requested connection is made. A Call request in the Prolog prototype reproduces this behaviour. But a request for further solutions produces a state in which the first connection is broken, with connection made to the calling party and the originally connected 'phone being queued as an outstanding request. We suggest that this more perverse behaviour was not an intended feature of the specification.

By applying the kinds of transformations described above, prototyping of the lift specification was practical. Every necessary transformation could be carried out using the tool. It was very tedious carrying out the same transformations entirely by hand. The animation of the lift system prototype was completed by adding a simple interface which explained simply in English where the lift was, and what it was doing, by examining the state of the lift between events. Using this animated interface, it was possible to validate the specification by trying out various situations.

The vending machine example contained several Z language extensions, which seemed to make it harder to make any headway on increasing efficiency. By choosing a small enough set of the natural numbers, though, a prototype that ran in minutes rather than hours was eventually created. With the right inference rules, we felt that transformation would have been considerably easier.

This work highlighted some difficulties with the structures used in the transformation system. In particular, it turns out to be difficult to apply inference rules to sequences of goals that lie inside another goal, like $not/1$, for instance. At present, the goal list is assumed to be a flat structure, and it is difficult to get at goals which are parameters of other goals. A more sophisticated approach would allow transformations to be more generally applicable.

It became apparent during these experiments, that some combinations of transformations occurred frequently. For instance, repeated unfolding of schema references followed by removal of duplicate goals. A language for describing transformational tactics would be an advantage.

The transformation that seemed most often to have a dramatic effect on efficiency was promotion/demotion of goals. Unfolding frequently allowed duplication to be removed, which also helped. Many of the other transformations often had little more than an aesthetic value, only slightly affecting efficiency on the examples we were trying.

## 8.    Conclusions and Further Work

When viewed as a logic language, Prolog is an obvious candidate to use for the rapid prototyping of a specification written in first order predicate logic. It is quite straightforward to generate a Prolog program from a Z schema, given an understanding of Z and the Prolog language. See for example [Stepney/Lord'87]. What we have tried to produce is a general environment whereby a Z specification may be compiled automatically into a Prolog program that correctly prototypes the formal specification. For reasons given, in general, a number of correctness preserving transformations need to be applied to the resulting Prolog program to improve its efficiency. It may well be that a more advanced control structure, as available in Mu-Prolog [Lloyd'84] or one of the concurrent logic languages [Ringwood'89], may allow a more straightforward approach without the need for program transformations. However, at present the program transformation system that has been described in this paper is an essential component in the animation of a formal specification.

The transformations that may be applied to the Prolog rules will in general depend on the required modality. As they are generated by the translation process, only the given sets need be instantiated. This enables the Prolog prototype to be used to fully explore the properties of a specification. All initial states that produce a given output may be generated, as well as all outputs for a given initial state. Any non-determinism in a specification will be quite naturally reflected by the non-determinism in a Prolog prototype. This may be an intended property of the specification, but on the other hand further solutions may show up an unintended underconstraining of the problem by a specification. An example of the latter case was demonstrated, as mentioned, in an experimental prototype of the Telephone Network specification given in [Hayes'87]. Unintented  non-deterministism is a common error in Z specifications, and can be detected as Prolog uses backtracking to generate all possible solutions to rules.

The execution of rules that prototype a Z specification can be used to explore its logical consistency. If, for example, the pre-condition of a schema can never be satisfied, the Prolog rule will always fail. Some of the transformations are forms of partial evaluation, and the simplification of schemas may be possible by studying the effect of transformations on the Prolog. In the case of unsatisfiability, a rule may reduce it to the single unsatisfiable goal, `false`.

Work is under way at Surrey to produce a general purpose interactive graphics front end that will enable the properties of a Prolog animation of a formal specification to be easily and fully explored. We have shown the feasibility and the value of automating the transformational part of a method for prototyping Z in Prolog.

The work has suggested the kinds of in-build knowledge required in such a system, such as modal knowledge relating to system and pmlibrary rules, and inference rules for the underlying set theory used in the specification language.    Useful investigations could be made into heuristics for the application of transformations, and a simple language devised for combining and repeating transformations.

# References

A. J. J. Dick & P. J. Krause [1989], "Computer Aided Transformation of Prolog Specifications", Tech. Report 10-1702, Racal Research Ltd., Worton Drive, Reading

I. Hayes (Ed.) [1987], "Specification Case Studies", Prentice Hall

R. D. Knott & P. J. Krause [1988a], "An approach to animating Z using Prolog" Report A1.1, Alvey Project SE/065, Dept. Maths, Univ. Surrey.

R. D. Knott & P. J. Krause [1988b], "LIBRARY SYSTEM: an example of rapid prototyping of a Z specification in Prolog" Report A1.2, Alvey Project SE/ 065, Dept. Maths, Univ. Surrey.

P. J. Krause, R. D. Knott & P. J. Byers [1989], "Lift System Animation" Report A2.1, Alvey Project SE/065, Dept. Maths, Univ. Surrey.

J. W. Lloyd [1984] "Foundations of Logic Programming", Springer Verlag

G. A. Ringwood [1989], "A Comparative Study of Concurrent Logic Languages", Knowledge Engineering Review, 4 (to appear)

J. M. Spivey [1988], "Understanding Z: a Specification Language and its Formal Semantics" Cambridge Univ. Press

J. M. Spivey [1989], "The Z Notation: a Reference Manual", Prentice Hall

S. Stepney & S. P. Lord [1987], "Formal Specification of an Access Control System", Software Practice and Experience, 17, pp. 575-593

L. Stirling & E. Shapiro [1986], "The Art of Prolog", MIT Press

# From Z Specifications To Functional Implementations

Michael Johnson        Paul Sanders

Systems and Software Engineering Division
British Telecom Research Laboratories

### Abstract

This paper examines work in the Systems and Software Engineering Division at British Telecom Research Laboratories which uses functional languages as part of a formal lifecycle. The use of functional languages allows programs to be quickly produced from formal specifications, and then enables the resulting program to be transformed into a correct implementation that meets the speed and size constraints of the specification.

The paper gives a small but complete example of how an initial functional program can be created from a Z specification, and demonstrates that the run-time behaviour of this program means that it cannot possibly be the final implementation. This initial program is then formally transformed into a program whose run-time behaviour could be considered acceptable.

The main advantage of this approach is that the engineer is working in an executable design language. This allows the benefits that are normally associated with prototyping to be gained in addition to the benefits that are associated with formal specification and program development.

The paper concludes that the use of functional programming technology is a valuable tool for the systematic construction of programs with regard to their specification.

## 1   Introduction

Formal Methods are currently receiving great interest as a means of specifying and implementing both hardware and software systems. The safety-critical and security-related industries use these techniques because of the need to improve the quality of systems, and because of customer demand. There is an increasing amount of evidence to suggest that the use of formal techniques can reduce development costs for other types of systems, since ambiguities are found during specification rather than during design, and reworks to correct faults found during testing are eliminated [2],[16].

Formal notations, and the process of producing a formal specification, are relatively well developed. The remainder of the lifecycle - developing an implementation which is guaranteed to meet the specification - is still a difficult operation, and suffers many limitations. Some of these stem from fitting a formal lifecycle into a traditional lifecycle, particularly taking an abstract specification through to an implementation in traditional imperative languages via a series of "refinement" steps [22]. Completing a formal proof that an implementation meets a specification can be a demanding and tedious task.

As a counter-point to these developments in specification technology, a programming language concept called functional programming [14] has developed to the extent that programs can be viewed as being executable formal specifications [18]. These languages can be manipulated using a technique know as "program transformation" which alters the form of the program but not it's behaviour [15]. Using program transformation it is possible to derive an efficient implementation from an inefficient specification.

This paper proposes that functional programming languages can be used for the design and implementations stages of the formal development lifecycle. The use of functional languages allows programs to be quickly produced from specifications, and facilitates the use transformation to "construct" an implementation which is correct with respect to the specification.

The next section presents an overview of some of the important technical issues involved in formal software development. Section 3 gives an overview of the approach using functional languages within the software development activity. Section 4 gives an example development illustrating the method the authors are advocating. Finally Section 5 contains a summary of the work and pointers to future work. An Appendix is provided to give a brief introduction to functional programming languages and to the notation used in this paper. Further appendices give definitions of all functions used in the paper and proofs of laws used for the transformation.

# 2  Technical Overview

Before introducing the details of our formal implementation approach, the work must be placed in context - a formal lifecycle must be established in which this approach can fit. This requires terms such as "formal specification" and notions of mathematical "proof" to be explored, concentrating on their relevance and importance.

## Formal Specification

The initial functionality of a system is created as a series of vague ideas; these ideas need to be documented to form a specification which can be used for communication with others. The process of producing such a specification helps crystalise the detailed system requirements. This specification then forms the baseline against which development occurs; similarly the final system is tested against this initial specification.

A specification must be clear, unambiguous and consistent; using natural language to express a specification in practice encourages ambiguity and allows inconsistent statements to be expressed - natural language is not a formal language. Ambiguities in a specification are usually discovered during development and testing phases, requiring expensive reworks.

A formal language with a mathematical basis can be used to solve the problem of ambiguous specification and also means that properties such as consistency can be proved of the specification. A formal notation also acts as a "mental tool" encouraging precise and accurate thinking to occur.

There are many examples of formal specification techniques - the example used in this paper is the Z notation [17] developed by the Programming Research Group at Oxford University.

## Non-Functional Requirements

Formal specifications are detailed descriptions of the functionality a system should possess. Formal specifications do not address the so-called non-functional requirements a system can possess. Examples of non-functional requirements include:

- Performance requirements eg. a system must make a response to a request within 10 seconds.

- Reliability/Safety requirements eg. a system should not be out of service for more than 1 hour in every month.

- Product/Marketing requirements eg. a program must run on a specific machine.

- Political/Corporate requirements eg. a program must comply with international standards or corporate technical strategies.

- Others - eg. a chess program must play up to a certain level of competence.

These types of requirements are the major influence on the design process that is used to implement a system that meets the formal (functional) specification.

## Implicit and Explicit Specification

Specifications of functionality can generally be stated using either an implicit or an explicit definition. An implicit specification states what properties a specification should possess whereas an explicit (or constructive) definition shows how a result can be computed. For a given specification an implicit specification will generally result in a specification that is considerably shorter than its explicit counterpart. However the use of implicit specifications creates a need to prove than an explicit definition (implementation) exists.

Whilst implicit specifications have many attractive features many specifications of computing systems are by their very nature explicit, for example calculating the cost of a telephone call, so often an explicit specification can be used in place of an implicit one. See [9] for a detailed explanation of implicit and explicit definitions.

## Refinement and Construction

Having obtained a formal specification, the question arises as to how an implementation can be developed so as to guarantee that the required specification is achieved and that the non-functional aspects of the system have been satisfied.

Several terms (transformation, refinement, reification, synthesis, derivation) are used to describe the processes involved in the creation of implementations from specifications. There are essentially two different approaches in the activity of deriving programs from specifications. For the purposes of this paper these different approaches will be known as "transformation" and "refinement". The use of either of these techniques depends upon whether the specification is explicit or implicit.

The first approach, transformation, manipulates an explicit specification using operations which are pre-proven to maintain correctness i.e. using the "toolkit" of available transformations it is impossible to produce an incorrect implementation. This is sometimes known as "proof by construction" - the way the system is built guarantees correctness.

The second approach, refinement, makes changes to an implicit specification which move it towards an explicit definition, and the correctness of the result must then be proved as a separate proof step.

Creative input is required from the engineer for both techniques. With transformation, improvements occur because of combinations of simple transformations. Knowing which transformations to apply and in what order is the creative input required of the engineer. With refinement, creative input is required to produce the refinement and then to prove that the refinement is correct.

The advantage of transformation is that the proof and the design activity occur in one step whereas two steps are required for the refinement approach. The disadvantage of transformation is that it requires specifications to be written explicitly[1]. Note that this section is a short overview on the subject of Refinement and Construction. The authors are not aware of a definitive reference on this subject. For information on this subject the following references can be consulted [9],[21].

## Proof and Verification

With traditional development techniques a large proportion of total effort goes into product testing, to demonstrate that the product meets the specification and actually works. However, testing cannot prove that a product is correct, only detect situations in which it does not work. To be a verification, testing must be complete in covering every possible operational situation. For real systems this is either prohibitively expensive or impossible.

Mathematical proof, on the other hand, can show that a product is correct with respect to the program's specification. The proof demonstrates that for all situations something is true. In practice, formal proofs might be completed for only the critical kernel of a system, with reasoned argument or proof outlines for the remaining parts.

Verifying that programs meet specifications does not address the question "does the specification describe what the customer wanted anyway?". Validating that a formal specification meets the customers requirements cannot, by definition, be a formal process. One technique that has some merit is to produce prototypes from formal specifications and demonstrate these prototypes to the customer. Unfortunately these prototypes will not generally take into account the non functional requirements the customer has and, as such, the prototype could result in a negative reaction from the customer.

---

[1]Note that the differences between refinement and transformation are not clear cut. Research is being undertaken on transforming (or synthesizing) explicit definitions from implicit specifications [7] and also on the refinement of implementations from specifications by correctness as opposed to proof after the refinement [3]

# 3    From Specifications to Programs

The process of deriving programs from specifications is complicated by the fact that the two activities are often performed in two separate languages. Programmers are faced with a choice in the development process: to model the programming language constructs in the specification language or to implement the specification constructs in the programming language. If the former approach is taken then program designs are written in the specification language and proofs that those programs satisfy the specification itself can be performed. If the latter approach is taken then specifications themselves become programs that can be executed.

A drawback of the first approach is that the programmer is working solely on paper and may have to revert to other techniques such as the creation of prototypes/simulations to explore the implications of various design decisions that have to be reached. From a customer perspective there is the problem that a long gap occurs between initial system specification and final implementation during which time it is likely that the customers requirements will have changed.

The drawback of the second approach is that the nature of a specification often means that they cannot be executed[2] and the execution of such specification-like programs will be very slow.

This paper proposes that a hybrid approach can gain the benefits (and hopefully lose the drawbacks) of both techniques. The hybrid approach is based around the use of an executable (and formal) design and implementation language (in this case a purely functional one). The overall picture of system development consists of the following stages

1. Produce a formal specification of the system to be built using a specification language such as Z.

2. Refine the formal model into an explicit (constructive) representation and carry out associated proof obligations.

3. Transliterate the refined model into a specification like functional program.

4. Using formal transformation techniques transform the functional program into a form that executes at a speed whereby the program can be assessed as a prototype or is itself the final implementation. This process will include data refinement [9] as well as algorithmic transformation.

5. Produce imperative programs that are implementations of the final functional program.

Using this approach programmers design within the framework provided by an executable language, This enables the benefits associated with prototyping to be gained [4]. Prototyping can

**increase** the confidence the programmer has of the system under construction

**enable** alternative designs to be visualised

**allow** customers to gain visibility of the progress of the project.

---

[2]although executable specification languages have been designed for example [6]

The use of a functional language allows the verification and software engineering benefits associated with functional languages to be realised [14]. In particular functional programming technology

**simplifies** the verification task

**allows** access to transformation theories [1] and tools [13].

**produces** fast implementations [11] (if written correctly)

## Stage 1 - Produce formal specification

This stage consists of the normal requirements analysis phase of the software development lifecycle. The product of this phase will be a formal specification of user requirements. Ideally this stage should not be influenced by the rest of the development. There is a danger in our approach that a specification statement is produced that is unnecessarily algorithmic in nature. The authors see no way of preventing this apart from ensuring that the specification has adequate quality review procedures applied to it.

## Stage 2 - Produce an Explicit specification

This is performed using the refinement techniques that are usually associated with formal software development. A different emphasis is however placed upon the refinement. The general method of refinement is to perform a data refinement or series of data refinements (i.e. choose a concrete representation for an abstract data type) and then to work on algorithm design. For the purposes of this approach a minimal refinement should be performed. Such a minimal refinement consists of keeping abstract types unchanged and selecting a simplistic algorithms that will satisfy the specification. It is this approach that enables a program to be developed quickly from a specification.

For example a *sort* specification can be written implicitly as

$$
\begin{array}{|l}
\hline
\_sort[X]_____ \\
in? : \operatorname{seq} X \\
out! : \operatorname{seq} X \\
leq : \operatorname{partialorder} X \\
\hline
out! \text{ isorderedby } leq \wedge out! \text{ permutes } in? \\
\hline
\end{array}
$$

This specification states that the output sequence (*out!*) must be a permutation of the input sequence (*in?*) and that the list must be ordered. Since the specification is generic the partial ordering relation on $X$ must be supplied (the abbreviation *partialorder* is defined in [5]). The relation *isorderedby* is defined by ensuring that adjacent elements of a sequence are ordered.

$$
\begin{array}{|l}
\hline
=[X]=\!\!=\!\!=\!\!=\!\!=\!\!=\!\!=\!\!=\!\!=\!\!=\!\!=\!\!=\!\!=\!\!=\!\!=\!\!=\!\!=\!\!=\!\!= \\
\_ \text{ isorderedby } \_ : \operatorname{seq} X \leftrightarrow \operatorname{partialorder} X \\
\hline
\forall xs : \operatorname{seq} X;\ po : \operatorname{partialorder} X \bullet \\
\quad xs \text{ isorderedby } po \Leftrightarrow \\
\qquad (\forall n : 1 \mathinner{\ldotp\ldotp} (\#xs) - 1 \bullet (xs\ n, xs\ (n+1)) \in po) \\
\hline
\end{array}
$$

To complete the specification the *permutes* relation is defined as follows

$$
\begin{array}{|l}
\hline [X] \\
\hline \_ \text{permutes} \_ : \text{seq}\, X \leftrightarrow \text{seq}\, X \\
\hline \forall\, r, s : \text{seq}\, X \bullet r \text{ permutes } s \Leftrightarrow items\ r = items\ s \\
\hline
\end{array}
$$

This relation is defined by turning each sequence into a bag (using the Z *items* function) and comparing the bags for equality.

An algorithm to satisfy this specification would be to generate all permutations of the input sequence and return a sequence that is ordered. This algorithm can be specified as follows

$$
\begin{array}{|l}
\hline csort[X] \\
\hline in? : \text{seq}\, X \\
out! : \text{seq}\, X \\
leq : \text{partialorder}\, X \\
\hline out! \in \{ s : \text{seq}\, X \mid s \text{ isorderedby } leq \wedge s \in perms\ in? \} \\
\hline
\end{array}
$$

The major intellectual activity required of this refinement is the definition of the *perms* function. The *perms* function can be defined explicitly as follows:

$$
\begin{array}{|l}
\hline [X] \\
\hline perms : \text{seq}\, X \rightarrow \mathbf{P}(\text{seq}\, X) \\
\hline \forall\, s : \text{seq}\, X \bullet \\
\quad perms\ \langle\rangle = \{\langle\rangle\} \wedge \\
\quad perms\ s = \{ a : \mathbf{N};\ p : \text{seq}\, X \mid a \in \text{dom}\, s\ \wedge \\
\quad p \in perms\ (\{a\} \lhd s) \bullet \langle s\ a\rangle \frown p \} \\
\hline
\end{array}
$$

The permutations of an empty sequence is a set containing an empty sequence. The permutations of a non-empty sequence is defined by by taking an element from the sequence and appending it to the permutations of the rest of the sequence.

The usual proof obligations associated with a refinement [20] should be discharged at this stage.

Note that the amount of effort required during this stage depends upon the initial specification. Internal studies have demonstrated that a considerable number of formal specifications are explicit [12] implying that this stage could be trivial or even omitted. However, in the case of very loose, implicit specifications this stage may require a considerable amount of work to achieve an explicit specification.

## Stage 3 - Transliteration

The authors have not produced a definition of the transliteration process (or indeed what constitutes the functional subset of Z). Several examples have been transliterated into functional programs and the experience of such transliterations are documented in [12]. The major concepts identified in the transliteration process were:

- Z schemas represent either states (with invariants) or operations. Operations can be viewed as functions that map the before state (and input values) to the after state and (output values).

- Polymorphism in a functional language is analogous to genericity in a Z specification.

- The basic Z mathematical toolkit can be implemented in a functional language.

- A restricted form of Z set expressions can be implemented using the list iteration expression.

- Non-deterministic specifications can be simulated by returning lists of solutions.

- Lazy evaluation allows potentially infinite lists of solutions to be executed.

For example the *csort* specification can be implemented using the following function (see A for details of the notation employed)

```
csort in? leq -> hd [ s | s <- perms in?; isorderedby leq s]
```

Note that the function takes the head of the list of solutions, this simulates the don't care non-determinism present in the original Z specification.

The *isorderedby* predicate can be transliterated to

```
isorderedby xs po
    -> forall [mem po ((ap xs n),(ap xs (n+1)))
                              | n <- [1..(len xs)-1]]
```

Note that the meaning of the universal quantifier is achieved by generating a list of booleans and ensuring that each boolean is True (the effect of **forall**).

## Stage 4 - Transformation

Program transformation is a methodology for formally manipulating programs using correctness-preserving techniques. These transformations can lead to an increase in efficiency (time, space or both) and thus allows programmers to write clear and understandable programs, with little regard for efficiency, in the knowledge that they can be transformed into more efficient versions.

The most widely used transformation style is the fold/unfold methodology of Burstall & Darlington [15] and is the style we shall use in this paper. The method consists of just six rules: definition, instantiation, unfold, fold, abstraction and law application. These are as follows:

A *Definition* introduces a new equation whose lefthand side does not conflict with an existing lefthand side. For example,

```
ex n k -> map (plusn n) (nat k)
```

One can *instantiate* an equation by giving a value to a variable. For example, the variable n in **ex** can be instantiated as 0 to give

```
ex 0 k -> map (plusn 0) (nat n)
```

To *unfold* an equation is to replace a function call in the right hand side of a definition by its definition (making the appropriate substitutions where necessary). For example, **nat** can be unfolded in

```
ex 0 k -> map (plusn 0) (nat 0)
    to get
ex 0 k -> map (plusn 0) (0 : nat (0 + 1))
```

*Folding* is the opposite of unfolding. That is, an instance of a right hand side of an equation in a clause is replaced by the equation's left hand side (making the appropriate substitutions where necessary). For example, our original definition of **ex** can be folded into the following,

```
foo -> 3 : 4 : map (plusn 3) (nat 5)
    to get
foo -> 3 : 4 : ex 3 5
```

*Abstraction* introduces a local clause into a definition. It is used where two or more clauses have a common subclause. This is not used in this paper so nothing more will be said about this.

One may assert *laws* giving properties about expressions and these (providing they are correct) may be applied to the right hand side of an equation as a rewrite rule. For instance, later on the law: $\mathbf{map\ f\ (map\ g\ l)\ ==\ map\ (f\ o\ g)\ l}$[3][4] shall be used.

```
baa -> map (plusn 3) (map (plusn 4) (nat 7))
    to get
baa -> map ((plusn 3) o (plusn 4)) (nat 7)
```

## Stage 5 - Produce Imperative Implementation

This stage consists of a hand translation from the functional program to an equivalent imperative language. The fact that the ultimate implementation would be done using an imperative language would of course affect the transformations that the programmer used. For example a data transformation may have been performed to produce a data type that simulates the behaviour of an array or a global data area in an imperative language.

Note that this stage has not as yet been attempted by the authors, indeed the state of the art in functional language compiler technology is advancing at a rate which may make such a step unnecessary for certain classes of applications.

# 4   An Example Development

To illustrate the previous section the development of the following example Z specification will be used. The example is a specification of the write procedure of the Unix[5] file system and is based upon the specification in [5] (it has been changed to conform with the definition of Z as stated in [17]).

---

[3]The '==' should be read as 'can be rewritten as'
[4]The 'o' is the function composition symbol
[5]UNIX is a trademark of AT & T, Bell Labs

## Stage 1

The specification is based upon a given set $[BYTE]$ and an assertion is made that $ZERO$ is an element of $BYTE$.

$$
\begin{array}{|l}
\_write _____ \\
\hline
\textit{file}, \textit{file}' : \text{seq } BYTE \\
\textit{offset}? : \mathsf{N} \\
\textit{data}? : \text{seq } BYTE \\
\textit{zero} : \mathsf{N} \to (\mathsf{N} \to BYTE) \\
\textit{pred} : \mathsf{N} \twoheadrightarrow \mathsf{N} \\
\hline
\textit{file}' = (\textit{zero offset}?) \oplus \textit{file} \oplus (\textit{data}? \circ \textit{pred}^{\textit{offset}?}) \\
\textit{zero} = (\lambda\, k : \mathsf{N} \bullet (\lambda\, n : \mathsf{N} \mid 1 \leq n \leq k \bullet ZERO)) \\
\textit{pred} = (\lambda\, n : \mathsf{N} \mid n > 0 \bullet n - 1) \\
\end{array}
$$

This specification writes the *data?* onto the *file* starting at the position *offset?* and produces the new *file'*. The function *zero* is used to create the padding necessary when the *offset?* is greater than the size of the *file*. The *pred* function is used to position the *data?* at the *offset?*. Finally the *file'* is created by overwriting the initial padding with the old file and the new data at the offset.

## Stage 2

The actual *write* operation is explicit and so can be left as it is. The only extra information that is required to be added to the specification is to define the given sets $BYTE$ and what will constitute a natural number. For the purposes of the example we will assume that the set $BYTE$ can be enumerated to be the set of all ASCII characters and that the the set of natural numbers starts at 0 and finishes at a constant called *maxint*.

This can be done by the following Z definition

$$CBYTE ::= a \mid b \mid c \mid d \mid \ldots \mid ZERO$$
$$Cnat == 0 .. maxint$$

The verification that *write* using $BYTE$ and the write that uses $CBYTE$ are the same has not been performed. It should however be a fairly straightforward activity.

## Stage 3

To transliterate this specification the following issues must be addressed.

- A programming representation for the given set $CBYTE$ and the element ZERO must be selected.

- The equivalent data structures for Z sequences and the concrete natural numbers must be implemented.

- A mechanism that enables $\lambda$-abstractions to be defined must be implemented. This will enable **zero** and **pred** to be defined.

- The functions for **override**, **composition** and **iteration** have to be implemented.

The simplest representation for the type $CBYTE$ uses the built-in character type of functional languages and hence $ZERO$ can be represented as the blank character. This is done by the following program

```
type BYTE = char
ZERO::char
ZERO -> ' '
```

The first statement defines a type synonym BYTE that is the same as char. The second and third statements define a constant function **ZERO** that always returns the blank character.

The implementation of a Z sequence is constructed in an identical way to the definition of a sequence in Z itself; it is a function from the natural numbers to the sequence type.

A Z function (more generally a relation) is defined to be a set of pairs. For example the square function would be displayed as $\{(1, 1), (2, 4), (3, 9), (4, 16), (5, 25)\,etc\}$. It is natural that the implementation should follow the definition. The first task is to represent a set in the functional programming language. The easiest way to do this is to use the list construct. A set is defined to be a list that has no repetitions.

```
type 'a set = 'a list
mkset::'a list -> 'a set
```

The first statement creates a type synonym **set** to be equivalent to a list. The **'a** is used to indicate that the type is polymorphic i.e. this can be a set of numbers, characters, lists of numbers etc. Note that this polymorphic property of functional programming languages allows Z generic structures to be implemented. The second statement gives the signature of the function **mkset** that turns a list into a set i.e. the repetitions are removed. The definition of **mkset** together with all the functions used in this paper is given in appendix C.

The Z definition of a relation is

$$X \leftrightarrow Y == \mathbf{P}(X \times Y)$$

Where the $X$ and $Y$ declare that this operator is generic.
The functional definition of a relation follows the Z definition

```
type 'x 'y rel = ('x,'y) set
```

A Z sequence can be represented simply as a relation from the non zero natural numbers to the element set [6]
A type definition suitable to represent a sequence can be defined as follows

```
type 'x seq = Nat 'x rel
```

---

[6] a Z sequence is actually a finite partial function whose domain is a contiguous subset of the natural numbers starting from 1

Note that this type declaration doesn't enforce the fact that the domain must start from 1 and be contiguous; operations using sequences must ensure this.

The other Z datatype used used in the example specification is the set of natural numbers *Cnat*. To implement this the functional language integer type **num** can be used.

```
type Nat = num
nat::'a set
nat n -> n:(nat n+1)
nats::'a set
nats -> take maxint (nat 0)
```

The functions **nats** and **nat** have been defined in order to generate a list of all numbers starting from **0** and ending at maxint (the take function returns n elements from the front of a list).

λ-abstractions of Z can be re-written as Z set comprehensions (page 61 of [17]). Hence *zero* and *pred* can be written as

$$zero\ k = \{n : \mathsf{N} \mid 1 \leq n \leq k \bullet (n, ZERO)\}$$
$$pred = \{n : \mathsf{N} \mid n > 0 \bullet (n, n - 1)\}$$

These Z set constructs can now be transliterated into list iterators as follows:

```
pred::Nat Nat rel
pred -> [(n,n-1) | n <- nats; n > 0]

zero::Nat->BYTE seq
zero k -> [(n,ZERO) | n <- nats; 1 <= n <= k]
```

The remaining functions must be given before the definition of write is complete. For example relational composition, as defined on page 97 of [17], can be transliterated into the following list iteration.

```
comp::'y 'z rel->'x 'y rel->'x 'z rel
comp s r -> [(x,z)|(x,y1)<-r; (y2,z)<-s; y1= y2]
```

Note that this definition requires two variables **y1** and **y2** to be used instead of just one in the Z definition. A more sophisticated list iteration construct such as that illustrated in [8] would be able to directly implement the Z definition.

The iteration function of Z (usually denoted by superscripting a number to a relation as in *pred*$^{offset?}$ can be defined (for the non negative cases) as follows

$$
\begin{array}{|l}
\hline
\rule{0pt}{2.5ex}[X]\\
\hline
iter : \mathsf{N} \rightarrow (X \leftrightarrow X) \rightarrow (X \leftrightarrow X)\\
\hline
\forall R : X \leftrightarrow X \bullet\\
\qquad iter\ 0\ R = idX \land\\
\qquad \forall k : \mathsf{N} \bullet iter\ (k + 1)\ R = (iter\ k\ R) \circ R\\
\hline
\end{array}
$$

where *id* returns the identity relation for a given set.

This can be implemented by the following function

```
iter::Nat->'x 'x rel->'x 'x rel
iter 0 r -> id (union (domain r) (range r))
iter (n+1) r -> comp (iter n r) r
```

Note that this definition uses the **id** of the **union** of the **domain** and **range** of the relation in the 0'th iteration case instead of the **id** of the type variable **X** in the Z definition. A better implementation of a Z relation would "carry" around the source and destination sets that the relation is defined on. This would allow a much closer correspondence to the notion of a mathematical relation. However, for the purposes of this example the implementation using just the pairs of the relation will suffice.

The functional override operation is defined in a similar manner.

Using these functions **write** can now be defined as follows

```
write::seq BYTE X Nat X seq BYTE -> seq BYTE
write (file,offset,data) -> file'
where file'
        -> override (override (zero offset) file)
                    (comp data (iter offset pred))
```

The input to the function is the old file, the offset and the data to be written. The output is the new file. This function can now be compiled by a suitable functional programming language implementation

## Stage 4

The definition of **write**, whilst being executable, is so inefficient as to be unusable for anything except demonstration purposes. The following execution times have been recorded [7].

| Test Call | Time (Seconds) |
|---|---|
| write "hello" 0 "there" | 0.36 |
| write "hello" 1 "there" | 4.86 |
| write "hello" 2 "there" | 9.18 |
| write "hello" 3 "there" | 13.41 |
| write "hello" 4 "there" | 17.59 |
| write "hello" 5 "there" | 23.04 |
| write "hello" 10 "there" | 42.93 |
| write "hello" 100 "there" | 341.51 |

This data suggests that the execution time increases linearly with respect to the size of the offset. Extrapolating these figures to a case when the offset is 1 000 000 (equating to a file that is 1 megabyte in size) the time to complete the test case would be approximately 46 days. Files of size 1 megabyte are not large by computing terms and hence this implementation cannot be considered finished. To derive a usable version of **write** program transformation is used.

The execution speeds indicate that the size of the offset directly affects the performance of the function. Examining the text of **write** shows that the part of the function that it is directly affected by the size of the offset is the following statement

---

[7]using the lml compiler on a Sun 3/60

```
iter pred offset
```

For ease of presentation a new function s will be defined as follows

```
s::Nat->Nat Nat rel
s offset -> iter pred offset
```

For the purposes of transformation the list iteration construct used in the last chapter is replaced with calls to the higher order functions map and filter. For example the pred function is rewritten as follows

```
pred::Nat Nat rel
pred -> map neg (filter nonzero nats)
        and nonzero n -> n > 0
neg::Nat->Nat Nat rel
neg x -> (x,x-1)
```

During the transformation the following laws will be used which are stated now so that they may be seen before they are used. Note that the justifications for these laws are in Appendix B.

The laws are stated in the form 'equation1 == equation2'. This means that an instance of equation1 can always be replaced by equation2, and vice versa, in a program clause and that the semantics of the clause will be unchanged. All variables in laws are universally quantified. The laws are defined for all instances of the appropriate argument type.

**Law 1** : pred == map neg (nat 1)
**Law 2** : (map f) o (map g) l == map (f o g) l
**Law 3** : fst o neg == plus1
**Law 4** : snd o neg == elem_id
**Law 5** : map elem_id l == l
**Law 6** : mkset ((mkset l1) ++ (mkset l2)) == mkset (l1++l2)
**Law 7** : mkset ((map plus1 nats) ++ nats) == nats
**Law 8** : iter pred (k+1) == map (plusn k) (drop k nats)

Proceed by considering all possible cases of the variable offset. Since it is numeric, these are 0 and n+1. Start with the first case, when offset is 0, ie. we instantiate offset as 0,

```
s 0 -> iter pred 0
```

Now, unfold the call to iter, using iter r 0 -> id(union(domain r)(range r)) we have

```
=> id (union (domain pred)(range pred))
```

And now unfold range and domain,

```
=> id (union (mkset (map fst pred))
             (mkset (map snd pred)))
```

The call to pred can be eliminated by applying law 1,

```
=> id (union (mkset (map fst (map neg (nat 1))))
             (mkset (map snd (map neg (nat 1)))))
```

This contains two function compositions (both involving only `map`) so the composition operator can be folded into this expression to give

```
=> id (union (mkset ((map fst o map neg) (nat 1)))
             (mkset ((map snd o map neg) (nat 1))))
```

Law 2 states that map distributes over the composition operator and so applying this law to the expression will give move the composition operator inside a single map call. Applying law 2 to the expression gives

```
=> id (union (mkset (map (fst o neg) (nat 1)))
             (mkset (map (snd o neg) (nat 1))))
```

Each of the function compositions can be transformed into a single, and more efficient, function. These transformations are encapsulated in Laws 3 and 4 [8] so now apply these laws to the definition. Firstly, applying Law 3,

```
=> id (union (mkset (map plus1 (nat 1)))
             (mkset (map (snd o neg) (nat 1))))
```

Now, apply Law 4,

```
=> id (union (mkset (map plus1 (nat 1)))
             (mkset (map id (nat 1))))
```

Applying the identity function to all the elements of a list will leave the contents of the list unchanged. Law 5 formally states this and is now applied,

```
=> id (union (mkset (map plus1 (nat 1)))
             (mkset (nat 1)))
```

Now unfold union,

```
=> id (mkset ((mkset (map plus1 (nat 1))) ++
              (mkset (nat 1))))
```

Here is a situation in which Law 6 may be applied which enables the removal of the nested `mksets`. Applying Law 6 gives,

```
=> id (mkset ((map plus1 (nat 1)) ++ (nat 1)))
```

Since the set of natural numbers contains no duplicates it would seem likely that it would be possible to remove the `mkset` from this expression. Law 7 tells how to do this and is applied to this expression,

```
=> id (nat 1)
```

This gives a definition for s when the argument is 0. Next, the case when `offset` is the general value, k+1, say, must be considered. So instantiate `offset` as k+1 in the original definition for s,

```
s    -> iter pred (k+1)
```

---

[8]Appendix B shows how the transformation was achieved

This can be transformed using a similar strategy to that used above. However, for the sake of clarity law 8 has been defined to express this result. The full transformation can be found in Appendix B. Our final result, then, is obtained by applying Law 8,

```
s::Nat->Nat Nat rel
s 0 -> id (nat 1)
s offset -> map (plusn offset)
                (drop offset nats)
plusn :: Nat->Nat->(Nat,Nat)
plusn n x -> ((n+x),x)
```

The new version of write can now be defined as follows

```
write::seq BYTE X num X seq BYTE -> seq BYTE
write(file,offset,data) ->
    override (override (zero offset) file) (comp data s)
    where s 0     -> id (nat 1)
          s (k+1) -> map (plusn (k+1)) (drop offset nats)
```

The timings for the new version of write using this are as follows

| Test Call | Time(Seconds) |
|---|---|
| write "hello" 0 "there" | 0.30 |
| write "hello" 1 "there" | 0.31 |
| write "hello" 2 "there" | 0.26 |
| write "hello" 3 "there" | 0.29 |
| write "hello" 4 "there" | 0.34 |
| write "hello" 5 "there" | 0.29 |
| write "hello" 10 "there" | 0.31 |
| write "hello" 100 "there" | 0.26 |

The figures differ due to the inaccuracies of the Unix time command. The figures show that the affect of the execution time upon the size of the offset is now negligible. We now have a program that runs at a speed which may be usable in the given application domain.

The function could be further transformed into a version that uses the built in list data type of a functional language instead of the Z style sequence. The same techniques as shown above can then be used to prove that the program with the changed data type still meets the specification.

# 5   Summary and Further Work

This paper has presented an approach to the implementation of systems using functional languages and transformation, rather than the traditional formal methods approach of refinement followed by proof. The technique has been successfully applied to a realistic example, including justifications of the transformation laws used.

The use of transformation demonstrated major improvements in both space and time performance. These improvements were achieved knowing that the final program still met its specification.

The performance of a functional language implementation could be acceptable in many situations. Functional language implementation technology is improving at a significant rate [11], making this approach increasingly viable.

If for performance, commercial or political reasons an implementation has to be achieved using an imperative programming language then the functional program can be "transliterated" into an imperative language. This has not yet been attempted but is one aspect of future work that needs to be done in the development and testing of this programming method.

Experience suggests that this method could be suitable for industrial usage, the "language-oriented" approach used in transformation is attractive to existing software engineers in that the formal specification/design language is a programming language.

A major advantage of this method is that executable programs exist early in the development life-cycle. This builds confidence in developers, and allows early demonstration to customers. This contrasts with refinement where nothing is executable until the very end of the process.

An initial stage of refinement may still be needed where specifications use an implicit style as the transliteration can only be applied to an explicit specificiation. Experience, however, suggests that many specifiers naturally use an explicit style, particularly when initially using formal techniques.

Sophisticated support tools are needed to make this approach viable. Collaborative research and development work is in progress with York University. Indeed much of the tranformation and proof work in this paper was completed using the Starship interactive transformation environment [13] from York. Current research in this area is concentrating on developing a "meta-language" which will allow programmers to create "meta-programs" that will perform transformation and proof of programs [10].

In conclusion, this method potentially has a great deal to offer in terms of both the introduction and practical use of formal methods within the software development lifecycle. Further work is required to develop/document the approach and to produce usable support tools.

# 6  Acknowledgements

The authors would like to acknowlege the contribution made by Siew Poh Lee to this work, to the Director of Communications Systems Technology, Research and Technology, British Telecom for permission to publish this paper and for comments made by Peter Breuer and Jonathan Bowen (of the Oxford PRG) and Sinclair Stockman (BTRL).

# References

[1] R.S Bird. Algebraic identities for program calculation. *The Computer Journal*, 32:122–126, 1989.

[2] I.H. Sorenson B.P. Collins, J.E. Nicholls. Introducing formal methods: The CICS experience with Z. IBM, Hursley Park, 1987. Technical Report.

[3] P. Gardiner C. Morgan, K. Robinson. On the refinement calculus. Oxford University Technical Monograph - PRG-70, 1988.

[4] Brooks F. P. No silver bullet - essence and accidents of software engineering. *Computer*, 1987.

[5] I. Hayes. *Specification Case Studies*. Prentice-Hall International, 1987.

[6] P. Henderson. The Metoo method of software design. Technical report, University of Stirling, 1985.

[7] M. Henson. Program development in the constructive set theory tk5. University of Essex - Technical Report.

[8] H. Pull J. Darlington, A. Field. The unification of functional and logic languages. Technical report, Imperial College, London, 1986.

[9] C.B Jones. *Systematic Software Development Using VDM*. Prentice-Hall International, 1986.

[10] M.Firth J.Patel, C.Runciman. Starship meta-language requirements - discussion document. University of York project Deliverable.

[11] T. Johnsson L. Augustsson. The Chalmers Lazy ML compiler. *The Computer Journal*, 32, 1989.

[12] S. P. Lee. Executing Z specifications. Technical Report RT31/009/88, British Telecom Research Laboratories, 1988. Research and Technology Memorandum.

[13] C Runciman M. Firth. Starship reference manual. Department of Computer Science, University of York, 1989.

[14] S. Peyton-Jones. *Software Engineering - The Decade of Change*, chapter 9. Peter Peregrinus Ltd, 1986.

[15] J Darlington R.M Burstall. A transformation system for developing recursive programs. *Journal of the ACM*, 24:44–67, 1977.

[16] S. J. Sadler. Nuclear reactor protection software - an application of VDM. Technical report, Rolls-Royce and Associates Limited.

[17] M. Spivey. *The Z Notation - A Reference Manual*. Prentice Hall International, 1989.

[18] D. Turner. Functional programs as executable specifications. *Phil. Transactions of the Royal Society*, 312:363–388, 1984.

[19] D. Turner. An overview of Miranda. *SIGPLAN Notices*, December 1986.

[20] J. Wilson. A case study in Z refinement. British Telecom Research Laboratories, 1989. Technical Report.

[21] T.S.E Maibaum W.M. Turski. *The Specification Of Computer Programs*. International Computer Science Series, 1987.

[22] J.B. Wordsworth. Specifying and refining programs with Z. In *Proceedings of Second IEE/BCS Conference on Software Engineering*, 1988.

# A    Functional Programming

Functional languages are members of the class of declarative languages; ie. languages in which programs have a declarative reading which asserts properties of the function defined by the program, as well as an algorithmic reading which describes how the functions are to be computed.

Programs consist of a set of function definitions and/or data structures which are to be computed. Executing a functional program involves reducing an expression using the equations as left to right rewrite rules until the original function call contains no defined functions, only constants or constructor functions (the equivalent of data structures).

The major feature of functional programming languages is that they do not allow side-effects. There are no equivalents of global variables or non-automatic local variables as found in imperative languages such as C. The variables a function operates on must be supplied to it via its parameter list and returned as its result.

In this paper a notation will be used that is similar to Miranda [9] [19]. Functions are defined by stating the signature of the function and then defining the function using sets of pattern matching equations. For example the **or** operation of Z can be defined as

```
zor :: (bool X bool) -> bool
zor (False,False) -> False
zor (False,True) -> True
zor (True,False) -> True
zor (True,True) -> True
```

This function can then be used in the following way

```
f :: num -> num
f x -> if (zor ((x=3),(5>6))) 4 6
```

Here **f 3** would return **4**, anything else will return **6**.

A function can take only one parameter and return one result. Functions that use more than one input must make a tuple of the input (as in the **zor** example) or use the higher order capabilities of functional languages as described later on.

Modern functional programming languages have a powerful and flexible type system. New data types can be defined using the following notation

```
data bool = True | False
```

Which declares the data type **bool** to be True or False. Data types can be recursively defined for example a list can be defined as follows

```
data 'a list = Nil | Cons ('a X 'a list)
```

---

[9]Miranda is a trademark of Research Software Limited

The 'a indicates that the list type is polymorphic. This means that the list can be of any type e.g. a list of number, a list of characters, a list of list of numbers etc. For example a list of numbers would be formed by the following statement

```
x :: num list
x -> Cons(3,Cons(4,Cons(6,Nil)))
```

For efficiency reasons most functional programming languages have the list type built into the language and use a clearer notation for lists. The expression [] is used to denote **Nil** and (x:xs) denotes **Cons(x,xs)**.

To examine elements in a list functions can pattern match on data types. For example a function that counts the number of elements in a list can be defined as follows

```
len :: 'a list -> num
len [] -> 0
len (x:xs) -> 1 + len xs
```

The function is defined by stating that the length of an empty list is **0** and the length of a non empty list is **1** added to the length of the tail of the list.

Type synonyms can be defined using the following notation

```
type BYTE = char
```

This is analogous to the abbreviation facility of Z mentioned in the last chapter.

Modern functional languages are termed higher-order. That is, functions may be both passed as parameters and returned as values. This enables generic functions to be easily constructed and functions to be defined that have more than one parameter. The previous **zor** function can be rewritten using a higher order function as follows

```
zor :: bool->(bool->bool)
zor False False -> False
zor False True  -> True
zor True False  -> True
zor True True   -> True
```

The signature of this function states that the function **zor** takes a **bool** as its parameter and returns a function that takes a **bool** as its parameter and returns a **bool** as the result. The function can hence be applied as follows

```
(zor (1=1)) (5>6)
```

or

```
zor (1=1) (5>6)
```

A commonly used higher-order function is called **map**. This function takes a list and a function and produces a new list by applying the function to each element of the input list. It can be defined as follows

```
map :: 'a list->(('a->'b)->'b list)
map [] f -> []
map (x:xs) f -> f x: map xs f
```

Map can for example be used to find the lengths of a list of lists

```
map len [[1,345,2,34],[4,5,6,7,8],[1]]
```

returns

```
[4,5,1]
```

A particularly useful construct that is found in some functional programming languages is the list iterator. This is similar to the set comprehension of Z. An example list iterator could return the list of lists that have more than three elements with the length of the list as the first element.

```
gtr3::num list list->num list list
gtr3 x -> [(len l):l | l<-x; len l > 3]
gtr3 [[1,345,2,34],[4,5,6,7,8],[1]]
```

returns

```
[[4,1,345,2,34],[5,4,5,6,7,8]]
```

The variable l in the list iterator takes the value of each element of x. The output will be a list whose elements are of the form (len l):l and these must satisfy the condition len l > 3.

List iterators are actually a syntactic device that can be replaced by calls to standard higher order functions. The above example can be replaced by

```
gtr3::num list list->num list list
gtr3 x -> map addlen (filter g3 x)
          where addlen l -> (len l): l
          and   g3 l -> len l > 3
```

Filter selects all elements of a list that satisfy the function passed to it (in this example g3).

Some functional languages have a function evaluation strategy called lazy evaluation. This means that a parameter in a function call will only be evaluated when it is known that it is absolutely necessary to do so, and it will only be evaluated as far as is required. This enables programs to be written that manipulate potentially infinite data structures. For example the following function will return the list of all numbers starting at n.

```
nat n = n : nat (n+1)
```

Using a lazy evaluation strategy this function can be used in the following program and will terminate.

```
take 3 (nat 10)
```

returns

```
[10,11,12]
```

where take n returns the first n elements of a list.

# B   Law Justifications

In this section, for completeness, the justification for each law used in the transformation is given. Where possible a formal proof of the law is given but in some cases such a proof is yet to be completed and as such the truth of the law is argued in an informal manner.

**Law 1:** pred == map neg (nat 1)

| **Proof** | Unfold pred | map neg (filter nonzero nats) == map neg (nat 1) |
|---|---|---|
| | Unfold nats | map neg (filter nonzero (0 : nat 1)) |
| | | == map neg (nat 1) |
| | Unfold filter | map neg (if (nonzero 0) |
| | | (0 : (filter nonzero (nat 1))) |
| | | (filter nonzero (nat 1))) |
| | | == map neg (nat 1) |
| | Unfold nonzero | map neg (if (0 > 0) |
| | | (0 : (filter nonzero (nat 1))) |
| | | (filter nonzero (nat 1))) |
| | | == map neg (nat 1) |
| | Simpllify and | |
| | Unfold if | map neg (filter nonzero (nat 1)) |
| | | == map neg (nat 1) |

□

**Law 2:** map f (map g l) == map (f o g) l

| **Proof** | By cases on l | |
|---|---|---|
| | **case (i):** | l = ⊥ |
| | ie. | map f (map g ⊥) == map (f o g) ⊥ |
| | Unfold map twice | ⊥ = ⊥ |
| | **case (ii):** | l = [] |
| | ie. | map f (map g []) == map (f o g) [] |
| | Unfold map twice | [] == [] |
| | **case (iii):** | l = l1:l2 |
| | ie. | map f1 (map g1 l2) == map (f1 o g1) l2 |
| | | ⊢ map f (map g (l1:l2)) == map (f o g) (l1:l2) |
| | Unfold map twice | map f1 (map g1 l2) == map (f1 o g1) l2 |
| | | ⊢ f (g l1) : map f (map g l2) |
| | | == (f o g) l1 : map (f o g) l2 |
| | Unfold (o) | map f1 (map g1 l2) == map (f1 o g1) l2 |
| | | ⊢ f (g l1) : map f (map g l2) |
| | | == f (g l1) : map (f o g) l2 |
| | Apply hypothesis | map f1 (map g1 l2) == map (f1 o g1) l2 |
| | | ⊢ f (g l1) : map (f o g) l2 |
| | | == f (g l1) : map (f o g) l2 |

□

**Law 3:** fst o neg == plus1

Rather than give an explicit proof of this law, the left hand side of the law will be transformed into the right hand side (Note that this does in fact consitute a proof of the law).

| Define | law3 x -> (fst o neg) x |
|--------|------------------------|
| Unfold (o) | law3 x -> fst (neg x) |
| Unfold neg | law3 -> fst (x+1,x) |
| Unfold fst | law3 x -> x+1 |
| Fold plus1 | law3 x -> plus1 x |

**Law 4:** snd o neg == elem_id

**Proof**

| Uncurry | (snd o neg) x == elem_id x |
|---------|---------------------------|
| Unfold (o) | snd (neg x) == elem_id x |
| Unfold neg | snd (x+1,x) == elem_id x |
| Unfold snd | x == elem_id x |
| Unfold elem_id | x == x |

□

**Law 5:** map elem_id l == l

**Proof** By cases on l

| case (i): | l = ⊥ |
|-----------|-------|
| ie. | map elem_id ⊥ == ⊥ |
| Unfold map | ⊥ == ⊥ |
| case (ii): | l = [ ] |
| ie. | map elem_id [ ] == [ ] |
| Unfold map | [ ] == [ ] |
| case (iii): | l = l1:l2 |
| ie. | map elem_id l2 |
| | == l2 ⊢ map elem_id (l1:l2) == l1:l2 |
| Unfold map | map elem_id l2 |
| | == l2 ⊢ elem_id l1 : map elem_id l2 |
| | == l1:l2 |
| By hypothesis | map elem_id l2 == l2 ⊢ elem_id l1 : l2 == l1 : l2 |
| Unfold elem_id | map elem_id l2 == l2 ⊢ l1 : l2 == l1 : l2 |

□

**Law 6:** mkset ((mkset l1)++(mkset l2)) == mkset (l1++l2)

**Justification** If one removes duplicates from each list and then joins them together the resulting list may still contain duplicates. Performing a mkset on this new list will then give a list equivalent to joining the two lists together having removed all duplicates. This is exactly what the right hand side of the law says.

□

**Law 7:** mkset ((map plus1 nats)++nats) == nats

**Justification** The map function call is going to return the (infinite) list of natural numbers bar the first. If the list of natural numbers is added (appended) to this list the result will be a list containing 2 copies of each natural number, except for 0 which will occur only once. Removing duplicates from this list will therefore leave one copy of each natural number.

□

**Law 8:** iter neg (k+1) == map (plusn k) drop k nats

**Justification**    Unfold iter to get

comp (iter neg k) neg ==

                    map (plusn k) drop k nats

Unfold iter again to get

comp (comp (iter neg (k-1)) neg) neg

                       == map (plusn k) drop k nats

`Self_comp` can be continually unfolded until the numeric
argument reaches 0. This will occur after k unfolds and
gives

comp (comp ... (comp (iter neg 0) neg) ... neg) neg. In the
transformation section the call to `self_comp` with zero
as the numeric argument was transformed to map pair nats,
and so this can be substituted into the subexpression above
to give

comp (comp ... (comp (map pair nats) neg) ... neg) neg.
Having eliminated `self_comp` work now on comp, working
innermost-first. Unfold the innermost call to comp,

comp (comp ...

    (forward_comp neg (map pair nats) neg) ... neg) neg.
This expression can be transformed to

comp (comp ... (map (plusn 1) nats) neg ... neg) neg.
Unfolding some more calls to comp reveals that 1 is added to
each number for each call. There are k of these calls so after
unfolding all of the calls to comp there will have been added
k to the each of the natural numbers. Each comp unfold
loses the first element of the list its being applied to.
Therefore, the first k numbers from the list shall be lost.

□

# C  Definitions

Z library functions and type definitions
used in this paper.

```
type 'a set = 'a list

type 'x 'y rel = ('x,'y) set

type Nat = num

nat::Nat->Nat set
nat n -> n : nat n + 1

nats::Nat set
nats -> nat 0

type 'x seq = Nat 'x rel

mkset :: 'a list -> 'a set
mkset [] -> []
mkset es
 -> mkset' [] es
   where
   mkset' acc (h:t)
     -> if (mem acc t)
          (mkset' acc t)
          (h:(mkset'(h:acc)
                    t))

mem :: 'a set -> 'a -> bool
mem [] e -> False
mem (h:t) e
  -> zor (e = h) (mem t e)

union :: 'x set -> 'x set
                -> 'x set
union x y -> mkset (x ++ y)

zor :: bool -> bool -> bool
zor False False -> False
zor False True  -> True
zor True  False -> True
zor True  True  -> True


pairs xs ys
  -> rfold (++) [] (map f xs)
```

```
   where
   f x -> map (pair2 x) ys
   and
   pair2 x y -> (x,y)

comp :: 'y 'z rel -> 'x 'y rel
                      -> 'x 'z rel
comp r1 r2
  -> map fstlast
        (filter sndtrdeq
                (pairs r2 r1))
     where
     fstlast ((x,y1),(y2,z))
        -> (x,z)
     and
     sndtrdeq ((x,y1),(y2,z))
        -> y1 = y2

domsub1 :: 'x 'y rel
            -> 'x -> 'x 'y rel
domsub1 [] s -> []
domsub1 ((ft,snd):tl) s ->
  if (ft = s)
    (domsub1 tl s)
    ((ft, snd)
          : domsub1 tl s))

domsubs :: 'x set -> 'x 'y rel
                      -> 'x 'y rel
domsubs [] r -> r
domsubs (ft:tl) r
    -> domsubs tl (domsub1 r ft)

override ::'x 'y rel ->'x 'y rel
                        ->'x 'y rel
override r1 r2 -> union new_r r2
   where
   new_r -> domsubs
              (domain r2) r1

elem_id :: 'x -> 'x
elem_id x -> x

fst :: 'x X 'y -> 'x
fst (x,y) -> x

snd :: 'x X 'y -> 'y
snd (x,y) -> y
```

```
domain :: 'x 'y rel -> 'x set
domain r -> mkset (map fst r)


range :: 'x 'y rel -> 'y set
range r -> mkset (map snd r)


id :: 'x set -> 'x 'x rel
id s -> map pair s


iter :: 'x 'x rel -> num
            -> 'x 'x rel
iter r 0
    -> id (union (domain r)
                 (range r))
iter r (k+1)
    -> comp (iter r k) r
```

Other functions used in the paper

```
append ::'a list -> 'a list
                 -> 'a list
append x [] -> x
append [] x -> x
append (x:xs) y
    -> x : (append xs y)

-- Note that
--   A ++ B
-- is equvalent to
--   append A B


upto :: num -> num -> [num]
upto x 0 -> []
upto x y -> x : upto x+1 y-1

map :: ('a -> 'b)
          -> 'a list -> 'b list
map f []-> []
map f (x:xs)
   -> f x : map f xs

rfold::('a -> 'b -> 'b)
       -> 'b -> 'a list -> 'b
rfold f z [] -> z
rfold f z (h:t)
      -> f h (rfold f z t)
```

```
forall:: bool list -> bool
forall = rfold (zand) True


take:: num -> 'x list
              -> 'x list
take 0 x -> []
take n [] -> []
take n (x:xs)
    -> x:take (n-1) xs


drop:: num -> 'x list -> 'x list
drop 0 x -> x
drop n [] -> []
drop n (x:xs) -> drop (n-1) xs


filter :: ('a -> bool) -> 'a list
                      -> 'a list
filter f [] -> []
filter f (x:xs)
   -> if (f x) (x:filter f xs)
               filter f xs
```

The write example

```
type BYTE = char
ZERO::char
ZERO -> ' '


pred::Nat Nat rel
pred -> map neg (filter nonzero
                        nats)
         where neg x -> (x,x-1)
         and nonzero n -> n > 0


zero:: Nat -> BYTE seq
zero k -> map z (filter inrange
                        nats)
         where
         z n -> (n,ZERO)
         and
         inrange n -> 1<=n<=k


write::seq BYTE X Nat X seq BYTE
                    -> seq BYTE
write(file,offset,data) -> file'
where file'
    -> override
         (override
```

```
                    (zero offset)
                            file)
              (data comp
                    (iter offset
                            pred))
```

The transformed version of write

```
write::seq BYTE X num X seq BYTE
                        -> seq BYTE
write(file,offset,data) ->
   override (override
                 (zero offset)
                         file)
             (comp data s)
   where
   s 0 -> id (nat 1)
   s (k+1)
       -> map (plusn (k+1))
              (drop (k+1) nats)

plusn :: Nat -> Nat -> (Nat,Nat)
plusn n x -> ((n + x), x)
```

# A Generalisation of Bags in Z

Ian Hayes*

Department of Computer Science,
University of Queensland,
St. Lucia, 4067
Australia

February 20, 1990

## Abstract

As a mathematical theory for use in specification, bags (in Z) are currently a poor cousin to the better known and more widely used theories such as sets, relations, functions and sequences. By both expanding the range of operators available on bags, and generalising the basic notion of bags themselves, bags can be turned into a more useful theory that is applicable to a wider range of problems.

The generalisation of bags introduced in this paper allows the frequency of occurrence of an element in a bag to be negative, as well as the usual zero or positive. The operators on bags generalise neatly to negative frequencies. Use of the generalised bags is illustrated by the examples of modelling a simple banking system and physical units.

# 1  Generalised Bags

The model used for bags, with elements taken from some set $X$, in both [Hay87, page 47] and [Spi89, page 127] is a function from $X$ to the strictly positive natural numbers. In addition, this function is

---

partial: it is only defined for those elements that occur in the bag with non-zero frequency.

$$\text{bag } X == X \nrightarrow \mathsf{N}_1$$

Our generalisation uses a model that maps to the integers (positive and negative). As before the function is partial: elements with zero frequency are not recorded explicitly.

$$\text{bag } X == X \nrightarrow (\mathsf{Z} \setminus \{0\})$$

We will use this model from here on.

The empty bag with items from the set $X$ is denoted $[\![\ ]\!][X]$, and is shorthand for the bag in which the occurrence of every element of $X$ is zero.

$$[\![\ ]\!][X] == \{\ \}[X]$$

Commonly, $[\![\ ]\!][X]$ is abbreviated to $[\![\ ]\!]$ when the set $X$ can be deduced from the context.

The function *count* defined in [Spi89, page 127] carries over to the new model, but is generalised to allow negative frequencies. To improve readability we have chosen to use an equivalent infix operator '$\#$' rather than the (curried) prefix function *count* used in [Spi89].

$$
\begin{array}{l}
\underline{\phantom{xx}}[X]\underline{\phantom{xxxxxxxxxxxxxxxxxxxxxxxxx}} \\
\quad \_\,\#\,\_ : \text{bag } X \times X \to \mathsf{Z} \\
\rule{6cm}{0.4pt} \\
\quad \forall B : \text{bag } X;\ x : X\ \bullet \\
\qquad (x \in \text{dom } B \Rightarrow B \# x = B(x)) \wedge \\
\qquad (x \notin \text{dom } B \Rightarrow B \# x = 0)
\end{array}
$$

The infix relation "in" [Spi89, page 127] is no longer quite as meaningful when negative frequencies are allowed. One could define it to mean elements with non-zero frequencies, and possibly restrict its use to bags containing only non-negative frequencies. We choose to omit it: we can use "$B \# x \neq 0$" for "$x$ in $B$".

## 1.1 Basic operations

Bag addition can be defined almost as it was in [Spi89, page 128]. In [Spi89] bag subtraction was not defined, no doubt due to the difficulty of defining what results when one subtracts 5 occurrences of an element from a bag that only has 3 occurrences of that element. This is no longer a problem: we end up with $-2$ occurrences. We can also define bag negation, bag multiplication and multiplication of a bag by a constant: the frequency of every element is multiplied by the constant.

$$
\begin{array}{l}
\rule{6cm}{0.4pt}\,[X]\,\rule{6cm}{0.4pt} \\
\quad \_\uplus\_ : \mathrm{bag}\,X \times \mathrm{bag}\,X \to \mathrm{bag}\,X \\
\quad \_\uplus\_ : \mathrm{bag}\,X \times \mathrm{bag}\,X \to \mathrm{bag}\,X \\
\quad - : \mathrm{bag}\,X \to \mathrm{bag}\,X \\
\quad \_\otimes\_ : \mathrm{bag}\,X \times \mathrm{bag}\,X \to \mathrm{bag}\,X \\
\quad \_\otimes\_ : \mathsf{Z} \times \mathrm{bag}\,X \to \mathrm{bag}\,X \\
\rule{6cm}{0.4pt} \\
\quad \forall B1, B2 : \mathrm{bag}\,X;\ x : X;\ n : \mathsf{Z} \bullet \\
\qquad (B1 \uplus B2)\,\#\,x = (B1\,\#\,x) + (B2\,\#\,x)\ \wedge \\
\qquad (B1 \uplus B2)\,\#\,x = (B1\,\#\,x) - (B2\,\#\,x)\ \wedge \\
\qquad (-B1)\,\#\,x = -(B1\,\#\,x)\ \wedge \\
\qquad (B1 \otimes B2)\,\#\,x = (B1\,\#\,x) * (B2\,\#\,x)\ \wedge \\
\qquad (n \otimes B1)\,\#\,x = n * (B1\,\#\,x)
\end{array}
$$

Other operators on the integers may be promoted to operate on bags. For example, unary operators, such as absolute value, may be promoted in a manner similar to bag negation, and binary operators, such as minimum, maximum and integer division, may be promoted in a manner similar to bag addition.

If $a$ is of type $X$ and $k$ is a non-zero integer, we write $[\![a \mapsto k]\!]$ for the bag

$$\{a \mapsto k\};$$

$[\![a \mapsto 0]\!]$ is equivalent to the empty bag $[\![\ ]\!]$; and $[\![a_1 \mapsto k_1, a_2 \mapsto k_2, \cdots, a_n \mapsto k_n]\!]$ is the bag

$$[\![a_1 \mapsto k_1]\!] \uplus [\![a_2 \mapsto k_2]\!] \uplus \cdots \uplus [\![a_n \mapsto k_n]\!].$$

Note that with this definition we do not require the $a_j$ to be distinct; for example,

$$[\![a \mapsto k_1, a \mapsto k_2]\!] = [\![a \mapsto k_1]\!] \uplus [\![a \mapsto k_2]\!] = [\![a \mapsto k_1 + k_2]\!].$$

A bag may also be specified via a lambda-notation expression which defines the frequency of occurrence of each item. We will introduce a more useful bag comprehension notation later.

**Laws** The laws for bag operators are similar to (and can be derived from) the laws for arithmetic on the integers.

$\forall B1, B2, B3 : \mathrm{bag}\, X;\ n, m : \mathbf{Z};\ x : X\ \bullet$

$\quad (B1 \uplus B2) \uplus B3 = B1 \uplus (B2 \uplus B3) \land$

$\quad B1 \uplus B2 = B2 \uplus B1 \land$

$\quad [\![\ ]\!] \uplus B1 = B1 = B1 \uplus [\![\ ]\!] \land$

$\quad B1 \uplus (-B1) = [\![\ ]\!] \land$

$\quad (B1 \uplus B2) \uplus B3 = B1 \uplus (B2 \uplus B3) \land$

$\quad B1 \uplus B2 = B1 \uplus (-B2) \land$

$\quad B1 \uplus B2 = -(B2 \uplus B1) \land$

$\quad B1 \uplus [\![\ ]\!] = B1 \land$

$\quad [\![\ ]\!] \uplus B1 = -B1 \land$

$\quad -[\![ x \mapsto n ]\!] = [\![ x \mapsto -n ]\!] \land$

$\quad (B1 \mathbin{\cap\kern-0.3em\cap} B2) \mathbin{\cap\kern-0.3em\cap} B3 = B1 \mathbin{\cap\kern-0.3em\cap} (B2 \mathbin{\cap\kern-0.3em\cap} B3) \land$

$\quad B1 \mathbin{\cap\kern-0.3em\cap} B2 = B2 \mathbin{\cap\kern-0.3em\cap} B1 \land$

$\quad [\![\ ]\!] \mathbin{\cap\kern-0.3em\cap} B1 = [\![\ ]\!] = B1 \mathbin{\cap\kern-0.3em\cap} [\![\ ]\!] \land$

$\quad B1 \mathbin{\cap\kern-0.3em\cap} (B2 \uplus B3) = (B1 \mathbin{\cap\kern-0.3em\cap} B2) \uplus (B1 \mathbin{\cap\kern-0.3em\cap} B3) \land$

$\quad 0 \otimes B1 = [\![\ ]\!] \land$

$\quad 1 \otimes B1 = B1 \land$

$\quad (n + m) \otimes B1 = (n \otimes B1) \uplus (m \otimes B1) \land$

$\quad (n - m) \otimes B1 = (n \otimes B1) \uplus (m \otimes B1) \land$

$\quad n \otimes [\![\ ]\!][X] = [\![\ ]\!] \land$

$\quad n \otimes [\![ x \mapsto m ]\!] = [\![ x \mapsto n * m ]\!] \land$

$\quad n \otimes (B1 \uplus B2) = (n \otimes B1) \uplus (n \otimes B2) \land$

$\quad n \otimes (B1 \uplus B2) = (n \otimes B1) \uplus (n \otimes B2) \land$

$\quad n \otimes (-B1) = (-n) \otimes B1 \land$

$\quad n \otimes (m \otimes B1) = (n * m) \otimes B1$

Of special note is the law

$$B1 \uplus (-B1) = [\![\ ]\!].$$

It shows that, with the generalisation of bags to allow negative frequencies, every bag $B1$ now has an inverse with respect to the operator '$\uplus$' of $-B1$.

One bag is contained in another if the frequency of every element in the first bag does not exceed its corresponding frequency in the second bag.

$$
\begin{array}{l}
\rule{0pt}{0pt}\\
\underline{\phantom{xx}} \ll \underline{\phantom{xx}} : \text{bag } X \leftrightarrow \text{bag } X\\
\hline
\forall B1, B2 : \text{bag } X \bullet\\
\quad B1 \ll B2 \Leftrightarrow (\forall x : X \bullet (B1 \# x) \leq (B2 \# x))
\end{array}
$$

It can be useful to be able to distinguish finite bags: those with only a finite number of elements with non-zero frequency.

$$\text{finbag } X == \{B : \text{bag } X \mid (\text{dom } B) \in \mathbb{F}\, X\}$$

Note that, if the type of the bag elements, $X$, is finite, then any bag of that type is finite.

## 1.2 Size and summation

The size of a bag is the total number of items in the bag taking into account the frequency of occurrence of each item. Negative frequencies may thus cancel out positive ones.

$$
\begin{array}{l}
[X]\\
\hline
size : \text{finbag } X \rightarrow \mathbb{Z}\\
\hline
size[\,] = 0\\
\forall x : X; \; n : \mathbb{Z} \bullet\\
\quad size[x \mapsto n] = n\\
\forall B1, B2 : \text{finbag } X; \; n : \mathbb{Z} \bullet\\
\quad size(B1 \uplus B2) = (size\, B1) + (size\, B2) \wedge\\
\quad size(B1 \sqcup B2) = (size\, B1) - (size\, B2) \wedge\\
\quad size(-B1) = -(size\, B1) \wedge\\
\quad size(n \otimes B1) = n * (size\, B1)
\end{array}
$$

It is convenient to define summation on bags of numbers. Defining summation on sets would not allow for a particular value occurring more than once, and summation on sequences may be inappropriate in some cases as it requires the elements to be put into order within a sequence. We define summation on bags of real numbers (**R**) and assume the arithmetic operators are defined on the reals and that the integers are a subset of the reals.

$$\Sigma : \text{finbag}\,\mathbf{R} \to \mathbf{R}$$

$$\Sigma[\![\,]\!] = 0$$

$$\forall x : \mathbf{R};\ n : \mathbf{Z} \bullet$$
$$\quad \Sigma[\![x \mapsto n]\!] = n * x$$

$$\forall B1, B2 : \text{finbag}\,\mathbf{R};\ n : \mathbf{Z} \bullet$$
$$\quad \Sigma(B1 \uplus B2) = (\Sigma B1) + (\Sigma B2)\ \wedge$$
$$\quad \Sigma(B1 \uplus B2) = (\Sigma B1) - (\Sigma B2)\ \wedge$$
$$\quad \Sigma(-B1) = -(\Sigma B1)\ \wedge$$
$$\quad \Sigma(n \otimes B1) = n * (\Sigma B1)$$

Summation is only defined for finite bags (bags with only a finite number of elements whose frequency is non-zero). With care, this can be generalised to allow infinite bags, as long as the sum converges; the domain of $\Sigma$ is widened considerably, but it is still not defined for all bags. For bags containing only integers, the restriction to finite bags is necessary.

## 1.3 Conversion to/from bags

We define *setof* to take a bag and give the set of elements in the bag that occur with non-zero frequency, and we define *bagof* to take a set and give the bag in which each element in the set occurs once.

$$[X]$$

$$setof : \text{bag}\,X \to \mathbb{P}\,X$$
$$bagof : \mathbb{P}\,X \to \text{bag}\,X$$

$$\forall B : \text{bag}\,X;\ S : \mathbb{P}\,X;\ x : X \bullet$$
$$\quad setof\,B = \text{dom}\,B\ \wedge$$
$$\quad \text{dom}(bagof\,S) = S \wedge \text{ran}(bagof\,S) = \{1\}$$

**Laws**

$$\forall B : \text{bag } X; \; S : \mathbf{P} \, X \bullet$$
$$setof(bagof(S)) = S \; \wedge$$
$$(\llbracket \, \rrbracket \ll B \Rightarrow bagof(setof(B)) \ll B)$$

The operation *items*, that takes a sequence of values and returns the bag containing those values with the same frequencies, can be generalised from that given in [Hay87, page 47] and [Spi89, page 129] so that it applies to any relation for which each range element is associated with only finitely many domain elements. As both functions and sequences can be considered as special cases of relations, *items* can be used on functions and sequences.

$$\begin{array}{l} =\!\!\!=[W, X]\!\!=\!\!=\!\!=\!\!=\!\!=\!\!=\!\!=\!\!=\!\!=\!\!= \\ \quad items : (W \leftrightarrow X) \rightarrowtail \text{bag } X \\ \hline \\ \quad \forall R : W \leftrightarrow X; \; x : X \bullet \\ \qquad (R \in \text{dom } items \Leftrightarrow (\forall x : \text{ran } R \bullet \\ \qquad\qquad\qquad \{w : \text{dom } R \mid (w, x) \in R\} \in \mathsf{F} \; W)) \; \wedge \\ \qquad (R \in \text{dom } items \Rightarrow \\ \qquad\qquad\qquad (items \, R) \# x = \#\{w : \text{dom } R \mid (w, x) \in R\}) \end{array}$$

**Laws**

$$\forall P, R : W \leftrightarrow X; \; w : W; \; x : X \bullet$$
$$items(\{ \, \}[W \times X]) = \llbracket \, \rrbracket[X] \; \wedge$$
$$items\{w \mapsto x\} = \llbracket x \mapsto 1 \rrbracket \; \wedge$$
$$items(P \cup R) = (items \, P) \uplus (items \, R) \setminus (items(P \cap R)) \; \wedge$$
$$(\text{dom } P \cap \text{dom } R = \{ \, \} \Rightarrow$$
$$\qquad\qquad items(P \cup R) = (items \, P) \uplus (items \, R))$$

$$\forall s, t : \text{seq } X; \; x : X \bullet$$
$$items(\langle \, \rangle[X]) = \llbracket \, \rrbracket[X] \; \wedge$$
$$items\langle x \rangle = \llbracket x \mapsto 1 \rrbracket \; \wedge$$
$$items(s \frown t) = (items \, s) \uplus (items \, t)$$

## 1.4 Bag comprehension

As with the set comprehension $\{x : X \mid P \bullet t\}$, it is useful to introduce a form of bag comprehension. If $B : \text{bag } X$, $P$ is a predicate and $t$ is a term of type $Y$ ($P$ and $t$ typically involve the variable $x$) the bag comprehension

$$[\![x : B \mid P \bullet t]\!]$$

is the bag we get by accumulating all the values of $t$, for $x$ ranging over all the items in the bag $B$ such that $P$ holds. If a value of $x$ occurs multiple times in the bag $B$ then we add the corresponding value of $t$ that many times to the resultant bag; if $x$ occurs with negative frequency, then the corresponding $t$ is added with the same negative frequency.

The following equivalence can be used to define the bag comprehension notation.

$$[\![x : B \mid P \bullet t]\!] \# y = \sum items(\lambda x : setof\, B \mid P \wedge y = t \bullet B \# x)$$

A comprehension is only well defined if each value of $t$ occurs only finitely often.

If the predicate part of the bag comprehension is omitted, the predicate is assumed to be true. For example, the following holds.

$$size\, B = \sum [\![x : B \bullet 1]\!]$$

With this new notation we can define the bag of the items in a sequence $S : seq\, X$ by the following expression.

$$items\, S = [\![i : bagof(\mathrm{dom}\, S) \bullet S(i)]\!]$$

If no confusion can arise, we allow the explicit conversion '$bagof$' to be omitted in writing bag comprehensions such as the above. For a relation $R : W \leftrightarrow X$ we have the following equivalence (omitting the '$bagof$').

$$items\, R = [\![(w, x) : R \bullet x]\!]$$

This forms the bag of range values in the relation with the frequencies that they occur in the pairs of the relation. Bag comprehension also allows one to select out the bag of domain items in a relation:

$$[\![(w, x) : R \bullet w]\!].$$

Multiple variables may be declared in the bag comprehension; each declared variable ranges over the values in the associated bag with the frequency of occurrence of the value in that bag. For example, if $B : \text{bag } X$ and $C : \text{bag } Y$ then

$$\llbracket x : B; \ y : C \bullet (x, y) \rrbracket,$$

is of type $\text{bag}(X \times Y)$, and the pair $(x, y)$ occurs in this bag $(B \, \# \, x) * (C \, \# \, y)$ times; this is the bag generalisation of Cartesian product. The general form of bag comprehension is

$$\llbracket x_1 : B_1; \ x_2 : B_2; \ \cdots; \ x_n : B_n \mid P \bullet t \rrbracket.$$

If the term $t$ is omitted, the default term is the tuple of the declared variables: $(x_1, x_2, \cdots, x_n)$.

# 2 A simple banking system

We illustrate the use of our generalised bags by modelling a bank as a bag of customer accounts. Each account is uniquely identified by an account number, and the balance of an account is represented by the 'frequency' of occurrence of the account number in the bag (an integer representing pennies in the account).

$$[AccNo]$$
$$Money == \mathbb{Z}$$

As our generalisation of bags allows negative frequencies, this model of a bank allows accounts to be in the red.

An operation to transfer money from one account to another can be specified by the following schema.

```
┌─ Transfer ──────────────────────────────────────────
│ bank, bank' : bag AccNo
│ from?, to? : AccNo
│ amount? : Money
├─────────────────────────────────────────────────────
│ bank' = bank ⊎ ⟦from? ↦ −amount?, to? ↦ amount?⟧
```

For comparison, the predicate of an alternative, almost equivalent specification, that represents a bank as a function from *AccNo* to account balance and does not use bag operators, follows.

$$bank' = bank \oplus \{from? \mapsto bank(from?) - amount?,$$
$$to? \mapsto bank(to?) + amount?\}$$

This differs from the specification using bags in that, if *from?* = *to?*, the bag specification is well defined, while the alternative is not. If *from?* and *to?* are allowed to be equal, the alternative needs to treat this as a special case.

The operations that follow have no simple alternative without using the equivalent of bag operators. The following operation corresponds to the updating of a bank's accounts with the total automatic teller withdrawals for all of the customer accounts for one day.

$\underline{\hspace{0.3cm}Update\_from\_AT\hspace{4cm}}$
$bank, bank'$ : bag *AccNo*
$withdrawals?$ : bag *AccNo*

$bank' = bank \uplus withdrawals?$

The bank provides a set of services, each of which has a cost; we can represent the service-cost relationship by a bag of services, where the frequency is the cost.

[*Service*]

$|\quad ServiceCost$ : bag *Service*

A customer of the bank makes use of a number of different services, each of which can be used a different number of times; again we can represent this as a bag of services (*use?*). An operation to return the total cost itemised on a per service basis (*usecost!*), as well as the overall cost of all the services (*totalcost!*), is given by the following schema.

$\underline{\hspace{0.3cm}Services\hspace{5cm}}$
$use?, usecost!$ : bag *Service*
$totalcost!$ : *Money*

$usecost! = ServiceCost \otimes use? \wedge$
$totalcost! = size\ usecost!$

## 2.1 Distributed bag addition

If we have numerous transactions, each of which may effect more than one account, then each transaction can be represented by a bag. As it is possible to have the same transaction occurring more than once (e.g., two withdrawals of £20 each from the same account on the same (busy shopping) day), the collection of all transactions is best represented as a finite bag of transactions: finbag(bag $AccNo$).

We can now define a distributed bag addition operator ($\uplus$), which allows us to accumulate all the transactions into a single transaction. For example, the result of accumulating the following bag of transactions

$$\uplus \begin{bmatrix} [\!\![ & a \mapsto 20, & & c \mapsto -15 & ]\!\!] \mapsto 1, \\ [\!\![ & & b \mapsto -20 & & ]\!\!] \mapsto 2, \\ [\!\![ & a \mapsto 10, & b \mapsto 50, & c \mapsto 5 & ]\!\!] \mapsto 1 \end{bmatrix}$$

gives the bag

$$[\!\![ a \mapsto 30, b \mapsto 10, c \mapsto -10 ]\!\!].$$

$$
\begin{array}{|l|}
\hline
\llbracket X \rrbracket \\
\hline
\uplus : \text{finbag}(\text{bag } X) \to \text{bag } X \\
\hline
\forall BB : \text{finbag}(\text{bag } X); \; x : X \bullet \\
\quad (\uplus BB) \# x = \sum [\!\![ B : BB \bullet B \# x ]\!\!] \\
\hline
\end{array}
$$

**Laws**

$$\uplus [\!\![ \;]\!\!] [\text{bag } X] = [\!\![ \;]\!\!] [X]$$

$$\forall B : \text{bag } X; \; n : \mathbf{Z} \bullet$$
$$\quad \uplus [\!\![ B \mapsto n ]\!\!] = n \otimes B$$

$$\forall BB1, BB2 : \text{finbag}(\text{bag } X); \; n : \mathbf{Z} \bullet$$
$$\quad \uplus(BB1 \uplus BB2) = (\uplus BB1) \uplus (\uplus BB2) \wedge$$
$$\quad \uplus(BB1 \cup BB2) = (\uplus BB1) \cup (\uplus BB2) \wedge$$
$$\quad \uplus(n \otimes BB1) = n \otimes (\uplus BB1) \wedge$$
$$\quad \uplus(-BB1) = -(\uplus BB1)$$

An operation that accumulates the transactions that have taken place at all the branches of a bank into one large transaction can be defined as follows.

[*BranchId*]

---
Accumulate
*branchtrans?* : *BranchId* $\nrightarrow$ (bag *AccNo*)
*transaction!* : bag *AccNo*

---
*transaction!* = $\biguplus$(*items branchtrans?*)

---

For each branch *b* we have a single transaction *branchtrans?*(*b*) representing all the transactions for that branch; we collect these into the bag of such transactions for all branches: *items branchtrans?*; and then merge all these transactions using distributed bag addition ($\biguplus$).

# 3   Physical units

This section outlines an approach to formalising physical units using generalised bags. The following basic units are sufficient for our example.

$$BasicUnit ::= metre \mid sec \mid volt \mid kelvin \mid celsius \mid fahrenheit$$

To represent physical quantities we need, not only basic units, but dimensionality. We can represent dimensionality by using a bag of basic units.

$$Units == \text{bag } BasicUnit$$

For example, velocity and acceleration can be represented as follows.

$$Velocity == [\![ metre \mapsto 1, sec \mapsto -1 ]\!]$$
$$Acceleration == [\![ metre \mapsto 1, sec \mapsto -2 ]\!]$$

The following abbreviations are useful.

$$Metre == [\![ metre \mapsto 1 ]\!]$$
$$Volt == [\![ volt \mapsto 1 ]\!]$$
$$Kelvin == [\![ kelvin \mapsto 1 ]\!]$$
$$Celsius == [\![ celsius \mapsto 1 ]\!]$$
$$Fahrenheit == [\![ fahrenheit \mapsto 1 ]\!]$$

Normal arithmetic operations on reals can be upgraded to work on physical quantities. Addition and subtraction are only defined for quantities with the same units; multiplication and division are defined for any units.

$$\_ + \_, \_ - \_, \_ / \_ : (\mathbf{R} \times Units) \times (\mathbf{R} \times Units) \nrightarrow (\mathbf{R} \times Units)$$
$$\_ * \_ : (\mathbf{R} \times Units) \times (\mathbf{R} \times Units) \rightarrow (\mathbf{R} \times Units)$$

$$\forall v1, v2 : \mathbf{R}; \; us1, us2 : Units \bullet$$
$$\quad ((v1, us1), (v2, us2)) \in \mathrm{dom}(\_ + \_) \Leftrightarrow us1 = us2 \land$$
$$\quad (v1, us1) + (v2, us1) = (v1 + v2, us1) \land$$
$$\quad ((v1, us1), (v2, us2)) \in \mathrm{dom}(\_ - \_) \Leftrightarrow us1 = us2 \land$$
$$\quad (v1, us1) - (v2, us1) = (v1 - v2, us1) \land$$
$$\quad (v1, us1) * (v2, us2) = (v1 * v2, us1 \uplus us2) \land$$
$$\quad ((v1, us1), (v2, us2)) \in \mathrm{dom}(\_ / \_) \Leftrightarrow v2 \neq 0 \land$$
$$\quad (v2 \neq 0 \Rightarrow (v1, us1) / (v2, us2) = (v1 / v2, us1 \uplus us2))$$

We can now perform arithmetic on physical quantities. In this context "$\uplus$" can be read as "per".

$$V : \mathbf{R} \times \{Volt\}$$
$$Scale : \mathbf{R} \times \{Volt \uplus Metre\}$$
$$Offset : \mathbf{R} \times \{Metre\}$$

$$Offset = V \,/\, Scale$$

An operation that takes a temperature expressed in either Fahrenheit, Celsius or Kelvin and converts it to Kelvin is given by the following.

$$absolute : \mathbf{R} \times \{Fahrenheit, Celsius, Kelvin\} \rightarrow \mathbf{R} \times \{Kelvin\}$$

$$\forall x : \mathbf{R} \bullet$$
$$\quad absolute(x, Kelvin) = (x, Kelvin) \land$$
$$\quad absolute(x, Celsius) = (x + 273 \cdot 15, Kelvin) \land$$
$$\quad absolute(x, Fahrenheit) = absolute((x - 32) * 5 \,/\, 9, Celsius)$$

# 4  Further extensions

The generalisation of bags presented in this paper allows one to use integers to measure the frequency of occurrence of values, rather than just natural numbers. A possible further extension is to allow real (or complex) values as the metric. The basic model then becomes a mapping from the element type to the real (or complex) numbers. The operators defined above can be carried over to these more general bags. However, size and summation need special consideration. If they are allowed on non-finite bags, they need to be considered as an integral and a weighted integral, respectively. (The current size and summation can be considered as an integral and weighted integral, respectively, by using a discrete topology.)

Another possible extension is to allow bag frequencies to be infinite. This would allow a function like *items* to be applied to a wider class of relations. If an element of the range of a relation corresponds to an infinite number of domain elements, we could still apply *items* to that relation, but the frequency for that element would be recorded as infinity. Care needs to be taken in redefining the operators for this extension; if we do not restrict ourselves to countably infinite sets we need to use the more complex model of cardinal arithmetic, rather than just adding an extra infinity value to the set of possible frequencies.

# 5 Conclusions

The new model of bags introduced above is more general than the model given in [Hay87] and [Spi89]. It can be used in all cases where the previous model can be used, as well as in new areas, as illustrated by the examples of the simple banking system and representing physical units. The new model is recommended as a replacement for future Z libraries.

# Acknowledgements

This work was completed while I was visiting the Programming Research Group of Oxford University and I would like to acknowledge the hospitality of the Programming Research Group and Wolfson College, and the financial assistance of the Special Studies Program of the University of Queensland. I would also like to thank Jonathan Bowen, Brendan Mahony, Carroll Morgan and Mike Spivey for useful comments on earlier drafts of this paper.

# References

[Hay87]  I. J. Hayes, editor. *Specification Case Studies.* Prentice Hall International, 1987.

[Spi89]  J. M. Spivey. *The Z Notation: A Reference Manual.* Prentice Hall International, 1989.

# Formaliser — An Interactive Support Tool for Z

Mike Flynn, Tim Hoverd, David Brazier

**Logica Cambridge Limited**
**Betjeman House, 104 Hills Road, Cambridge CB2 1LQ**
**Tel: (0223) 66343**

Formaliser is a software tool which supports the interactive editing, syntax, scope and type checking of Z specifications. The tool uses windows and a mouse, operating in a "WYSIWYG", point-and-click style. Unconstrained text may be interspersed with syntax-enforced formal utterances. The tool is generic, in that it may be configured for formal languages other than Z. The software runs on low-cost desk-top machines. This paper illustrates the use and implementation of the tool.

## Introduction

The days in which files were painstakingly prepared and tentatively submitted to a monolithic compiler, only to be bounced back with some terse error message, are thankfully drawing to a close. Increasingly, the computer is viewed by users as an interactive accomplice in the creative aspects of their work, rather than as some final obstacle — the user and computer arrive together at the finished result. This has been brought about, in part, by significant improvements in low cost desk-top computers and work-stations.

With this philosophy in mind, we have produced a prototype support tool, called "Formaliser", for writing formal specifications in the Z notation [Z]. Formaliser provides a highly interactive document editing facility which:

- displays mathematical symbols and constructions as they will appear on the printed page;

- ensures correct syntax, as specifications are written;

- enforces compliance with the scope and type rules of Z, on the fly;

- supports queries about scope and type, interactively;

- edits ordinary text and structured mathematics, as found in typical Z specifications;

- provides a persistent environment which specifications inhabit — files are not visible.

This paper illustrates a typical session with Formaliser, discusses its architecture and then describes the implementation. Lastly, the current status and plans for the future are discussed.

# A Typical Session

In this part of this paper we will try to give a flavour of the use of the Formaliser tool. This is not easy for such a user-oriented tool and we have therefore adopted an approach based upon a copious quantity of screen dumps, with commentary alongside.

From the beginning of the Formaliser development we were conscious of the need to provide a highly interactive tool and much of our effort has gone into user-interface issues. We had always intended to produce a tool operating in a "windows and mouse" environment, where the user could easily designate parts of the formal or informal text for processing in some way. Such a direct manipulation style of user interface is now recognised as one of the keys to usable tools and also fits well with an object-oriented implementation technique, such as that chosen for the Formaliser development. Furthermore, we have found that the style of user interface adopted has had deep implications for the implementation of the rest of the tool — the lesson of this being that user interfaces are not something that can be "tacked on" at the end of a development.

## *The Specification Library*

One of our objectives has been the elimination of the requirement to consider machine details such as files and fonts. The principal manifestation of this is the specification library. This appears to the user as a window containing a list of the specifications that are known to the system:

Each specification is tagged with a short description of its purpose, which appears in the window's right-hand pane when the specification in question is selected.

Given this representation of specifications, the user has merely to select a particular specification and select a menu option in order to place that specification in an editing window for further manipulation. Formaliser takes care of any required housekeeping details, such as loading the specification from a disk file if required.

We have gone through several alternative approaches to the display of an external representation of a Z specification before settling on the current practice. This is to present specifications in a style closely representing their appearance on the printed page. Although this might seem the obvious approach there are many other possibilities, such as presenting Z specifications as a number of separated Z schemas, each tagged with some informal text.

At the top of the window there are some small panes that provide the user with some extra information (see overleaf). These include some arrow buttons for moving about the internal abstract syntax tree, a description of the currently selected part of the specification and a description of the contents of the paste buffer. It is our objective to remove entirely the requirement for the buttons, as they require a knowledge of a specification's internal structure that is unreasonable to expect of all users. However, we have not yet totally achieved this objective; although the buttons are now very seldom used — their function having largely been replaced by using the mouse in the "clicking and wiping" style so familiar to, for example, Apple Macintosh users.

A Z specification on the Formaliser screen now looks like this:

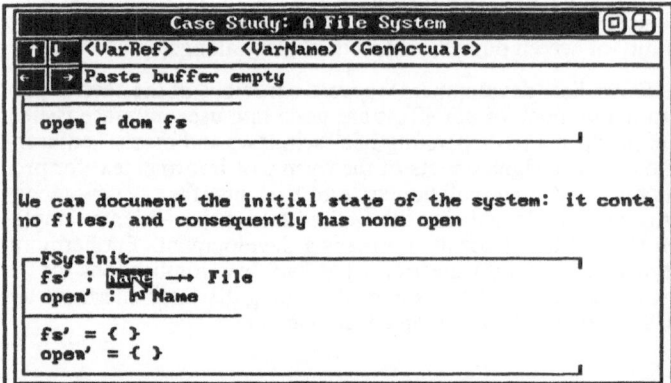

The specification is presented in a single window, and appears to the user in a form closely resembling the printed page. As described later, this is by no means the only external form of a specification, but is undoubtedly the one that will be used for most editing operations.

## Basic Editing

With the specification in an editing window a number of simple operations are immediately available, such as the following:

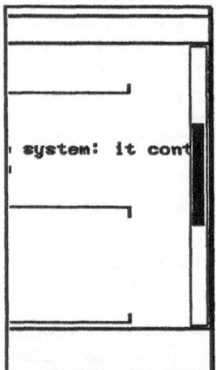

The window may be scrolled in order to reveal the required part of the specification, during which operation a scroll bar is displayed on the screen. Notice the scroll bar also gives a visual indication of the amount of the specification that is visible in the current window.

The user interface to Formaliser uses a mouse and menu style of interaction. In this case the menus are of the "pop-up" variety, in that they appear at the point where the mouse cursor is currently positioned, rather than the "pull-down" variety. The content of the menus varies depending upon the currently selected object.

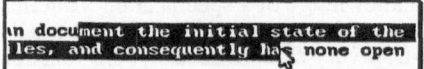

The textual parts of the specification may be edited using conventional mouse-style editing: double-clicking to select words, clicking and wiping to select arbitrary parts of text, and so on.

## Mathematical Editing

If the user attempts to select a piece of the formal text in the same manner as unstructured text then Formaliser exhibits a different behaviour:

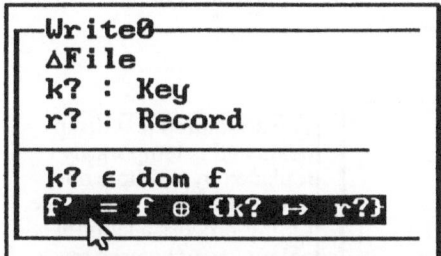

A portion of the mathematical text that represents a single production of the underlying grammar is selected — which from the user's point of view should represent a well-understood object, such as the predicate shown selected here.

In situations where the user has not yet entered a complete specification, Formaliser displays the name of an unfinished component of the specification in angle brackets:

In this situation, the tool has created a new paragraph and the user may now define the sort of paragraph that is required. This is done by a menu selection.

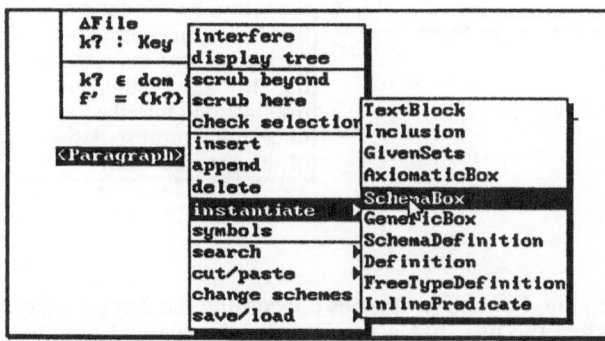

The user selects the type of paragraph that is required (such as a schema box) ...

... and Formaliser inserts as much of that part of Z as may be achieved without further reference to the user. In this case this is equivalent to inserting the *pro forma* schema box.

This scheme operates throughout Formaliser's structured editing. In general, the tool fills in as much of the structure as it can without recourse to the user.

## Typing an Expression

Although this menu mechanism could be used for entering all of a Z specification into Formaliser it would be unbearably tedious. The mechanism works well for such things as schema boxes and text paragraphs but to use it for, say, arbitrary expressions would be excessive. For these situations Formaliser provides an integrated parser and the user may just select the component of the formal text that is to be entered and type the required text:

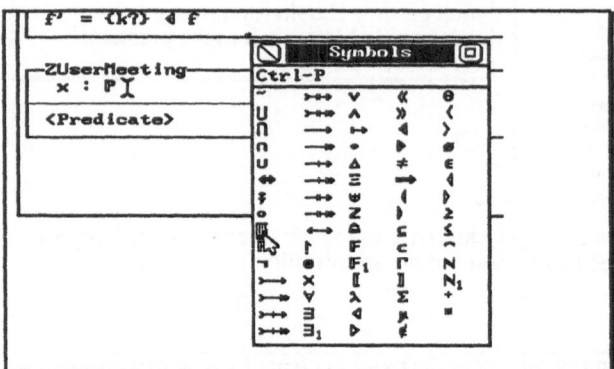

The structured text disappears and is temporarily replaced by a simple one line text editor. During the typing process a symbol palette[1] may be used to enter one of the many symbols that does not appear on the keyboard.

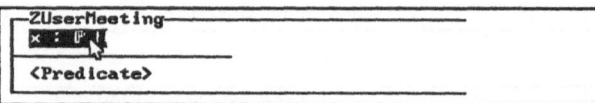

At the completion of this process the user just types the return key and the text that has been entered is parsed and the corresponding structured representation inserted into the underlying representation of the specification.

## Checking Scope and Type

During the entry of a specification into Formaliser queries concerning the Z type system may be made. For example, when the user has a particular mathematical structure selected[2] then a "check" operation may be selected which checks that structure for compliance with the Z scope and type rules. Whether this is the right mode of operation for such a tool has been the subject of much discussion. It would be possible to invoke the type-checker automatically, perhaps after the user had finished entering a complete schema, instead of adopting the user-driven approach that the current version of Formaliser exhibits. We are still experimenting with this particular aspect of the tool and

---

[1]This device allows for the use of function keys to represent the common symbols. The function key that could have been used is displayed whenever the symbol palette is used so that the keyboard equivalents for common symbols will become familiar.

[2]This operation is available on all of the mathematical components of a specification. However, it is most likely that the user will only invoke it at the "paragraph" level — on a schema, for example.

it likely that the "best" answer to this question will only emerge after a period of continuous use of the tool.

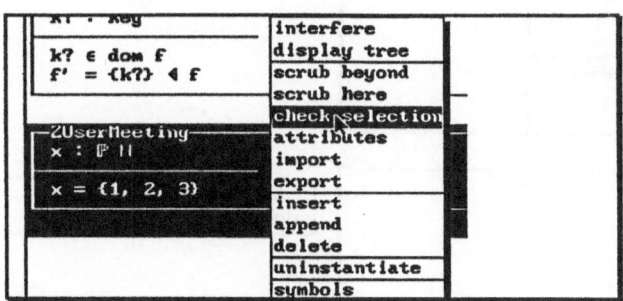

The user selects a schema and invokes the check operation...

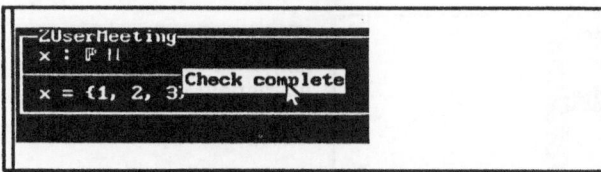

... which could result in Formaliser informing the user that there are no errors in the currently selected structure...

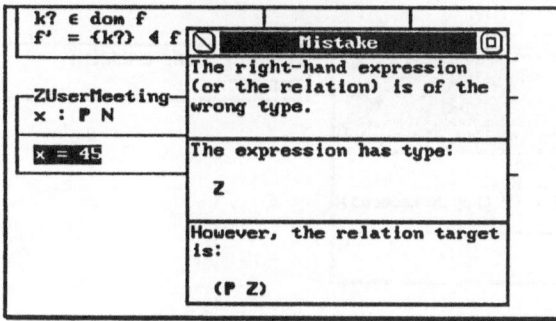

...or an error message that is relevant to a particular error could be produced

We have provided the same style of interaction during type-checking that is apparent while entering a specification. This is a very different approach from the more usual batch-oriented type-checker. Indeed, type-checking is an integral part of Formaliser, and appears as an ordinary menu operation. These operations, some of which are illustrated overleaf, provide some of the most useful features of Formaliser.

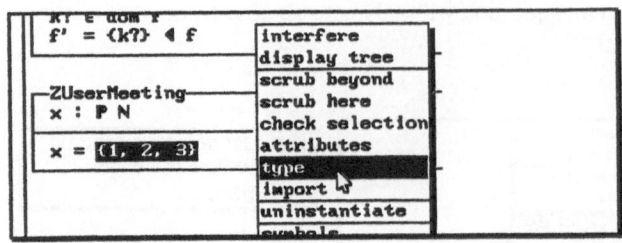
Selecting some part of the specification and enquiring as to its type...

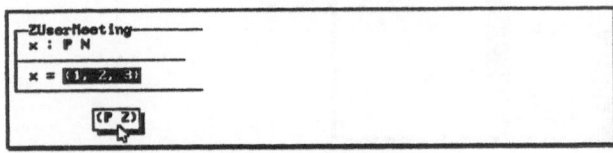
...and receiving a prompt and meaningful response

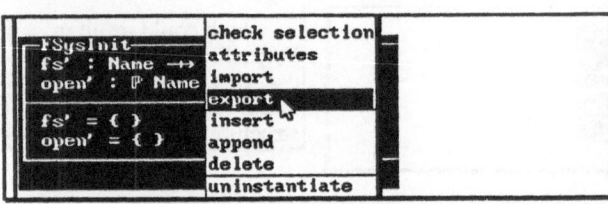
Enquiring about the exported bindings from a paragraph...

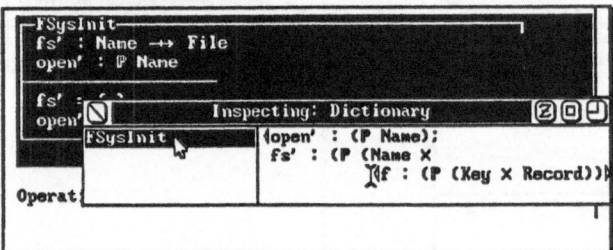
...and getting a useful answer

## Document Inclusion

With Z, for the type checker to work correctly it requires the Z basic library. We did not want to build this into the tool directly, as this would have adversely affected the generic capabilities of the system, and so opted for defining the library as just another Z specification under the control of Formaliser.

In order to make its type environment available we defined a new kind of specification paragraph, the document inclusion. This is the one extension to the grammar defined in [Z] that we have made and allows one specification to include the exported environment of any other known to Formaliser.

# The Architecture

The architecture of Formaliser is illustrated below; there follows a discussion of the components: the grammar, tree and view.

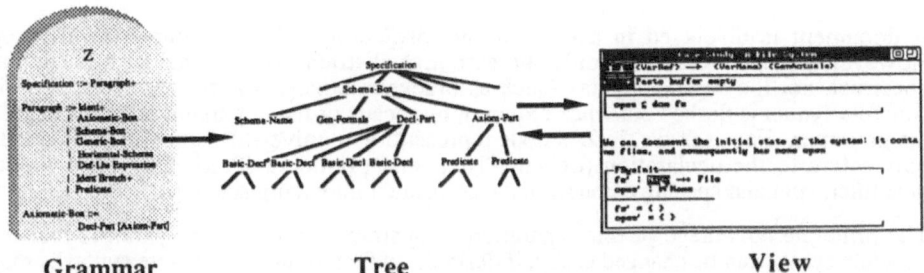

Grammar                    Tree                              View

*Figure 1—The Architecture of Formaliser*

## The Grammar

The Grammar defines the formal language upon which Formaliser operates — so far, we have tried Pascal and a miniature Lisp, in addition to Z. It contains four closely related kinds of information (examples are shown later):

- a context free grammar, which defines the abstract syntax.

- 'unparse schemes', which define the concrete syntax.

- predicates, which define the context conditions for each production — the scope and type rules in the case of Z.

- *pro forma* error reports, for reporting violations of the context conditions.

In addition to conventional productions, the grammar may include special 'free text' productions which allow informal commentary in otherwise formal documents[1].

## The Tree

The centre of all activity is the Abstract Syntax Tree ("the tree"), which is an internal representation of the document being edited. The nodes of this tree represent steps in the derivation of the document, according to the supplied context free grammar. For example, a tree fragment such as this:

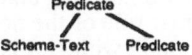

would represent a derivation according this grammar rule:

    Predicate ::= Schema-Text Predicate

---

[1]Currently, these productions can only be used as whole 'paragraphs' within a document, not as 'comments'.

At any given moment, at most one of the tree nodes is considered 'selected'. The selected node decides what to do with input, what menu options are available and how to implement them. Nodes which represent different kinds of productions (choices, lists, fixed sequences, free text etc.) are implemented by subclasses of general nodes, thereby providing appropriate specialised behaviour.

## The View

A document is displayed in a window by "projecting" the tree into textual form. However, the tree represents only the essential abstract components of a particular construct, not the detailed syntax (such as brackets, boxes, spaces etc). Instead, this concrete syntax is fleshed out when required, by means of the unparsing schemes held in the grammar. For example, in Z, a node representing a universally quantified predicate only refers to the declaration (Schema-Text) and predicate (Predicate) parts — the quantifier, spot and spacing come from the associated unparsing schemes.

The principle advantage of this separation of abstract and concrete syntax is that the concrete syntax can be changed easily, if desired. In fact, multiple concrete syntaxes may be defined, leading to a simple language translation facility. For example, in the case of Z, documents are prepared for high quality printing by translation into L^TEX [L^TEX]:

> Predicate ::= Schema-Text Predicate
>> Unparse as Normal with '∀ @1 • @2'
>> Unparse as LaTeX with '\forall @1 \spot @2'

The portion of text represented by the selected node appears highlighted in the view. As the mouse is clicked on formal utterances, the lowest node whose textual form contains that point (i.e. the "tightest enclosing node") is selected. "Wiping" the mouse across the text, causes the node whose projection contains both the starting point and the current point to become selected. The overall effect is very natural to use: an identifier may be selected just by clicking on it; a predicate by clicking on the principal connective; a schema by its box; a list of declarations just by wiping over them, and so on. By restricting selection to nodes, only syntactically sensible selections can ever be made. However, for free text, a text insertion cursor appears by clicking, and some part of the text may be selected by wiping, in time-honoured fashion.

## The Parser

As described above, the user can construct new portions of a document either by means of the menus, with little typing, or by typing directly 'at' a selected node. The node attempts to parse this input according to its own grammar production and concrete syntax. Thus, the unparsing schemes not only dictate the form of output, but also guide the parsing process.

Currently, the parser uses a simple backtracking algorithm, laboriously examining all the possible alternatives for the grammar rule of the node in question. This makes parsing very slow (at least for Z). In common with similar algorithms, this one exhibits poor error reporting[1] and recovery, since context is lost whilst backtracking. However, the parser is still useful for small amounts of input, such as a simple declaration or expression. Fortunately, this is the level at which the menus become tedious to use, making this a natural place to change between menus and typing.

---

[1]There is one error message, the ubiquitous "Parse Error"

## Context Conditions

Predicates associated with each production define the context conditions of the language. For Z, these are mainly scope and type restrictions. For example, the bare grammar might state that an expression can be an identifier, but there may exist a restriction that the identifier be in scope, and of a type appropriate to the context of the expression.

In order to express the predicates formally, some formal theory was required, together with a suitable interpretation which would model the Z scope and type system. We constructed such a theory in Z itself [Formaliser]. Briefly, this theory contains a graph of schemas, interpreted as the abstract syntax tree. The variables of each schema are interpreted as "attributes" of each node, and the predicates as the context conditions imposing restrictions on their values[1]. The interpretation is such that all the schemas in the graph are consistent if and only if the abstract syntax tree represents a well formed formula of Z.

For example, at a node representing a universally quantified predicate, assuming Import and Export are attributes representing type environments, and that $Child_1$ and $Child_2$ refer to bindings for the children of this node, then we can write:

```
Predicate ::= Schema-Text Predicate
         Unparse as Normal with '∀ @1 • @2'
         Unparse as LaTeX with '\forall @1 \spot @2'
     Child₁.Import = Import
     Child₂.Import = Import ⊕ Child₁.Export
     Export = {}
```

Formaliser operates incrementally, checking consistency and determining the values of attributes on the fly. The attributes typically contain useful information regarding scope, type, representatives, characteristic tuples and so on. This information is readily available to the user, through the menus.

If Formaliser discovers an inconsistency, revealed as a false predicate, then an error report is constructed from any *pro forma* reports which are associated with that predicate in the Grammar. Since Formaliser operates incrementally, building up information as a specification is constructed, this report is usually very pertinent to the problem, and the reports can have arbitrary attribute information embedded in them. A large repertoire of reports can be accommodated, one per predicate.

## Documents and the Environment

Documents are simply instances of a document class, and have their own behaviour, such as the ability to be opened, closed and included in other documents. The concept of 'file' is entirely hidden within this class, so that the user neither knows nor cares where the contents of a document really reside[2]. Access to documents is through a browser, providing further insulation form the operating environment. There is no need to 'save' documents, as they have an independent existence which persists from one Formaliser session to the next — restarting Formaliser brings the user back to the *exact* situation in which it was left.

---

[1]The predicates must determine a unique value for each attribute, and quite explicitly so.

[2]Actually, each document transparently maintains a copy on disk, both for safety and to save memory space.

## *The Symbol Palette*

The Z notation contains symbols not found on standard keyboards. Formaliser displays a "palette" of these symbols which can be chosen with the mouse, without typing. Each time a symbol is chosen, the palette displays equivalent key strokes which may typed instead (e.g. the symbol Δ with Control-D). After a while, the common symbols tend to be typed and the obscure symbols chosen from the palette. The boxes of Z are just part of the concrete syntax (defined by the unparsing schemes), which are drawn automatically, net typed or chosen.

# The Engineering

To date, Formaliser has consumed just two staff-years of effort. Some of the techniques used to achieve this are discussed below.

## *Object Orientation*

Object oriented techniques [Meyer] were used throughout, and were found to be very beneficial. Classes such as Node, Grammar, UnparseScheme, Document etc. exist explicitly within the implementation, and are understandable in isolation. Much use was made of inheritance; for example, initially we constructed a tool which only understood context free grammars, with no context conditions or attributes. Once we were happy with that, we introduced AttributedGrammar as a subclass of Grammar, and AttributedNode as a subclass of Node, inheriting almost all their behaviour and adding attributes, to yield the more sophisticated tool.

Formaliser is implemented in the object-oriented system Smalltalk [Smalltalk], from which many of its characteristics derive. The Smalltalk class library saved much effort too, especially in the user interface. Great advantage was taken of the so-called "Model-View-Controller" mechanism, to provide the user interface — windows, panes, menus, selection, scrolling etc. all came for little effort. The immediate, interactive nature of Smalltalk made development more fun, and certainly influenced the ethos of Formaliser.

## *Constructing Grammars*

The generic nature of Formaliser was exploited in its own production. The Grammar from which it works is itself defined in a formal language. So, as soon as the syntactic parts were working, we defined a grammar for grammars, and used Formaliser to prepare its own future grammars (and even to edit the grammar-grammar to accept attribute grammars).

Also, we exploited to the full Formaliser's ability to use multiple concrete syntaxes, providing a simple translation facility. For example, when a new grammar has been prepared using the grammar-grammar, it is normally displayed as a conventional-looking attribute grammar. However, merely by swapping concrete syntaxes it can be displayed as a tract of Smalltalk code, which, when executed, builds the appropriate Smalltalk objects to represent the new grammar. (Using a Lisp grammar, one of the authors devised an alternative concrete syntax for Lisp expressions, which produced equivalent executable Smalltalk code, turning Formaliser into a Lisp interpreter!)

## Attribute Evaluation

The attribute predicates are implemented and checked in a rather incestuous manner. As explained above, Formaliser uses Z itself to express these predicates, and must interpret these to determine consistency and find the values of attributes. To simplify the task, predicates must be stated such that eager evaluation with unification can determine their truth. So we are left with the problem of interpreting simple Z predicates and expressions.

Originally, the approach taken in Formaliser used "meaning" functions, as in denotational semantics [Stoy]. These functions, when given an environment mapping variables to their values, yielded the interpretation of the particular construct. Interestingly, these functions were themselves expressed as attributes on those constructs, again using Z. As with denotational semantics, these highly recursive definitions 'bottomed-out' in a few elementary constructs — in this case the meaning of constants, variables, function application, set membership and equality[1]. At these points Formaliser executed equivalent trivial fragments of Smalltalk code, mimicking the denotational semantics[2]. This approach worked well but had several disadvantages: the "tree-lets" representing the predicates consumed considerable space; it required the Z grammar to be resident even when editing documents in other languages; interpretation was slow.

The new approach exploited Formaliser's simple translation facility, once again. A new concrete syntax for Z was devised to translate simple expressions and predicates into appropriate Smalltalk code, which is then compiled and stowed away. Once the predicates have been translated, their tree-lets can be discarded, the Z grammar is no longer needed for interpretation. The result is considerably faster and uses very little space. (For Z there are about four hundred predicates, and each compiles to less than one hundred bytes.)

Equality is translated to unification; attributes which Formaliser cannot determine (for any reason) are given an 'unknown' value. By default, unification of objects is implemented as Smalltalk equality, whilst unknowns literally take on the identity of the unified object. This nicely implements the generics of Z without the attribute grammar explicitly coping with them. Thus, unification may be used in determining any attribute, not just 'type' — indeed Formaliser makes no distinction between attributes, they are all determined blindly in the same manner. In this way, the commonly found unification type checking algorithms are subsumed by this more general mechanism.

## Attribute Caches

Each node maintains a cache of attributes determined on demand. So, for example, if the user asks for the type of an expression, only the necessary predicates are checked and all intermediate results are cached. By this means, acceptable performance is maintained for incremental development of documents. However, this incremental policy can be a little slow when, for example, early definitions are modified by the user, potentially invalidating a large proportion of the cached information. A more sophisticated cache updating mechanism may be required, such as that described by Reps [Reps].

---

[1]Later, we found lambda abstractions to be very useful.

[2]These translations are so straightforward that they are now done automatically.

## The Status and Future

Formaliser exists, and is demonstrable now. Development is proceeding with the general intention of making the prototype tool available to interested users in the near future. We are currently working on a number of upgrades, including:

- the removal of a few annoying characteristics of the tool;

- performance improvements (especially to the parser);

- the display of types in a more useful manner;

- a "seamless" interface to the L^TEX text formatter and *f*UZZ macro package, used for printing the specification produced by Formaliser;

- better recovery from errors, especially in definitions;

- on-line help.

Currently, Formaliser runs on an IBM PC/AT platform.

Of most importance is the need to obtain feedback from some *real* users of Formaliser from their day-to-day work with the tool.

## Summary

We have presented a prototype Z support tool, called Formaliser, for low cost desk-top personal computers.

Formaliser provides an environment in which specifications can be developed interactively, with immediate feedback regarding syntax, scope and type information. Specifications are constructed using a system of menus or directly by typing, with the aid of a palette of symbols.

Although the tool is currently configured for Z, it is implemented in a generic fashion. Formal languages other than Z can be accommodated, by supplying a suitable attribute grammar. The attribute grammar specifies the syntax of the language and its context conditions, such as the scope and type rules of Z. Error reporting is tailored to the language by associating *pro forma* error reports with any such context condition.

Formaliser was used heavily in its own construction and used object oriented techniques throughout, to good effect. The effort expended so far has been remarkably low, and much of this was spent considering design issues, rather than coding.

Through development this prototype, we have gained many valuable insights into formal languages, their support tools, object oriented techniques and human computer interaction. We hope to gain further insights through the continued development of Formaliser.

## Acknowledgements

We would like to thank many of our colleagues at Logica for all the help and advice that they have given. In particular, our thanks go to Rosalind Barden, Ian Clowes and Robert Worden for their comments on the user interface, Colin Grant for his early implementation work, Alistair Wardell and Dick Perkins for their bug reports and Roy MacLean for having to pick up the reins.

141

# References

[Z]            J. M. Spivey, *The Z Notation: A Reference Manual*, Prentice-Hall International, 1989.

[L^TEX]        Leslie Lamport, *L^TEX: A Document Preparation System*, Addison Wesley, 1985.

[fuzz]         J. M. Spivey, *The fuzz Manual*.

[Formaliser]   Mike Flynn, *Attribute Grammar Specification*, *An Attribute Grammar for Z*, and *Design of an Attribute Evaluator*, Formaliser project internal documents, Logica Cambridge Limited.

[Smalltalk]    Adele Goldberg and David Robson, *Smalltalk-80: The Language and its Implementation*, Addison Wesley, 1983.

[Reps]         Thomas W. Reps, *Generating Language-Based Environments*, MIT Press, 1984.

[Stoy]         Joseph E. Stoy, *Denotational Semantics*, MIT Press, 1977.

[Meyer]        Bertrand Meyer, *Object-oriented Software Construction*, Prentice Hall, 1988.

# Using Z to Develop a CASE Toolset

David Brownbridge

PRAIS Systems plc

20 Manvers Street, Bath, Avon, UK. BA1 1PX
(Telephone: 0225-444700,
International: +44 225 444700,
e–mail: drb@praxis.co.uk)

## Abstract

A medium-scale commercial software project which used Z extensively is described. The project developed a CASE toolset to support SSADM. A large specification was produced which was then implemented using the object-oriented language Objective-C. Using Z undoubtedly made the system specification more precise and less open to misinterpretation. The conclusion is that Z can be used as a tool for better system specification with real gains in clarity of expression without requiring formal refinement.

## 1    INTRODUCTION

This paper is about using Z in a commercial environment as part of a standard software development process. A new, medium-sized, software system was specified and then implemented. The system specification consisted of a large document containing Z and explanatory text; the implementation was performed in Objective-C[1].

The requirements given by the client were to develop a complete CASE toolset for SSADM[2]. CASE (Computer Aided Software Engineering) is the generic name for interactive software which supports a particular method of systems analysis or design. SSADM is a paper-based systems analysis method used extensively in government computing (and soon to become mandatory for some classes of work).

A common problem with SSADM is difficulty in managing the volume of documents produced. Small changes to documents, especially diagrams, require tedious manual re-drafting. Over time, documents which depend on each other become inconsistent. These problems can be reduced by the computerisation of SSADM using interactive workstations to edit documents and a central file server to maintain project consistency. The initial system is based on Sun UNIX machines connected over Ethernet.

Work on the project began in July 1987. The specification phase was completed by February 1988 and implementation delivered in June 1989. The project team was 4–7 people, most with some background in maths and/or formal methods.

The key software engineering features of the project were:

1. *clean sheet* design with no requirements for backwards compatibility, only the requirement to automate SSADM;

2. software structured in two parts: tools and infrastructure;

   the tools contain all things specific to SSADM such as the layout of forms and the role of particular documents in the SSADM analysis process;

   the infrastructure provides general facilities to store, display and edit documents;

3. SSADM information is shared amongst users with strong consistency requirements, to ensure a coherent picture of the analysis is always available;

4. information is distributed, using individual workstations and a central document server connected by a network;

5. the system is interactive, using large display screens with a mouse for direct manipulation of diagrams etc.

6. all of the SSADM method is to be automated, not just preparation of individual documents but all aspects of SSADM projects including management and delegation of work items.

The project consisted of three phases:

Phase 1 – in which the facilities of the infrastructure were specified;

Phase 2 – in which the infrastructure software was built;

Phase 3 – in which the SSADM tools using the infrastructure were built.

On completion of Phase 1, Phases 2 and 3 were carried out in parallel. Phases 1 and 2 were carried out at Praxis and Phase 3 was carried out mainly by client staff. Phase 1 (specification) delivered a document called the 'Abstract Specification', a Z specification containing 945 fragments of typechecked Z in a 340 page narrative. Phase 2 (infrastructure) delivered 37,000 lines of documented tested code (excluding comments and test suites). This paper covers work on Phases 1 and 2 and not the work of Phase 3.

The work of the whole project team is described here and I am grateful for their advice in preparing this paper; any opinions, errors or omissions are of course my own, not those of the team, nor of Praxis.

## 2    PROJECT ISSUES

This section describes non-technical issues raised by the use of Z. They are relevant to Z in a commercial software development context.

At the proposal stage before the contract was let, Praxis decided the that best way to approach the project was to use formal specification followed by object-oriented design and programming. A formal notation was felt to be the right way of structuring the specification of a completely new and possibly complex piece of software. Object-oriented design and programming was the key to providing the kind of highly interactive window-based environment required.

## 2.1   Why Z?

Given the decision to use a formal specification, the decision to use Z was made early in the specification phase of the project. Some of the team had previous practical experience with Z or VDM. All had training in one or the other. At the time the choice was balanced between Z and VDM but two factors resulted in Z being chosen:

1.   the ability to structure large specifications using the schema calculus;

2.   availability of a typechecker.

Both these factors remedied shortcomings found with VDM on a previous Praxis project where a similar-sized specification was produced. In that project, it was found difficult to review the specification because of the lack of structure and some reviewing time was wasted on trivial faults that a typechecker would have detected. We have no regrets in choosing Z.

Z played a number of roles in the project. In Phase 1, specification notes were used to communicate ideas between the team. The Abstract Specification, containing Z, was the major deliverable of Phase 1. As such it was used as the basis for building the infrastructure in Phase 2 and the tools using the infrastructure in Phase 3.

## 2.2   Early Specification

At the earliest stages of the project, Z provided a *vocabulary* making it easier to communicate ideas. The act of selecting Z *given sets* was important in setting the boundary of the specification. The given sets define the level of abstraction and provide a basis for discussion. Once we had decided that the basic components of the system were objects called documents, we could discuss and eventually specify their properties.

As the specification progressed, a series of *specification notes* were produced. Each covered a single aspect of the system and used Z to specify that aspect *eg Z Specification of the System Administration Facilities*. A specification note was typically a 3 or 4 page document describing the specification of a single aspect of the system. Notes were issued and retained as project documents but not formally reviewed. As ideas became clearer some of the notes were improved and reissued, perhaps incorporating informal input from other team members or coming into line with other parts of the emerging specification.

## 2.3   The Abstract Specification

Towards the end of the specification phase, work was begun on the final consolidated specification documents. These were written as a whole, using the ideas from the various specification notes. The large Z specification document was called the *Abstract Specification* and a shorter *Concrete Specification* was also produced. The Abstract Specification contained the main parts of the system specification including the system state and operations expressed in Z. The Concrete Specification provided a programming language definition of the main system objects expressed in Objective-C.

The Abstract Specification had three purposes:

1.  to document the specification;

2.  to communicate the specification to the implementors;

3.  to communicate the specification to the users.

It was very successful in the first and second of these and to a lesser extent in the third. The specification was undoubtedly better for the use of Z. Implementors had a precise and comprehensive description of the system. The users were programmers employed by the client, writing code to use an interface we specified. There was a tendency for them to rely on the Concrete Specification. This meant that some aspects of the *meaning* of operations were hidden to them and required further explanation. Clearly there is a training obligation if Z is to be delivered to a client.

## 2.4 Team Issues

Team members must have some formal Z training. This can be achieved either through a full-length Z course or by a shorter conversion course from, say, VDM.

Typically, a week of basic training in Z was supplemented by advice from more experienced team members and feedback through the formal review process. It was found that a 3–5 day course in writing Z was sufficient for staff to begin writing useful specifications. The Z notation itself is indeed easier to learn than some programming languages. Although the notation is straightforward, it is harder to choose the right level of abstraction in a specification. The team was steered by the experience of a technical leader practiced in writing Z. It is not enough for the team to be proficient in Z in-the-small – writing good correct fragments of Z; someone is needed who can set the right level of abstraction and ensure the specification fits properly with the rest of the project. The tasks of this technical leader include:

1.  direct early specification;

2.  guide the team to correct level of abstraction in specifications;

3.  advise on details of Z (less important);

4.  act as editor for the completed specification.

The technical leader can be full-time team member or part-time consultant who has already been involved in the use of formal specification.

## 2.5 Maintaining The Abstract Specification

For the specification to be of any use to implementors, it must be maintained throughout program development. It becomes a major piece of the documentation of the delivered product. Changes during implementation arise for a number of reasons:

1.  client change-requests which alter the way the system works;

2.  internal changes: reconsideration of specification decisions;

3.  clarifications: expanding the specification to explain things better.

All these changes resulted in periodic reissue of the specification. The specification was expanded to cover some areas in greater detail. An example was concurrency control which was extended to take account of network delays.

## 2.6 Productivity

Specification occupied about a quarter of the total effort of Phases 1 and 2. This covered both the Abstract and Concrete Specifications. Within the specification effort, Z was produced at a rate of a little over one schema per day's effort. A further half of the total effort was spent on code development, the remaining quarter being taken up by requirements analysis, project management, system testing etc.

It was felt that the effort of producing a formal specification was repaid by a relatively short time needed for lower-level design which proceeded with little reworking. This saving was offset by unexpected complexity in parts of the user interface code which had not been formally specified. The overall rate of code production over the whole of Phases 1 and 2 was higher than would be expected without a formal specification. Measuring in lines of code (excluding comments) specified in Z, written, documented and tested per day, the overall production figure was 17 lines per day. This is 1.5 times the figure Boehm predicts for a *semi-detached* project of this size[3].

The conclusion of the team was that Z allowed real problems to be brought forward and dealt with earlier, and thus more efficiently, than would otherwise have been possible.

Nonetheless, specification can be hard to do and review. It is very different from informal specification and can require as much management effort as writing a program of the same size. No great productivity gains can be claimed but there is a strong feeling that a better job was done by using Z. It is too early to assess the rate of residual fault detection in the delivered code although this will be useful for comparison with code not formally specified.

## 3    TECHNICAL ISSUES

This section covers technical issues relating to Z usage when specifying a large system whether in a commercial project or elsewhere.

### 3.1    Standards

Two kinds of standards are needed to use Z effectively:

1.   a standard for the Z notation;

2.   a standard defining how the notation is to be used.

Currently, Spivey's Reference Manual[4] is the recommended candidate for the first class of standard. Previously there was no single definitive description of Z widely available.

Standards for Z usage are more a matter of taste and local preference. They are needed for the same reasons as coding standards are needed in software development: to define a uniform 'house-style' and promote clarity and maintainability.

For the CASE project a two-part project standard for Z usage was used. The first part provided a basis for formally reviewing documents containing Z and is now being adopted as a company-wide standard. It defined standard practice as observed in the literature and dictated by experience in using Z. For example:

- each fragment of Z is preceded by explanatory text;

- given sets are spelt in UPPER CASE, schema names Capitalised and variables in lower case;

- For every schema S

$$\Delta S \cong S \wedge S'$$

and

$$\Xi S \cong [\, S \wedge S' \mid \theta S = \theta S' \,]$$

The second part of the project standard provided guidance specific to the project. We were sure the implementation would be an object-oriented language but uncertain how far to make this apparent in the Z specification. Guidelines were prepared for specifying objects, classes and inheritance. These are described in a separate paper[5] and will not be described here.

On a multi-person project it is important to discourage over-clever use of Z. This is hard to define in a standard; reviews are the main weapon against such practices. Some published Z specifications have been 'neat' at the expense of simple readability.

## 3.2 Structure

The Abstract Specification was a large document requiring careful structuring to avoid becoming unwieldy. It was divided into thirteen chapters each describing a relatively self-contained part of the system. Specifications from successive chapters were combined using the schema calculus.

The first six chapters defined the configuration management facilities on the server and workstation, culminating with a schema defining the entire system state and its operations. Five more chapters described the abstract objects from which SSADM documents could be built and the facilities for display and editing them. Another two chapters described administration of the system as a whole including backup, archiving and retrieval. Finally an appendix was used to contain a library of Z constructs used throughout the specification. These were general extensions to the mathematical library, such as the specification of a 'tree' data structure.

The implementation had a different structure, determined by programming constraints and recorded in the *System Architecture* document. In order to implement a single top-level schema correctly, all of its included schema must be understood. During the implementation it would have been useful to have some sort of high-level road-map of the specification allowing the schema inclusion hierarchy to be traced. Some help was given by including a summary of operations at the end of each chapter. In future projects a road-map should be produced, probably in the form of a diagram.

## 3.3 Tools

Use of checking tools increases confidence in a specification. It must be considered irresponsible not to use whatever tools are available. In many cases, theorem proving will be less important than simple typechecking. (No proofs were included in the Abstract Specification.) For example, use of a simple typechecker helps formal reviewers to concentrate on higher-level aspects of the specification, instead of getting lost in the details.

We used an early version of the FORSITE parser and typechecker. FORSITE normally operates in conjunction with the QED screen-based editor. A specially adapted 'ASCII' edition was obtained from Racal Research[6], not requiring QED, enabling standard editors to be used. Documents were prepared using the UNIX *troff* formatting program. Each document contained *troff* source plus fragments of Z in FORSITE syntax bracketed by **startZ ... endZ** keywords. A UNIX command was developed to extract the Z from a document and pass it to FORSITE for checking and another to process FORSITE Z syntax into printable *troff* form.

In addition to typechecking, there is a clear need for a simple tool to expand and merge schemas and provide other editing and browsing facilities. A typechecker tends to concentrate attention on low-level details of Z. This is especially bad at early specification stages when ideas are being sketched out – one tends to become more worried about correct placement of semi-colons. It would have been useful to have a way of partially typechecking an incomplete specification.

The Abstract Specification was a 340 page document consisting of Z embedded in English language commentary. As a rough measure of the amount of Z used, there were 945 **startZ ... endZ** pairs each representing a distinct fragment of Z. A total of 619 schemas and 52 given sets were used .

Whilst there were problems with the resources needed to typecheck large documents it was important to be able to have confidence in a basic level of consistency before beginning to formally review documents. (The Abstract Specification took more than 30 minutes to typecheck on an otherwise idle Sun 3/50.)

No really serious defects were uncovered by typechecking alone. On the other hand, most chapters of the Abstract Specification were found to have real type inconsistencies, or at least mistakes in the use of types such as using 'DOC' (document identifier) where 'DOCV' (document *version* identifier) was intended.

### 3.4  Refinement

Experience on the CASE project has shown that Z can be used to specify and implement a new system without formal refinement. It is sufficient to have an informal relationship between the specification and the software which implements it. By using an object-oriented language, the gap between specification and implementation is narrower than with conventional languages. This is partly through the use of high-level libraries providing data structures and screen management, and partly by the nature of object-oriented languages which allows software to be re-used.

Even without refinement, the specification can be used as the reference when constructing test suites. Test suites were independently constructed by referring to the specification, not low-level code documentation. For example tests on a Text class can be derived from the Text schema, rather than the class description of the Objective-C Text class.

### 4  CONCLUSIONS

Z was especially useful in specifying the configuration management aspects of the CASE system. This part of the specification was essentially a distributed database with associated integrity constraints. An *ad hoc* approach to refinement worked well; time did not permit a rigorous refinement. Use of an object-oriented language ensured the gap between specification and code was relatively narrow. A separate program design phase is necessary, in place of refinement, once system specification is complete. After that, system tests were derived direct from specification independent of the code.

If embarking on a similar project again, we would use Z. Z can be a useful specification tool without requiring the whole of a formal development method. When a system specification is relatively complicated, problems are exposed and dealt with earlier, and more efficiently, than in informal specification. Although code metrics are notoriously approximate, we believe code was produced faster than would have been expected otherwise.

**REFERENCES**

1    Cox, B J, *Object Oriented Programming,* Addison-Wesley, London ISBN 0-201-10393-1, 1986.

2    Longworth, G and Nicholls, D, *SSADM Manual,* NCC Publications, Manchester, 1986.

3    Boehm, B W, *Software Engineering Economics,* Prentice Hall, 1981.

4    Spivey, J M, *The Z Notation, A Reference Manual,* Prentice Hall  ISBN 0-13-983768-X (paperback), 1988.

5    Hall, J A, *Using Z as a Specification Calculus for Object-Oriented Systems. (To appear in Proceedings of 'VDM90')*

6    Lowe, C, *ASCII Forsite: Users Guide,* Racal Research Ltd.

# Using Z to Describe Large Systems

T.C. Nash

TPMS Project

ICL

Wenlock Way

West Gorton

Manchester M12 5DR

Tel. 061-223-1301 extn. 2495

## Abstract

This paper deals with the problems of using Z on a large software product. The specific aim is to show how Z can be used to describe a large system, where the number of refinement steps from a single abstract view to implementation is large, i.e. significantly more than one or two as assumed by the average textbook. The method described is currently in use for respecifying TPMS, ICL's Transaction Processing monitor for VME.

We intend to concentrate on the design method, avoiding discussion on why we are applying it to TPMS and what the consequences might be. This could be the subject of a future paper, after we have given the method prolonged exposure and used the results on the actual product. The current paper deals with the subject from a practical point of view: it is aimed more at an audience of software designers than mathematicians.

The primary feature of the method described is that it allows for an arbitrary number of refinement steps between initial specification and implementation, without requiring that we re-describe the entire system at every level. This avoids duplication, and in so doing helps to prevent the introduction of inconsistencies between levels (given that proof of consistency is not economic). The resulting design record consists of a tree-like structure of individual specifications, each of which is complete in its own right. Each design step requires the consideration of a single specification, either as an isolated entity or as an abstract view of a small number of lower level specifications. Thus the complexity of the design task does not increase with the size of the system.

We show that despite having an arbitrary number of levels of abstraction, a design produced using this method still has four parts corresponding to the traditional Requirements - Specification - Design - Implement split, but that

# 1 Introduction

This paper deals with a method by which the Z notation, in conjuction with other techniques, can be used to design large systems. The underlying principle is that of structural modelling (data driven functional decomposition) as employed by ICL in the design of VME.

Most text books on the subject of refinement deal with small examples and generally take you from a fairly small specification down to implementation in a small number of steps. The process by which a single operation can be turned into a number of operations or code modules, and the result shown to be equivalent to the original specification, are explored in great detail. However, there is usually the implicit assumption that the representation of the system at any level is always a single specification.

This clearly cannot be the case for a large software system, where the number of operations near the implementation level is likely to number in the hundreds if not thousands. This paper therefore deals not with the refinement issues such as operation decomposition and proof, but rather with the specific problems of how to organise the specification and development of an arbitrarily large system.

Section 2 outlines a method of structuring the development process and its documentation which is capable of dealing with an arbitrarily large product. This is then expanded upon by §3, which deals with specific techniques and approaches required to make the method work. Some observations about the work carried out so far at ICL are discussed in §4.

Finally, the appendix contains some annotated extracts of a fictitious set of design documents. Although on the surface this is a 'toy' example, it is constructed to demonstrate problems found in the specification of a real large system, namely TPMS, and to show possible methods of solving these problems.

# 2 Method Overview

The basic approach is to start with a single very high level abstract specification, but then rather than refine individual operations we divide the specification into subsystems[1], typically 4–6, each containing some part of the state plus all the *basic* operations which interact with it. By basic operation we mean one defined as an individual schema rather than in terms of previously defined operations. We deliberately leave out the other operations: The basic premise is that having defined once that $A \cong X \land Y$ there is no reason to repeat the fact in the lower level descriptions of $X$ and $Y$.

In order to do this we assume a specification written in the style whereby each function is described as the combination of a number of basic operations, each of which uses a small part of the overall system state. The state is therefore also made up from parts rather than being declared all at once.

We then take each subsystem and produce a more detailed specification of it,

---

[1]We use the term subsystem in this document in a general sense — a subsystem is some self contained group of functions which may be divided into further subsystems in less abstract descriptions. In some environments (ICL CADES in particular) subsystem has a stricter definiton, where these logical divisions have to be given some other name such as 'mini-subsystems'.

by redefining the single state component as a number of parts, and producing refinements of the original basic operations again in terms of operations made up of several parts. In this way we obtain further specifications which can themselves be divided using the same technique.

Notice that these subsystems taken together do *not* add up to the complete system, because they represent only the *basic* operations from the higher level. We still have to combine them according to the rules expressed in the higher level specifications. On the other hand, the state description at each level may actually get larger as we introduce data to do with aspects of the implementation.

The complete system specification will therefore be in the form of a tree of specifications, each of which is a self contained definition of some subset of the system at a given level of abstraction. The important feature is that when describing how two subsystems at the same level interact we do it in terms of a more abstract view of those subsystems rather than at the same level. Thus the level of understanding required at any time is restricted to the order of complexity of a single specification, rather than all of the specifications at a particular level. The corollary of this is that in implementing the system we need to refer to the entire network of specifications, not just the lowest level.

We have introduced the Specification part of the conventional development route, and that is the part we concentrate on in this paper. But how does this relate to the other three phases: Requirements Capture, Design and Implementation?

We believe that the Requirements statement should have the same structure as the specification, and as a result will be produced in parallel with it. The order would be:

- Produce abstract requirements document for the whole system.

- Produce abstract specification for the whole system.

- Decompose that specification into subsystems. This involves making design decisions about the logical structure (architecture) of the eventual implementation.

- For each identified subsystem re-examine the abstract requirements and add further details which arise from design decisions made in the abstract specification and it's decomposition.

The Requirements document for each subsystem could be called the user view of that subsystem, where 'user' could represent some other part of the system as well as an actual end user. As such these documents will normally contain more than one view of the subsystem.

The alternation between specification and requirements is a formalisation of a familiar process: as the result of making design decisions we have to go back to the originator to 'clarify' the requirements. The benefit of mirroring the structure of the specification in the requirements statement is that we can record which design decisions gave rise to the lower level requirements.

The design phase produces a mapping from the complete specification onto a particular implementation. This will similarly work a level at a time, but in general this will be bottom up. The lowest level specifications will contain operations that can be directly translated into code — but remember that since each level redefines only the basic operations of the level above, we produce only a set of procedures and data which are as yet not connected to each other in any way. We must progress to the next level up in the specification, where we will find a set of rules for how the procedures we have created so far should interact. This may result in new procedures (but not new data), or in modifications to the ones we already have. This must continue until we reach the most abstract level where we finally obtain a complete system.

It is important to realise that this process *does not* imply that the physical structure of the resulting product (in terms of the procedure calling hierarchy) has to resemble the logical structure of the specification in any way. In a transaction processing system for example, the top level may well contain an operation called 'process message'. It would be naïve to expect to find a procedure in the product which carried out this operation, as this would imply that 'process message' could be carried out synchronously, without reference to anything else going on in the system. And we all know that TP systems were invented exactly because this cannot be done. What we *should* have is a description of how the system contrives to make it *look* like 'process message' is a synchronous operation. This is what the design method described in this paper gives you.

The design method can therefore accomodate any number of levels of abstraction, but still results in the four basic types of document present in traditional methods: Requirements, Specification, Design and Implementation. The difference is that we do not consider each of these four as a different level of abstraction. Instead we say that for each level of abstraction there is a description made up of the four parts. Thus the existence of the four phases of development no longer limits the number of refinement steps, and so in theory there is no limit to the complexity of system which can be described. Using this as a basic principle, the following sections now explore the method in more detail.

# 3  Method

## 3.1  A Document Structure

Figure 1 illustrates how the various documents described in the overview fit together. The boxes labeled 'U' represent the requirements documents (U is for User view), 'S' represents specification and 'R' refinement. These documents make up the design model. Then we have the low level design documents labelled 'N' (for narrative) which enable us finally to produce the implementation. The arrows indicate that the number of documents at each level increases—try to imagine that you are looking at a set of tree-like structures side on, where the structure of each tree is the same.

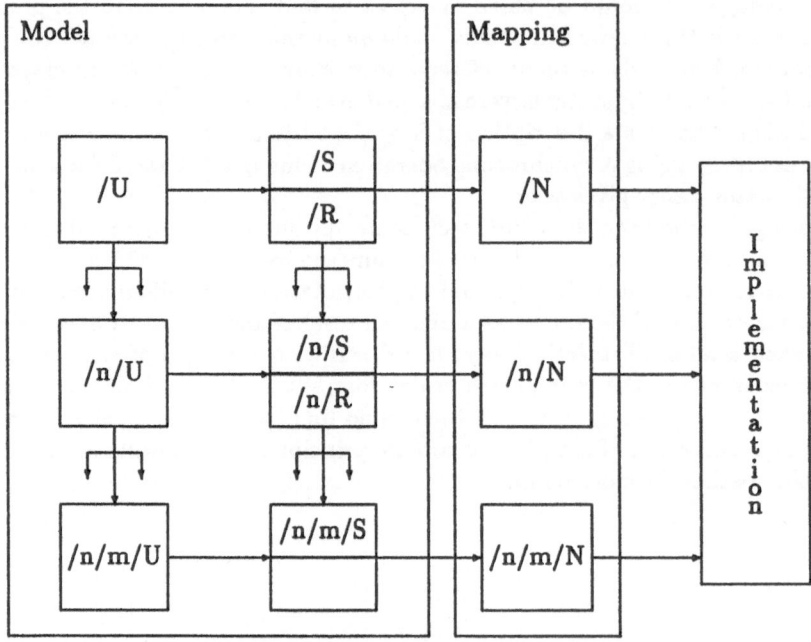

Figure 1: Document Structure

The top level documents simply have letters as a reference, there being only a single set of these. The next level will contain several subsystems, with a set of documents for each, and these will be numbered from 1 upwards. The ordering of the numbers is not significant, and need not be consecutive—we are just giving ourselves a key for a filing system. Subsequent levels then gain additional numbers, derived from their parents. TP/2/5/S would be the specification document from the fifth subsystem derived in TP/2/R for example, and would therefore refine some selection of operations from TP/2/S. The 'TP' prefix is simply some tag for the system being described.

There is no rule which states that every branch of the tree has to extend to the same depth. You simply stop when you get to something which can be implemented directly. There is also no requirement that the network be a strict tree: if the same function is required in a number of places (a storage manager say) then the node representing that function will have more than one parent. From the point of view of numbering, in this case it would probably be best to start a new tree with a different name, rather than arbitrarily choose which parent determines the shared subsystem number.

## 3.2   Requirements

The requirements documentation has these features:

- Requirements are stated in terms of interfaces to the system, so the user is told not only what the system does, but how to access each function. As such we are describing a mapping between requirement and specification rather than pure requirements.

- We document requirements of one part of the system on another within the same structure. This includes requirements on components outside the actual product we are considering: in a description of a transaction processing system we would expect to find requirements on terminal hardware and device driving.

- Interfaces are described according to their logical functionality rather than their physical implementation. The actual syntax of an interface will be described in the lowest level requirements documents: at the higher levels different parameters from the same physical interface may well be described in different documents.

At the top level we should describe a function rather than a product. In that way as the specification process develops we will obtain requirements documents which describe parts of the system which are used to provide the functionality sought by the user, but are not parts of the product: they are descriptions of system components which the product makes use of. When we discuss our requirements with the owners of the other system components, we can present them with our model of what their component does—they do not have to try to understand how our product operates. In this way the boundary between the product and its environment develops naturally as the design progresses, rather than being artificially forced on the abstract view of the system.

We are dealing with only part of the requirements process here: that part which states what needs the system will satisfy, and by what means. In practice we should also provide information about non functional requirements concerning aspects such as performance.

The very top level contains an abstract description of what the system will do, described from the point of view of each type of user. If we take a particular interface expressed in the top level, we will find it linked to one or more less abstract interfaces at the next level down: each of these lower level interfaces will reveal in more detail how some particular piece of information is to be communicated. The use of the system is therefore described in a hierarchical fashion according to logical functionality—which is the sort of input we require for producing well written user documentation.

As an example, if the top level informs us that we are allowed to 'make a phone call', then we would expect a lower level to describe 'dialling the number' and 'speaking into the handset' in *separate* documents. Only at the very lowest level would we discover that there are two ways to dial a number (buttons or dial) and that the handset is physically attached to the same piece of equipment.

When re-implementing an existing product (or working to a predefined interface) it is important to avoid describing the logic of the system in terms of the target syntax of the interfaces. Otherwise you will find yourself describing operations which simply copy information from one place to another without needing it for anything else.

The requirements documentation presents interfaces in a structured way. The idea is that for each available function we present the information required or supplied first in the abstract and then in progressively more detail, presenting alternatives in a logical fasion where a given function may be implemented in more than one way.

## 3.3   Specification

A specification document must describe what must be done to provide the interfaces decribed in the corresponding requirements document. That is, it must produce operations whose signatures include the parameters declared for the defined interfaces, and whose behaviour is compatible with the various user views of the system. A specification is the internal view of a subsystem, which must be shown to be equivalent to the various user views contained in the corresponding Requirements document.

A specification must be capable of being split up into a number of small pieces which can then be grouped together into subsystems to form the basis for producing lower level specifications. This demands rather than encourages a modular style. In our experience Z is a particularily good language in this respect, provided certain conventions are adopted to avoid the semantic problems with some parts of the schema calculus (negation is not generally a good idea for example).

The key to success is to be aware of the different information requirements in the system, and to reflect this in the way the state and operations are defined. That is, construct the specification with the rules of information hiding in mind. This may well lead to a division of the system which is orthogonal to a functional split: this is certainly true of TPMS. Whereas the top level requirements document for TPMS concentrates on transporting a message from A to B as a single function, the specification splits this up into parts:

- the physical transport of a message

- the decision making process which determines the destination of a message (i.e. which application is required)

- controlling whether an application is able to recieve a message

Further, we try to separate out consideration of the fact that we have to carry out these processes for many users simultaneously. Each operation is therefore made up of a number of basic operations, each dealing with some aspect of one of the areas listed above.

By describing the operations in this way we produce a specification of the right form to be split up according to information visibility. Or to put it another way we are beginning to develop the rules defining the architecture of the system, which control the visibility of information within it.

We should not let the requirement for this sort of granularity get in the way of producing a readable specification. Where it is natural to describe an operation which uses more than one state component (such as $Decode_0$ in the example, C.2) then it should be described in this way. It is for reasons such as this that we have a separate 'refinement' document which formally records the division of a specification, including any adjustments to the original form of basic operations—see the next section.

Notice that each specification document is a full Z specification in its own right, and can therefore be understood without reference to the rest of the system. Essentially each specification says

> "If I assume that these basic operations (which I specify as schemas) can be implemented, then I can combine them together thus and so to provide the functions I have been asked for in the corresponding requirements document."

At the top level the functions requested are the functions required of the system—at lower levels they are the basic operations assumed at the next level up.

If the reader having understood a particular specification then wishes to see how it fits in to the 'larger picture' he reads the corresponding specification in the next level up—*not* the other specifications at the same level. Here he will find an abstraction of the specification he has just read (in the form of a number of basic operations) combined with other operations from other subsystems to provide some higher level functionality. Similarly if he wishes to see how a particular basic operation is implemented he reads *one* specification from the next level down. In this way the level of understanding needed to work through the system is restricted to the order of magnitude of one specification, regardless of the size of the total system.

The importance of this can be seen if we consider a conventional Z specification in which only the schema calculus is used to express modularity. If the component schemas are well chosen, there is no problem in communicating an intuitive idea of the meaning of a particular operation. However, to obtain a formal understanding of the operations one must unravel the schema calculus to get at the fundamental mathematical objects. As a specification gets larger, this becomes progressively more difficult—the 'distance' between an idea and the mathematics which represents it increases. The method described in this paper avoids this problem essentially by introducing intermediate abstractions of parts of the specification, thus enabling the distance between idea and mathematics to be kept constant.

Taking the network of specifications as a whole, there are a number of techniques which are used to control the size and complexity of specifications in the higher levels;

- The more abstract specifications tend not to deal with error handling. We simply specify pre-conditions, and allow the design at the lower levels to strengthen the pre-conditions by generating error messages. This is most applicable to declarative type interfaces, where we are providing the system with information rather than actually carrying out work.

- Similarily we tend not to specify system status displays. These can safely be introduced at lower levels as valid refinements of $\Xi SystemState$.

- The given types used at the higher levels need to be *very* abstract, and therefore when used on an interface represent a large amount of information. Almost inevitably lower level specifications will use more restricted types, and so strictly speaking they are not true implementations of the higher level. This could be dealt with mathematically by use of arbitrary functions representing the translation of the internal view of an object to that of the particular user, but this would confuse rather than clarify the specification. There has to be a trade-off between readability and absolute rigour.

Specific techniques are required to move the design towards implementation. The most important one is to do with parallelism and divisibility of operations. We may well have specified an operation which in practice requires the allocation of some resource which may incur a delay, e.g. the aquisition of space in which to store something. Where an operation described in the parent specification might simply state that a copy of a piece of information is made in the system state, in practice we know that resources are always limited, and therefore

1. There may be a delay before the operation can complete

2. During that delay other events may occur in the system which introduce conditions which did not have to be considered at the abstract level (since there the operation was indivisible, or atomic).

3. We may therefore have to arbitrate between multiple processes which were totally independent in the abstract.

Thus we wish to refine a single operation into a sequence of operations separated in time, so we might state

$$A \sqsubseteq X \longrightarrow Y \longrightarrow Z$$

where $\longrightarrow$ is a non-Z symbol[2] which may be read as 'then' or 'followed by'. This is used instead of the natural alternative $\,\natural\,$ because the latter is too strict. Schema composition says that the after state on the left is *identical* to the before state on the right—and we specifically need it to change (typically $X$ says we are waiting for a resource, $Y$ says we have aquired it, $Z$ then uses it). Similarly we might write

$$\natural\ \Delta State\ \natural$$

but this would be too weak—we would expect the state to remain unchanged with respect to the process that is waiting.

We can then construct a 'system' which can execute any particular operation one at a time:

$$System \cong X \vee Y \vee Z$$

and we can show that this will indeed perform the sequence $X \longrightarrow Y \longrightarrow Z$ under all circumstances. You can expect to deduce from reasoning like this that the system

---

[2]There is a subtle typographical difference between the CSP '$\longrightarrow$' and the Z '$\rightarrow$'.

only works if some other process will release the resource that $A$ is waiting for. It is no accident that the symbol $\longrightarrow$ is borrowed from CSP: that algebra will no doubt prove useful in producing formal arguments in this sort of specification.

A consequence of this sort of refinement is that we will introduce additional state components to keep track of where we are in the sequence of sub-operations implementing the more abstract operation—we need to know that we have done $X$ and $Y$ but not $Z$. Since these intermediate states have no equivalent in the abstract description, it follows that the usual refinement proofs can only be applied when these extra state components have particular values: specifically, those values that represent states in which there are no partially completed operations as defined by the parent specification.

We can see therefore that the implementation of a basic operation may not be a simple combinatorial affair. But what the lower level specification must contain is an explanation (if not a proof) of how the system is made to appear as if operations are being carried out indivisibly. This is of course a crucial aspect to the TPMS project, where data integrity in a multiprocessing environment is vital.

Each specification is one step in a transformation of an abstract logical view of the system to an implementable physical view which can potentially have a markedly different structure. This method is therefore equally applicable to sequential systems and reactive / interrupt driven systems, such as are found in transaction processing.

## 3.4 Refinement

We have already discussed refinement in the context of the specification documents, where we were considering how to refine particular operations. In the refinement *document* we consider the relationship between subsystems as a whole rather than between individual operations. It is the refinement documents which contain the full architectural definition of the system—that is, they define completely what information is allowed to pass from one part of the system to another.

The refinement process begins with an analysis of the specification. We are particularily interested in the operations that are defined directly as schemas rather than as combinations of other operations: what we call *basic* operations as opposed to *compound* operations. We look for ways of grouping these together with components of the system state to form independent sub-systems. This process will only work if we have written the specification with a particular structure in mind, as discussed in the previous section—the refinement process can only reveal a structure that is already there, it cannot create one out of nothing.

There may be operations which use more than one part of the state. In these cases we define an interface so that we can refine the one operation in the abstract specification into two operations in the lower level, each belonging to different sub-systems but sharing information through the specified interface. The interface is described by a schema containing a number of data types. (Or of course we can modify the original specification if that seems appropriate.)

Thus we might write

```
┌─ Interface ──────────────────────────────────────
│  declarations defining information carried
└──────────────────────────────────────────────────
```

$$Abstract \sqsubseteq (Concrete_1 \wedge Concrete_2) \setminus Interface^3$$

What we are doing by this is breaking the system into a number of parts, and defining their relationships to each other in terms of their interfaces, or rather the information that may be exchanged. This can be thought of as a specification or set of constraints which will help to determine the physical structure of the final product. Notice that we avoid making any statement about who is the initiator in the transaction, even to the extent that there are no ! or ? decorations: the implementation of the information sharing is therefore unconstrained.

The general strategy should be to deal with only the basic operations, and make no use of the compound operations at all. This will lead to the most flexible implementation, since by definition you would subsequently be able to introduce or modify compound operations in the top level (leaving the basic operations alone) in the knowledge that the changes to the implementation would be just as simple. For most real world systems, it is not that easy, and some additional techniques are required.

The typical situation is that we wish to take advantage of the fact that certain operations only occur in given combinations, e.g. there are three operations $A$, $B$, $C$ which only ever appear as $A \wedge B$ or $A \wedge C$—never in other combinations or by themselves.

We might then be able to optimise the implementation by producing different versions of $A$ according to the context. We then allow refinement relations of the form

$$A \wedge B \sqsubseteq X_{a1} \wedge Y_b$$
$$A \wedge C \sqsubseteq X_{a2} \wedge Y_c$$

where the various $X$ and $Y$ operations are in different subsystems.

This technique allows us to express design optimisations without polluting the specification proper. Notice that we are not just stating what optimisations we are making, we are explicitly and precisely stating the assumptions under which they operate.

To summarise, the refinement document does these things:

- It defines the target architecture of the system, by specifying information ownership. In so doing it may present an alternative view of certain operations and interfaces in the specification.

- It provides the formal definition of which basic operations go in which subsystems at the next level. This link is actually used in both directions, to find out how an operation is implemented and to discover what some part of the implementation is for.

---

[3] This is not legal Z according to Spivey, but it is very useful. For '*Interface*' read '(List of names declared by *Interface*)'.

- It states the assumptions (if any) that may be made in the lower levels in the form of dependencies on what is in the parent specification.

## 3.5  Implementation

When it comes to implementing a system decribed in this way, obviously we do not just consider the bottom level specification. Although this describes all of the system state, in terms of functionality it defines only a set of 'building block' operations which have to be put together according to rules defined in the higher level specifications.

The process for implementing the bottom level specifications is the same as that presented in standard texts on the subject. Similarly where the higher level specifications simply combine operations using plain schema calculus the options are fairly obvious: given $A \triangleq B \wedge C$ you can either create a procedure which calls the implementations of $B$ and $C$ (in either order) or if $B$ and $C$ are never used independently you might change one to call the other.

The real work comes when we have to consider more complex constructions, such as that in 3.3 which deals with resource allocation in a multiple process environment. The specification itself is easy enough to implement, since its higher level (compound) operations will always be expressed in terms of sequential combinations of its basic operations. But these are not direct representations of operations found in the parent specification—when we come to implement this we find that we have to combine operations which are no longer implemented as simple procedure calls: instead we have instructions as to how to initiate a process and how to find out if it is finished. The method we choose for ensuring that the higher level operations are carried out in the right combinations then depends on what method we have chosen for controlling processes within the system. This may be free (in which case we have to design it) or it may already be provided in the target environment.

When we are developing a new product it is clear that we can do little work on the implementation of the design until the bottom level of the design has been reached, because the implementation of each level relies on information about how the lower levels are realised.

There is one way in which the implementation does match the specification, and that is in the area of information hiding. We stated above that in working our way back up from the lowest level specification we are only linking existing procedures together: although this linking may involve passing data across interfaces, it will not introduce direct access to any data structures: all such access is limited to the code resulting from the bottom level specification. From the architectural point of view therefore, the implementation obeys rules which are contained in the entire model.

This aspect is important when we are respecifying an existing product, as is the case for TPMS. It means that the specification can guide future developments even though the specification is not yet complete: you can still test proposed changes against the specification to see if they break any rules regarding access to data.

# 4 Conclusion

## 4.1 Current State

The TPMS project are currently re-specifying the product using the method described above. This new specification will eventually replace the existing design documentation, giving us greater control over the product architecture in preparation for large developments in the future.

The current state is that we have produced the top level requirements, design and refinement documents and are working on two subsystems out of the five identified at the next level.

## 4.2 Refinement

By far the hardest part has been producing the initial refinement step from the top level specification, both from the point of view of developing the technique and actually doing the work. There are a number of reasons for this:

- This part of the procedure is not widely dealt with in the literature, and at the same time few people have much experience of it.

- You are forced to think very precisely but very abstractly about the target architecture of the system. This is not something that comes naturally to many designers.

- There are no tools to support this part of the process. For specifications we can make use of type checkers, but for refinements everything is hand crafted.

The refinement process proved to be very worthwhile in that the analysis of the specification structure led us to make improvements and simplifications which we might not otherwise have come up with. It has also had a significant effect on the architecture we had developed informally, in that it exposed weaknesses that were not at all obvious without a detailed examination.

## 4.3 Document Structure

Because of the granularity in both individual documents and in the document structure as a whole, a good document processing system is almost mandatory. As a minimum you need indexes to every document, preferably there should also be global indexes which will reveal the relationships between documents at the various levels.

## 4.4 Summary

It is early days yet to make categorical statements, but generally the method seems to work although it is not easy for everyone to assimilate—it requires a particular attitude of mind which takes time to develop.

There are two areas which could benefit from some theoretical investigation

- The well known concurrency problem, which gives rise in this method to the introduction of intermediate system states which do not correspond to any of the more abstract states, and which cannot therefore be investigated with conventional retrieval relations. While the method can handle concurrency adequately, there is still scope for improving the formalisms used.

- The derivation of implementations from the higher levels of the design model.

## 4.5 References

A method such as the one presented here obviously draws on earlier work from many sources—we only quote the following two which are particularily relevant to the techniques presented:

PRG-62   The Formal Documentation of a Block Stoarge Device
         Roger Gimson

PRG-63   Specifying System Implementations in Z
         Jonathan Bowen, Roger Gimson, Stig Topp-Jørgensen

# A   Example

As an example we introduce extracts from a simplified specification of a transaction processing monitor. This example is deliberately constructed to demonstrate how the design method is applied to specific sorts of problems. The design decisions made may therefore seem a little perverse from time to time, and of course the design itself is incomplete.

Each of the following sections (starting with section B) represent what would be a separate document in a real system. The section titles start with the document reference—the numbering system we use is explained below. The specifications have been cut down to show the relationships between the various bits of mathematics, and are therefore not complete. Proper specifications would be expected to contain much more in the way of descriptive material, diagrams etc and there are few initialisation operations or error cases. Footnotes are used to record information about the method itslef, and to say something about extra items that would appear in a normal specification. These should probably be omitted on first reading.

## A.1   Document Structure

There are three types of document in the design model, covering the requirements, specification and refinement. These are labeled U (User Interface) S (Specification) and R (Refinement). The top level documents have no numeric reference (e.g. EX/U), while the first level documents are numbered according to the subsystem (EX/1/x, EX/2/x). Each subsystem inherits the reference of its parents plus a number to distinguish it from its siblings.

There has not been time to include a mapping to an implementation, but this would be contained in documents numbered in the same way.

# B  EX/U: System User View

## B.1  Introduction

The EX TP monitor takes messages from users and passes them to applications according to a predefined mapping which allows the system to determine which application is to process each message. We are describing only the input path of the system, omitting the fact that a reply should be generated.

## B.2  Users

There are two types of external users, one simply called 'user' who is the user of the system (i.e. of applications) and the other is the application itself.

## B.3  Concepts

We use the names *USER* to represent the application user, and *APP* to name applications.[4] The message passed from a *USER* to an *APP* is *MSG*. This represents both the actual message content and the necessary information to allow it to be routed to the correct destination, i.e. *MSG* embodies everything we know about a specific message.[5]

## B.4  Function

The basic function of the system is to process messages. This involves two users (a message taken from a user is passed on to an application) and so the functionality is described in terms of two different views of the same operation, which must then be related to each other.[6]

### B.4.1  User Interface

Users submit messages for processing.[7]

$$\underline{\quad Process_U \rule{7cm}{0.4pt}}$$
$$msg? : MSG$$
$$user? : USER$$

---

[4]The users and concepts sections generally introduce what will be the given sets in the specification document, hence the syntax.

[5]*MSG* is an example of a *very* abstract data type. The use of such abstraction is crucial to the method, as it allows us to present a very simple (but still complete) view of what is in practice a very complex system.

[6]It may seem a bit artificial to describe the functionality this way. The reason is that when we come to describe the system in more detail we will start to differentiate between the form of message as seen by the user and the application. In the abstract we are saying that the application and the user agree on the meaning of a particular message, while in the concrete we will acknowledge that the physical presentation will be different.

[7]We use subscripts in interface names when there is a relationship between interfaces belonging to different users. In this case *Process_U* and *Process_A* are different ends of one pipeline.

## B.4.2  Applications Interface

Applications are given messages for processing.

```
┌─ Process_A ──────────────────────────────────
│  msg! : MSG
│  adr! : APP
└──────────────────────────────────────────────
```

## B.4.3  Interactions

A message from a user always results in a message for an application.

$$Process \cong Process_U \ldots Process_A{}^8$$

The message submitted by the user is passed unchanged to the application, i.e. in the abstract $msg!$ of $Process_A$ is the same as $msg?$ of $Process_U$.[9]

---

[8]The symbol ... is invented. The statement leads us to expect that in the specification document we will find an operation *Process* which has the parameters of both *Process_U* and *Process_A*.

[9]We could of course define this formally, but we choose not to for economic and practical reasons.

# C  EX/S: System Specification

TP systems receive messages, store them, and subsequently despatch them to somewhere else (i.e. an application).[10] All the information about a particular message is collectively known as:

$$[ \; MSG \; ]$$

## C.1  Single User View

Each user of the system thinks he has the applications to himself, so we first describe the system like that.

For each user we require somewhere to put the message while it is in transit between the user and the application.[11] *Msg* records the current message being processed for a particular user.

```
┌─ Msg ────────────────────────────────────
│ msg : MSG
└────────────────────────────────────────────
```

*Read*$_0$ represents the users half of processing a message, i.e. the capture of a message in the system state.[12]

```
┌─ Read₀ ──────────────────────────────────
│ ΔMsg
│ in? : MSG
│─────────────────────────────────────────
│ msg' = in?
└────────────────────────────────────────────
```

A message is despatched to a destination supplied by another part of the system (see *Decode* later). We are separating the issues of deciding where a message should go, and actually delivering it there.[13]

```
┌─ Despatch₀ ──────────────────────────────
│ ΔMsg
│ out! : MSG[14]
│─────────────────────────────────────────
│ out! = msg
└────────────────────────────────────────────
```

---

[10]In a normal specification we would expect somewhat more descriptive material than this. It is important to give an informal 'top down' view of the system so that the reader is not puzzled by the Z when it starts to construct the system 'bottom up'.

[11]We have already started making design decisions: we could produce a more abstract specification which uses no intermediate storage, but then we would be making no progress from the requirements document. Such a specification could be used in place of section B.4.3 if we were to do the requirements document more formally.

[12]In a real specification there would of course be replies from the application, and we would probably make the user and application take turns. This is an unnecessary complication for the purposes of the example.

[13]This again makes the point that in this specification we are beginning to *design* the system rather than purely specifying it. Thus it is important to structure the specification according to the logical subdivisions we expect to see in the next level of specification.

[14]Although we are sending a message to an application we make no mention of which application it is—this will be supplied by the *Decode*$_0$ operation described later. We might expect that the message and destination would appear on the same interface, but that is an aspect of the implementation which we should not introduce at this point.

Note that once the message is sent we do not need to keep it, hence we write $\Delta Msg$ rather than $\Xi Msg$. That is, $msg'$ is undefined.

## C.2 Routing

The required destination is decoded by a function of $MSG$ yielding the name of an application, $APP$.[15]

$$[\; APP \;]$$

```
┌─ Map ──────────────────────────────────────────
│ map : MSG \nrightarrow APP
└────────────────────────────────────────────────
```

We now require an operation which looks at the current message and determines the application to which it is to be delivered.[16]

```
┌─ Decode₀ ──────────────────────────────────────
│ Msg
│ ΞMap
│ app! : APP
├────────────────────────────────────────────────
│ app! = map msg
└────────────────────────────────────────────────
```

In this case we specify $Msg$ rather than $\Xi Msg$ or $\Delta Msg$ because we wish to leave it to another operation to determine the value of $Msg'$, without suggesting to the implementor of $Decode_0$ that he is permitted to change $Msg$.

## C.3 Complete System

There are in fact many users, represented by:

$$[\; USER \;]$$

For each one we maintain a separate copy of $Msg$. We actually only need this for users which are connected, so $msg\_n$ is partial.[17]

```
┌─ AllMsg ───────────────────────────────────────
│ msg_n : USER \nrightarrow Msg
└────────────────────────────────────────────────
```

---

[15] Any real TP monitor would provide some means to specify/modify *map*, but the resulting operations would be of little interest for our purposes.

[16] Notice that we have chosen to ignore our own advice to construct operations which use only one part of the state. To split $Decode_0$ into two bits piped together would detract from the readability of the design, so we choose to handle this in the refinement document instead (see the discussion in D). One should probably be suspicious of operations which *update* more than one part of the state, particularly if they occur in any numbers. This might be an indication that the state components have not been properly chosen. This is an example of the way this method prompts the iterations necessary to get a design right.

[17] This example does not include connection and disconnection, which would maintain this map.

Each operation refers to a particular user. We therefore write an operation $Sel_0$ which defines which $Msg$ we are talking about for a particular user. Notice that we deliberately choose a form which is independent of the definition of $Msg$.[18]

$$
\begin{array}{|l}
\hline
\_Sel_0 _____ \\
\Delta AllMsg \\
\Delta Msg \\
u? : USER \\
\hline
u? \in \operatorname{dom} msg\_n \\
\theta Msg = msg\_n\ u? \\
msg\_n' = msg\_n \oplus \{\ u? \mapsto \theta Msg'\ \} \\
\hline
\end{array}
$$

The total system state is made up from $AllMsg$ and $Map$, where we had better disallow messages for which we do not know the address.

$$
\begin{array}{|l}
\hline
\_TP _____ \\
AllMsg \\
Map \\
\hline
\forall u : \operatorname{dom} msg\_n \bullet (msg\_n\ u).msg \in \operatorname{dom} map^{19} \\
\hline
\end{array}
$$

To process a message, we read it, then decode it and despatch it. Reading the message does not change $map$.

$$Process_0 \cong ((Read_0 \wedge \Xi Map)\ \S\ (Decode_0 \wedge Despatch_0))$$

The definiton of $Process$ generalises the operation for any user.

$$Process \cong (Sel_0 \wedge Process_0) \wedge \Delta TP$$

$\Delta TP$ is included to capture the existence of the invariant: it does not help the reader of the specification much, but it could come in handy for automated theorem provers etc.

---

[18]This is an example of how good specification style leads to improved structure in the implementation. In early specifications of TPMS we did not use schema promotion, which meant that every operation contained function applications to extract data for a particular user. You can get some idea of the results by expanding $Sel_0 \wedge Read_0$ and then re-writing it without making use of $Msg$. Using promotion not only leads to a cleaner specification, it also prompts the idea that we should have a separate subsystem of the implementation which looks after the totality of the map $msg\_n$ but does not understand the individual $Msg$ elements, while another knows about an individual $Msg$ but not how we contrive to have many of them.

[19]We record here any invariants which need reference to more than one element of the state to express them. Such invariants should be guaranteed by this level of the specifcation, because they cannot be repeated in the lower levels—by definition no lower level specification will contain *both* the state components necessary to express the invariant.

# D  EX/R: First Level Refinement

Table 1 shows the analysis of the schema operations defined in EX/S against their use of the state components *AllMsg*, *Msg* and *Map*.[20] The rows tell you what parts of the state are used by a particular operation, the columns record what operations use a particular part of the state.

| Data | | | |
|---|---|---|---|
| *AllMsg* | | • | |
| *Map* | | • | |
| *Msg* | • | | |
| Operations | Data Usage | | Components |
| $Read_0$ | Δ | | *Transport* |
| $Despatch_0$ | Δ | | |
| $Decode_0$ | Ξ | Ξ | *Decode* |
| $Sel_0$ | $S$ | Δ | *Connect* |

Table 1: State *vs.* Operation Analysis

We have recorded Ξ for $Decode_0$ vs. *Msg* even though the definition of $Decode_0$ contains simply *Msg*. This is because $Decode_0$ does not in fact change *Msg* but does use it, so use of Ξ represents the true situation. The $S$ recorded against $Sel_0$ represents *select*. It notes the fact that $Sel_0$ selects an instance of *Msg*, but does not access it as such. The interface between subsystems implied by this will be defined by a schema (specifically *Msg*) whereas other interfaces will be in the form of given types.

We can see that if it were not for the $Decode_0$ operation which accesses *Msg*, we would be able to divide the specification into three pieces as indicated by the lines in the table. That is, we really want a table of the form of table 2. The 'S' is allowable since this represents an interface rather than access to shared data—one side knows the contents of an individual *Msg* while the other maintains a collection of them without having any knowledge of the individual contents.

So we need to produce a refinement of $Decode_0$ which involves both *Transport* and *Decode*.

We do this by defining an interface schema which describes the information to be provided by one sub-system to another. We could simply make the interface consist of *MSG*, but this would be making rather too much of the message visible to *Decode*. We want to break *MSG* into separate components representing the content of the message (*TEXT*) and the information which yields the destination (*TAG*).[21]

---

[20]Notice that we analyse against state schemas rather than individual state items. In the example there is only one field to each schema, but that is not typically the case. The extra complexity of analysing individual fields in a normal sized specification is probably not worth it, considering that fields are only collected together in a schema because they have some relationship with each other, and are usually used together.

[21]It turns out that type refinements like this are more important than one might think to the design process, and they deserve more than passing thought. We are in fact laying ground rules for the architecture of the system, by defining what information is visible to each part. Note that we are not excluding the possibility that the next level specification might further refine the types in use. We only do refinements here when they are needed to resolve interface problems between subsystems.

| | Data Usage | | | Components |
|---|---|---|---|---|
| Data | | | | |
| *AllMsg* | | | • | |
| *Map* | | • | | |
| *Msg* | • | | | |
| Operations | Data Usage | | | Components |
| $Read_0$ | Δ | | | Transport |
| $Despatch_0$ | Δ | | | |
| $Decode_0$ | | Ξ | | Decode |
| $Sel_0$ | S | | Δ | Connect |

Table 2: State *vs.* Operation Analysis

$$MSG \sqsubseteq TEXT \times TAG$$

We can then restrict the interface between *Decode* and *Transport* by specifying that it should contain only *TAG*.

```
┌─ D_T_Tag ──────────────────────────────
│ tag : TAG
└─────────────────────────────────────────
```

We now name the operations in *Decode* and *Transport* which together will refine $Decode_0$, and also name the interface by which they will communicate. The prefixes to the operations determine which sub-system they belong to. Thus *T_Give* belongs to *Transport*, and extracts *tag* from *msg*.[22]

$$Decode_0 \sqsubseteq (D\_Decode \wedge T\_Give) \setminus D\_T\_Tag \qquad (1)$$

*Transport* looks like a separate component which need know nothing about users, but we want to introduce delays in what are described so far as indivisible operations. *Transport* will need a method of referring to users so that it can implement some form of queuing.[23] This will not be the external representation of user, but some internal form.

We therefore invent an internal identifier for users:

[ *UID* ]

*Connect* will know the correspondence between these and *USER*. We do not define how this is to be done; we simply use the name *C_TakeUser* to represent an

---

[22] We do not consider it necessary to actually rewrite the operations: the statement of the interface plus the original operation is enough to make it clear to the designer of the next level what is required. The choice as to whether we alter the main specification or define the interface in the refinement is based on what makes the specification easier to read. If we do it in the main specification then we are treating it as a statement about the structure of the problem. If we do it in the refinement then we consider it to be a statement about the structure of the implementation.

[23] This type of refinement was dicussed in section 3.3.

operation which will translate between the two, and leave the actual definition to the designer of *Connect*.

We can now introduce the interface between *Connect* and *Transport*. $\Delta Msg$ derives from the $S$ access by $Sel_0$; $id$ is required because of the need for queueing.

```
┌─ C_T_State ────────────────────────────────────
│  id : UID
│  ΔMsg
└──────────────────────────────────────────────
```

We can now write the refinement relation covering the *Transport* operations and $Sel_0$, equations 2 and 3 below. Notice that the left hand side is a compound statement: this is necessary because we are altering the interface between two basic operations: this refinement is *only* valid where these two operations occur together. We rely on two things:

- The operations being refined occur only in the combinations shown — if they were to occur separately we would need to introduce other refinements in those cases.

- $Read_0 \wedge Sel_0$ does not appear directly in the specification — refer to the definitions of *Process* and *Process_0*. What we in fact have is a definition of the form

$$Sel_0 \wedge (A \mathbin{;} B)$$

which we are treating as equivalent to

$$(Sel_0 \wedge A) \mathbin{;} (Sel_0 \wedge B)$$

This is not generally true, but in this particular case it *is* true given the form of $Sel_0$.

$$Read_0 \wedge Sel_0 \sqsubseteq (C\_TakeUser \wedge C\_Sel \wedge T\_Read) \setminus C\_T\_State \qquad (2)$$

We choose to divide the $Sel_0$ function into two parts, $C\_TakeUser$ which converts *USER* to *UID*, and $C\_Sel$ which provides an instance of *Msg* corresponding to a *UID* rather than a *USER*.[24] We can then use the same $C\_Sel$ in the refinement:

$$Despatch_0 \wedge Sel_0 \sqsubseteq (C\_Sel \wedge T\_Despatch) \setminus C\_T\_State \qquad (3)$$

---

[24] Again, we are making a statement about the desired structure of the implementation.

It is useful to represent the derived structure of the lower level components in terms of tables similar to the one we started with: as an example we include the one for the *Transport* component. The numbers refer to the refinement equations in which the particular operations are involved.

| T | Data | |
|---|------------|------------|
| | *Msg* | ● |
| | Operations | Data Usage |
| 2 | *Read* | Δ |
| 3 | *Despatch* | Ξ |
| 1 | *Give* | Ξ |

Table 3: *Transport* Definition

# E   EX/1/U: Transport User View

## E.1   Users

There are two types of external users, one which submits messages (*USER*) and one which processes them (*APP*). *USER* represents the terminal user, *APP* the application.

## E.2   Concepts

Messages are made up of two parts, *TEXT* which is the actual message content and *TAG* which is information necessary to determine the destination of the message.[25]

## E.3   Function

### E.3.1   User Interface

Users submit messages for processing. A message consists of two parts: [26]

```
┌─ Read ──────────────────────────────────────────
│  msg? : TEXT
│  tag? : TAG
└──────────────────────────────────────────────────
```

### E.3.2   Applications Interface

Applications recieve messages for processing. Notice that the *TAG* is not included in the information passed to the application.[27]

```
┌─ Despatch ──────────────────────────────────────
│  msg! : TEXT
└──────────────────────────────────────────────────
```

### E.3.3   Decoder Interface

Decoder obtains the *TAG* for the current message via the *Give* operation.[28]

```
┌─ Give ──────────────────────────────────────────
│  tag! : TAG
└──────────────────────────────────────────────────
```

---

[25]This implies that the user is aware of how the destination is derived, which is not necessarily a good choice for a generalised TP system. Alternatively we could introduce a different type (*SCREEN* say) and relate this to *TEXT* and *TAG* by means of functions introduced in the specification.

[26]We have used the same name, *Read*, as the design specification, rather than the name in the higher level U document because otherwise we would run into uniqueness problems. Typically each interface will resolve to several interfaces at the lower level. See section E.3.5 for how this sub-systems' interfaces relate to those of other sub-systems.

[27]This is an example of where we do not seem follow the requirements of the parent specification to the letter—we are supplying only *TEXT* when the parent specification of $Process_U$ gives *MSG*, which implies we should supply *TAG* as well.

[28]Note the relationship between the interface defined in the R document and the one given here. The R interface has no decoration of fields, while the one here categorically states that the information flow is from *Transport*. There must be a matching interface (decorated with ?) in the interface document of *Decode*.

## E.3.4 Interactions

None.[29]

## E.3.5 Refinement

This section shows the relationships between the interfaces in this document, the interfaces defined in other documents at the same level, and EX/U. Letter prefixes denote interfaces defined in other documents at the same level. [30]

$$Process_U \sqsubseteq Read \land C\_TakeUser$$

$$Process_A \sqsubseteq Despatch$$

---

[29]We deliberately *do not* discuss here that there is a relationship between messages coming in and messages going to applications, as that has already been dealt with in EX/U. From the point of view of Transport we should not be aware of this relationship, much less take any advantage of it. If we did we would be breaking the information hiding rules around which this design method is built.

[30]Note the correspondence between these refinement relations and those in EX/R. $T\_Read$ and $C\_TakeUser$ derive from $Read_0$ and $Sel_0$ respectively (equation 2). $Read_0$ and $Sel_0$ are both parts of the implementation of *Process*, which is the operation in EX/S which contains the interface $Process_U$. It would be useful to have some tool support for checking these statements for consistency — a sort of global type checker.

# F    EX/1/S: *Transport* Specification

Do not be distracted by the details of this specification—the point being demonstrated is that specifications can be expected to contain abstract views of other software (or hardware) components that are to be used by the product being described.

For each owner we have the current *TEXT* and *TAG*.

```
┌─ Msgc ─────────────────────────────────────────
│  m : TEXT
│  t : TAG
└─────────────────────────────────────────────────
```

This corresponds to *Msg* in EX/S. The proof is simple because we have already stated that $MSG \subseteq TEXT \times TAG$.

$$Msg \subseteq Msgc$$

The message is communicated from the user to the TP system by a communications network which simply deals with packets of data. That is, we wish to hide from the communications sub-system the structure of our messages in terms of *TEXT* and *TAG*.

$$[ PACKET ]^{31}$$

We know how to turn messages into packets and back again; making a message into a packet will be the responsibility of the terminal software, unpacking the data will be done by the TP system.[32] We represent these with two functions:

```
│  pack : (TEXT × TAG) → PACKET
│  unpack : PACKET → Msgc
├────────────────────────────────────────────
│  ∀ p : PACKET; msg : Msg •
│      pack(msg.m,  msg.t) = p ⇔ unpack(p) = msg
```

That is, packing and unpacking messages results in no change.

There will be delays in the communications sub-system. We represent this by inventing a queue and arranging for message input to be a two stage process. Elements within the queue are identified by the user identifier.[33]

---

[31]This is an example of a type introduced in a lower level specification. The apparently arbitrary introduction of complications into what started out as a simple operation is typical of the higher level specifications of a large system.

[32]Here we have the beginnings of a statement of requirement on an external system. We tell the user what the screen looks like, then the communications subsystem turns this into a packet using the function *pack*. We must understand *pack* because we have to untranslate the packet using *unpack* to retrieve what the user input.

[33]Here we have an example of the introduction of a state component which is not represented *at all* in the abstract. This is only possible because we have introduced intermediate states by splitting operations up into parts separated by time (see 3.3). It follows that we can only prove equivalence between the abstract and concrete states when the concrete system is in a quiescent state, i.e. it is not half way through some operation. In these cases the extra part of the state will have a particular value — in this case $q = \varnothing$. We should be able to show that given any concrete state where $q \neq \varnothing$ the system will find its way back to a quiescent state, i.e. where $q$ once again becomes $\varnothing$.

$$
\begin{array}{|l}
\hline
\_\,Iq \phantom{xxxxxxxxxxxxxxxxxxxxxxxxxxxxxxxxxxxxx} \\
\hline
q : UID \nrightarrow PACKET \\
\hline
\end{array}
$$

*Input*$_0$ represents the idea that messages are accepted by the communications sub-system and put into the queue for processing.

$$
\begin{array}{|l}
\hline
\_\,Input_0 \phantom{xxxxxxxxxxxxxxxxxxxxxxxxxxxxxxxxx} \\
\Delta Iq \\
u? : UID \\
m? : TEXT \\
t? : TAG \\
\hline
q' = q \cup \{\; u? \mapsto pack(m?, \; t?) \;\} \\
\hline
\end{array}
$$

At some time the communications sub-system will give us an indication that data has arrived for us. This is represented by the precondition of *IpReady*$_0$ becoming true. Note that we do not restrict the order in which input is notified to us. This is only a notification: a separate operation must be invoked as a result of this one to actually retrieve the packet.

$$
\begin{array}{|l}
\hline
\_\,IpReady_0 \phantom{xxxxxxxxxxxxxxxxxxxxxxxxxxxxxxxxx} \\
\Delta Iq \\
u! : UID \\
\hline
u! \in \mathrm{dom}\, q \\
\hline
\end{array}
$$

Capturing the data removes it from the queue and records it in the state proper.

$$
\begin{array}{|l}
\hline
\_\,Capture_0 \phantom{xxxxxxxxxxxxxxxxxxxxxxxxxxxxxxxxx} \\
\Delta Iq \\
\Delta Msgc \\
u? : UID \\
\hline
\theta Msgc' = unpack(q \; u?) \\
q' = \{u?\} \lhd q \\
\hline
\end{array}
$$

The *Read* operation is implemented by the occurrence if *Input*$_0$ followed at some later time by the *IpReady*$_0$ signal which causes *Capture*$_0$. Note that these two halves of the operation *must apply to the same user*. [34]

$$
Read \sqsubseteq (Input_0 \land \Xi Msg) \longrightarrow (IpReady_0 \gg Capture_0)
$$

A correctly operating system can then be defined as:

$$
Readops \mathrel{\widehat{=}} (Input_0 \land \Xi Msgc) \lor (IpReady_0 \gg Capture_0)^{[35]}
$$

---

[34]The notation used here is introduced in 3.3

[35]The specification would go on to derive an implementation of *Despatch*$_0$ which would introduce similar constructions because of the need to wait for applications which were not available, since in general there are fewer applications than there are users.

# G   Summary of Example

The example has demonstrated these points.

- We have presented a possible way of structuring the overall design in terms of documents. This overall structure might benefit from being described less formally, e.g. using Yourdon, especially as there are tools around to help draw pictures using these methods.

- A structured description of user interfaces may be produced (§B, §E). We touched on the idea that two formal descriptions of each subsystem might be appropriate, one to give the user model and one the design model.

- §D shows the techniques required to derive subsystems from a specification, in particular how we produce a tightly defined structure. We also gave examples of how we record engineering choices, which are necessary to either improve performance or reduce cost.

- §F demonstrates how to introduce temporal aspects into the design, by extending the system state.

# CICS/ESA 3.1 Experiences

Mark Phillips
CICS Products
IBM United Kingdom Laboratories Ltd.
Hursley Park
Winchester SO21 2JN

**Abstract**

The paper describes the use of the Z notation and method throughout the development cycle of IBM's CICS/ESA 3.1 [1] software product. Included is a description of IBM Hursley's experiences with the Z notation in terms of educational requirements and changes to the development process. There is a description of development benefits achieved from using Z specifications, including a comparison of components specified with Z and those developed without Z. The paper also describes measurements made during development in terms of lines of code produced per schema, number of schemas produced, and number of schema variables used. The final section in the paper describes plans for the use of the Z notation and methods in future CICS products and releases.

## Introduction

CICS/ESA 3.1 is the largest CICS release IBM has produced to date. CICS/ESA 3.1 was the first release of any IBM product to use the Z specification notation during its development cycle. The release consists of 268,000 lines of new and modified code of which 37,000 lines were specified using the Z notation and 11,000 lines were partially specified using the Z notation. Part of the CICS/ESA 3.1 release consisted of an internal restructure of the product to provide a platform for future development. As CICS is a product which is 20 years old, some investment in the infrastructure of CICS was required to allow development activity of the product to continue in the future.

## Objectives

The primary objectives of introducing the Z notation into the CICS/ESA 3.1 development cycle were to allow the identification of errors as early as possible in the cycle and in doing so reduce development costs. It is known that the later errors are detected in the CICS development cycle, the more expensive they are to fix.

---

[1]Trademark of the IBM Corporation.

An overall objective was to reduce the total number of errors detected both in the development cycle, and by our customers and, thereby produce a better quality product.

We also had secondary objectives in introducing the Z notation and they were to introduce software engineering technology into CICS and to give IBM the ability to produce designs that could be reused by other CICS products.

# Experience

Before the use of the Z notation could be introduced into the CICS development process, an amount of environmental activity had to take place. CICS programmers were trained in the introduction of software engineering techniques, on a two week course run by IBM. In addition a series of Z courses were run which introduced the Z notation, taught designers and developers how to use and write Z and a Z readers course. The readers course allowed the non-programming community to read and understand documentation produced in Z. Training of CICS personnel in the Z notation reached a peak in 1984 with 130 students taking part in the *Writing Z* specification courses, 33 students attending the *Reading Z* specifications and 51 students attending the *Refining Z* specification courses.

At the same time a consultation and research contract was initiated with the Programming Research Group (PRG) in Oxford. This allowed IBM to get advice and guidance with technical problems with the Z notation, specifically in techniques employed in specifying CICS function in Z. A research contract was initiated to provide IBM with an understanding of how Z could be used to describe more complex situations such as program concurrency and specification refinement. Because the Z notation uses many mathematical symbols CICS made a significant investment in terminals which could display Z symbols.

Once Z specifications had been produced for a function these were formally reviewed as part of the design inspection process. Simple tools were developed to allow names used within Z specifications to be cross referenced in the documentation. During the development of CICS/ESA 3.1 some 2000 pages of specifications were produced. There was some use of formal refinement techniques, although as these techniques were in their infancy during the CICS/ESA 3.1 development time-frame this use was limited. Case studies and publications were produced both by IBM Hursley and by the PRG, which has provided an invaluable source of education and discussion in the software engineering community.

The following chart is based on measurements that were made on the CICS/ESA 3.1 release, and show errors detected at major stages of the process.

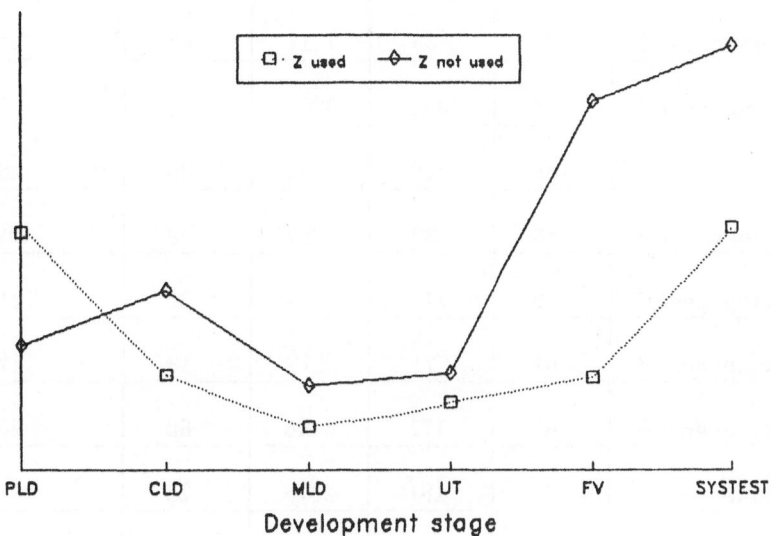

**The stages defined are as follows:**

- **PLD - Product Level Design**
- **CLD - Component Level Design**
- **MLD - Module Level Design**
- **UT - Unit Test**
- **FV - Functional Varifioation**
- **SYSTEST - System Test**

Figure 1: CICS/ESA 3.1 Comparison of development methods

|  | No. of schemas | No. of schema variables | Lines of code | Lines of code per schema | Lines of code per schema variable |
|---|---|---|---|---|---|
| Component 1 | 22 | 27 | 885 | 40 | 33 |
| Component 2 | 25 | 33 | 1117 | 45 | 34 |
| Component 3 | 114 | 464 | 3201 | 28 | 7 |
| Component 4 | 88 | 119 | 3036 | 35 | 26 |
| Component 5 | 43 | 39 | 4267 | 99 | 109 |
| Component 6 | 70 | 117 | 2494 | 36 | 21 |
| Component 7 | 61 | 71 | 818 | 13 | 12 |
| Component 8 | 81 | 177 | 6446 | 80 | 36 |
| Component 9 | 94 | 181 | 2376 | 25 | 13 |
| Component 10 | 43 | 84 | 2469 | 57 | 29 |
| Component 11 | 82 | 125 | 7448 | 91 | 60 |
| Component 12 | 28 | 53 | 377 | 14 | 7 |
| Component 13 | 39 | 67 | 2138 | 55 | 32 |

Figure 2: Measurements for components of CICS/ESA 3.1 that were *specified* using Z.

At the first stage of the specification process, the total number of schemas and schema variables produced was 790 and 1557, which produced 37,072 lines of code. An average of 47 lines of code were developed corresponding to 1 schema and 24 lines of code were developed corresponding to 1 schema variable.

|  | No. of schemas | No. of schema variables | Lines of code | Lines of code per schema | Lines of code per schema variable |
|---|---|---|---|---|---|
| Component 1 | 21 | 41 | 885 | 42 | 22 |
| Component 2 | 79 | 118 | 1117 | 14 | 10 |
| Component 3 | 179 | 358 | 3201 | 18 | 9 |
| Component 4 | 24 | 65 | 3036 | 127 | 47 |
| Component 5 | 207 | 356 | 4267 | 21 | 12 |
| Component 6 | 171 | 393 | 2494 | 15 | 6 |
| Component 7 | 76 | 152 | 818 | 11 | 5 |
| Component 8 | 64 | 237 | 6446 | 101 | 27 |
| Component 9 | 180 | 445 | 2376 | 13 | 5 |
| Component 10 | 45 | 111 | 2469 | 55 | 22 |
| Component 11 | 83 | 208 | 7448 | 90 | 36 |
| Component 12 | 41 | 86 | 377 | 9 | 4 |
| Component 13 | 14 | 105 | 2138 | 153 | 20 |

Figure 3: Measurements for the *refinement* of the components in CICS/ESA 3.1 that were specified using Z.

In the refinement or last stage of the specification process, the total number of schemas and schema variables produced was 1184 and 2675, which resulted in 37,072 lines of code. An average of 31 lines of code were developed corresponding to 1 schema and 14 lines of code were developed corresponding to 1 schema variable.

# Benefits

The initial conclusions from using the Z notation in the development of CICS/ESA 3.1 were that Z specifications are appropriate both in new components and where large changes involve rewrites. Measurements indicate quality improvement of CICS/ESA 3.1 throughout the development process. There is also an improvement in development costs, and the number of errors detected was reduced.

The initial development benefit has been assessed to be a 9% improvement in the *total development cost* of the release, as opposed to developing the 37,000 lines without Z specifications. The assessment of cost benefit was based on the reduction of programmer days fixing problems.

# Planning

There is initial planning that needs to be done before the Z notation and formal methods can be employed in developing a software product. If the Z notation is being introduced for the first time, consideration has to be given to training. This includes training designers and programmers, as well as testers, technical writers and support personnel. This training will take time and it will also take time for the designers and developers to become fluent in Z and, therefore, this has to be allowed for in product development schedules.

There needs to be a clearly defined standard for the documentation containing the Z specifications. A ratio should be agreed of formal notation and supporting commentary. Because the use of formal notation is so different from previous design techniques it is recommended that selected members of the development groups are given the role of consultant. This is to provide support and advice to development personnel as they write and use specifications written in Z. Specific steps should be defined so that the Z specifications created are formally refined to provide a concrete version of the function. A verification stage is then performed to ensure the refinement is a true derivation from the initial specification. One very important aspect of using formal methods and the Z notation is to review and measure the benefits at all stages of a product development cycle. The use of the Z notation may not provide benefit in all environments and therefore it needs to be used selectively.

# Future

In the future it is envisaged that IBM Hursley will continue to use Z specifications when new code is being developed. A significant piece of work being undertaken is to formally specify in the Z notation the CICS Application Programming Interface. This will introduce Z notation to the IBM customer environment and provide further exposure of the use of the Z notation within the CICS organisation. Significant investment is being made in workstation tools to allow developers to create and update documents which include Z notation more effectively than they can currently. IBM Hursley is sponsoring reverse engineering activity, to allow Z specifications to be created from existing code. IBM will continue to sponsor PRG research activities and see the PRG as a partner in improving the acceptability of the Z notation.

# References

[1] Hayes, Ian J. (editor), Flinn, L. William, Gimson, Roger B., Morgan, C. Carroll, Sørensen, Ib H., and Sufrin, Bernard A., *Specification case studies*, International Series in Computer Science, Prentice Hall, Hemel Hempstead, Hertfordshire HP2 4RG, UK, 1987.

[2] Collins, B.P., Nicholls, John E., and Sørensen, Ib H., *Introducing Formal Methods: the CICS Experience with Z*, IBM Technical Report, TR12.260, IBM United Kingdom Laboratories Ltd., Hursley Park, Winchester, Hampshire SO21 2JN, UK, December 1987.

[3] Nix, C.J. and Collins, B.P., "The use of Software Engineering, including the Z Notation, in the Development of CICS," *Quality Assurance*, vol. 14, no. 3, pp. 103-110, September 1988.

[4] Wordsworth John B., "Teaching Formal Specification Methods in an Industrial Environment," in *Software Engineering '86*, Peter Peregrinus, London, UK, 1986.

# Structural Metrics for Z Specifications*

Robin Whitty
CSSE
South Bank Polytechnic
Borough Road
London SE1 0AA

## 1. Introduction

The most compelling arguments for introducing the Z notation into software development are those which concern traditional mathematical guarantees of consistency and hence of the users' safety and satisfaction [HOAR84]. However, it is clear that Z is not always used as are mathematical techniques in other disciplines of engineering construction. In building a bridge, for example, a relatively small amount of precisely targeted mathematics provides a foundation for the entire construction effort. By contrast software developers expect to replace a complete phase of their operation by mathematical work; at one stage a complete software system may exist in a purely formal and abstract representation.

Z is indeed in use on a 'complete system' scale. On this scale the mathematics is not a collection of ingenious, back-of-the-envelope calculations, although such calculations may have a place. Rather it is hundreds or even thousands of pages of Z, involving thousands of schemas and, perhaps, dozens of engineers. Much of the confusion often associated with software development will have been removed from these engineers' mathematical work. Nevertheless, the inherent problems in managing a large engineering development of any kind will remain: the development of a large specification must be supported by configuration management, resource allocation and scheduling and cost control via productivity measurement. One suspects that these issues are antipathetic to the scientific spirit of Z, as they are to mathematics in general; they smack of Dijkstra's creation 'Mathematics Inc.' [DIJK82], where productivity measurement is applied to the development of a proof of the 4-colour theorem! Unfortunately, these issues are a reality for industrial users of Z.

In this paper, we bite on the bullet and tackle the problem of measurement for Z specifications. In particular we present a technique for quantifying the amount of structure in a first order predicate, using a graph theoretic model. This technique was originally applied to non-quantified logic and has been extended to include quantification by the author and other members of the so-called 'Grubstake Group', working in formal measurement under NATO funding [BAKE89]. The model is based on a canonical form and a theory of composition.

---

*Work supported by NATO under Collaborative Research Grant 0343/88, and by the European Commission under ESPRIT Project 2686 (COSMOS).

## 2. Measurement for Z - Choice of a Model

Deriving and applying measurements for software systems is a thriving technical area of research, broadly termed 'software metrics'. It is an area particularly fraught with hazards and pitfalls, arising from poorly understood concepts in software engineering and doubtful analogies with other engineering disciplines. At least it can be said that the difficulties in this research are recognised and general strategies have been mapped out for overcoming them. Perhaps the most promising strategy is the use of Measurement Theory [KYBU84, ROBE79]. Measurement Theory concerns the properties which should be satisfied by mappings from the real-world into number systems in order that universal measurement concepts (for example, 'scale') can be applied. Another strategy, which is consistent with Measurement Theory is the well-known Goal Question Metric (GQM) approach of Basili and Rombach [BASI88]: a clear definition of the goals of measurement (say, improved reliability or greater maintainability) is required. Questions are then formulated to help achieve these goals (say, "what is the impact of the use of Z on reliability?" or "is configuration management significant in increasing maintainability?"). Finally, specific measurements are defined to address the questions (perhaps, metrics for Z specifications, failure rates, change data and upgrade times).

We shall be concerned with techniques for deriving measurements from Z specifications. We shall not follow GQM completely; rather we shall postulate that there are some aspects of Z specifications which are intuitively important, so that it is inherently worthwhile providing measurement techniques for these aspects of Z. The techniques will, we postulate, repeatedly be employed whenever an approach such as GQM has identified specific questions about the use of Z in the development of software systems. We are not going to produce numbers from Z schemas and proclaim them to measure the 'quality' of Z. Instead we produce numbers from Z schemas which, we claim, will be useful to anyone who is tackling the issue of quality in Z (and this is an important issue, by no means as simple as 'mathematically correct' versus 'mathematically incorrect') by a trustworthy approach such as Measurement Theory or GQM.

The aspects of Z which we will address are those concerning 'structure'. This is itself a concept that requires careful interpretation. We have to be explicit about the assumptions which we make. Following the line proposed in [BAKE89] we proceed thus:

i.     We are free to concentrate on structure of single schemas, **provided we acknowledge that we are failing to address all other aspects of Z specifications.**

ii.    We are free to concentrate on structure for the predicate parts of schemas, **provided we acknowledge that signatures are not addressed.**

iii.   We are free to concentrate on a particular model of a predicate expression, **provided we acknowledge that other models may be equally valid and, in some cases, may be more appropriate to particular questions about Z.**

In accordance with this line of reasoning, we shall propose a model of structure in predicate expressions which, we feel, exhibits non-trivial structural properties of predicate expressions and, therefore, of Z schemas.

## 3. An Example

Before giving our model of structure, we will show how some of the above ideas apply to a more standard model of predicates, the syntax tree. For example, the predicate

$$P \equiv a \wedge b \vee g$$

is represented by the syntax tree in Fig. 1.

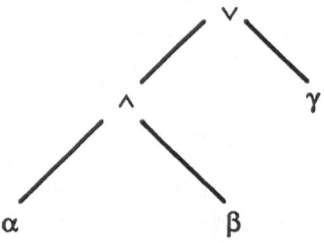

Fig. 1

No controversial assumptions are being made in this model. In fact, it is unexciting, in so far as, it is isomorphic to the algebraic form of P - the only additional information that is revealed in the syntax tree is the precedence which is implied by the semantics of predicate logic. This is useful since it may suggest some non-algebraic measurement techniques.

Let us take a specific example of a technique which we can apply to Fig. 1. The axiomatic theory of structural metrics [PRAT86, FENT86, DARO88] is essentially a proposal that, wherever structure can be represented as a syntax tree, it should be meaningful to give a definition of 'structural complexity' in terms of
a)   the complexity of the primitive operands (leaves), and
b)   the combining effect of the operators (internal nodes) on this complexity.
In the present instance, we are free, within these axioms, to propose any metric for primitive clauses in predicate expressions, and to propose functions which combine these metric values when $\wedge$ and $\vee$ are applied to clauses. In Z the primitive clauses will normally be set-theoretic expressions. Suppose we define the 'complexity' of such set-theoretic expressions to be the number of different sets referenced. Suppose we further define $\wedge$ to have a multiplicative effect on complexity and $\vee$ to have an additive effect. Given the following instances of primitive clauses in P:
a     is     $X \cap Y = \emptyset$,
b     is     $A \cup B \supset C$,
g     is     $|X| = 0$.

Then a glance at the syntax tree in Fig. 1 allows us to compute the complexity of the predicate, **within our chosen scheme**, to be

$$2 \times 3 + 1 = 7.$$

We are not concerned with the merits or demerits of axiomatic structural metrics here. There are an example of how we can use a structural model to propose a measurement technique. In the end, this measurement technique is only as good as its applicability to real problems, within an approach such as GQM. But in itself we can ensure the objectiveness and consistency of the technique, and that is what we are doing here.

## 4. The Short-Circuit Evaluation Model

The model of predicate expressions which we propose now is not, itself, any more of an innovation than syntax trees. In nearly all imperative programming languages, the evaluation of predicate expressions is carried out from left to right according to what is often called the 'short-circuit' rule. This decrees that, if the first operand of an $\wedge$ operator is evaluated to FALSE, then the second operand is not evaluated. Similarly, if the first operand of an $\vee$ operator evaluates to TRUE then the second operand is not evaluated. This is a labour saving device and allows expressions such as

if (x <> 0) and (y/x > 1.0) then ....

to be programmed without needing to worry about whether or not the second operand is defined.

It follows, that using the short-circuit mode of evaluation defines a 'flow of control' through any predicate expression. This flow may be represented graphically in the usual way, with directed edges denoting, in this case, continuation of evaluation from one operand to the next, in left-to-right order. The predicate P represented in Fig. 1 gives the graph shown in Fig. 2.

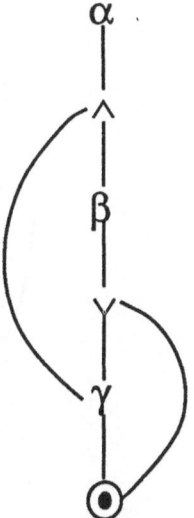

Fig. 2

We have omitted arrows in our drawings, adopting the convention that all arrows go from top to bottom of the page. It can be shown that there is no inconsistency in this convention. The final, encircled node represents return of a Boolean value from the evaluation of the predicate. The key features of the model are the forward branching edges, followed if a is FALSE or if a$\wedge$b is TRUE in Fig. 2.

Now, this short-circuit model is a perfectly legitimate model of structure in predicates, whether they arise in a programming language such as FORTRAN 77, or a formal specification notation such as Z or VDM. Of course the *interpretation* of this structural model will be very different. It may even be impossible to give a usable interpretation. Or proposition is, that we should be able to find useful application of these flowgraphs in the measurement of formal specifications. It is intuitively reasonable to assume that such flowgraphs offer an acceptable cognitive model of how complex predicates are read by humans, or reflect the nature of the application domain, or have some such useful purpose.

We re-iterate: it is not our purpose to try and justify the short-circuit model in terms of such purposes. We merely wish to explore its theoretical possibilities, *on the assumption* that it is a useful model.

We conclude by mentioning how the short-circuit model can be extended to address quantified logic, as discussed in [BAKE89]. Here we are taking a step beyond what occurs in imperative languages such as C or FORTRAN, since these languages cannot directly implement quantification ($\forall$ and $\exists$). When quantifiers are implemented in imperative languages, they are evaluated by loop structures, and this is how we extend our short-circuit model: a universally quantified expression, $\forall P$, loops until it has checked that P is true for all the values of all the variables bound by $\forall$. An existentially quantified expression, $\exists P$, loops until it is checked that at least one set of values of the bound variables makes P true. As with $\wedge$ and $\vee$, evaluation only continues until the truth or falsehood of the quantified expression is determined. The short circuit model with quantifiers is illustrated in Figure 3. Here the convention is adopted that all branches on the left are backward loops (from the quantifier to 'A') while the branches on the right are forward branches; again it can be shown that there is no inconsistency in this convention, that is all quantified predicate expression models can be drawn in this way. The different effect of $\exists$ and $\forall$ is captured by the different destinations of the forward branch from $\vee$.

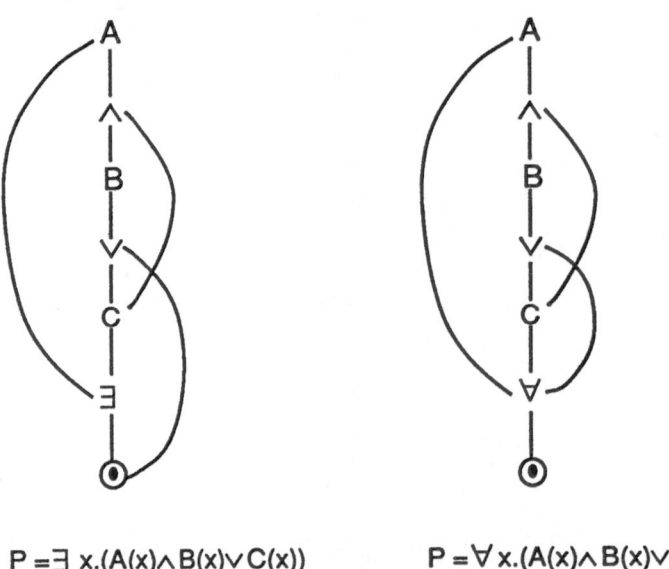

$$P = \exists\, x.(A(x) \wedge B(x) \vee C(x)) \qquad P = \forall\, x.(A(x) \wedge B(x) \vee C(x))$$

Fig. 3

# References

[BAKE89]   Baker, A., Bieman, J., Fenton, N.E., Gustafson, D., Melton, A. and Whitty, R., "Report on NATO Research Collaboration 0343/88, 1989.

[BASI88]   Basili, V. R. and Rombach, H.D., "The TAME project: towards improvement-orientated software environments", *IEEE Trans. Software Eng.*, 14 (6), 1988, pp 758-773.

[DARO88]   Daroczy, Z. and Varga, L., "A new approach to defining software complexity measures", Acta Cybernetica, vol. 3, 1988, pp 287-291.

[DIJK83]   Dijkstra, E.W. *Selected Writings on Computing: a Personal Perspective*, Springer-Verlag, 1982.

[FENT86]   Fenton, N.E. and Whitty, R.W., "Axiomatic approach to software metrication through program decomposition", Computer J., 29 (4), 1986, pp 329-339.

[HOAR84]   Hoare, C. A. R., "Programming: sorcery or science?", *IEEE Software*, April 1984,  pp 5-16.

[PRAT86]   Prather, R.E., "An axiomatic theory of software complexity measure", *Computer J.*, 27 (4), 1984, pp 340-347.

[ROBE83]   Roberts, F.S., *Measurement Theory with Applications to Decision Making, Utility, and the Social Sciences*, Addison Wesley, 1979.

[KYBU84]   Kyburg, H. E., *Theory and Measurement*, Cambridge University Press, 1984.

# Educating Management in Z

*David Cooper*
*CITI*
*Pitfield*
*Kiln Farm*
*Milton Keynes*

The Z community is a steadily growing group of people with an interest in the theoretical basis of Z and the practical application of Z to software development. We have a lot of experience in teaching technical people what Z is, and how to use it, and in general we are successful in this teaching process. But there is considerable scope for improvement in the teaching of Z to industrial management, rather than technical staff.

In this paper I will look at the way in which Z and other formal methods should be presented to industrial management. I will do this in three steps. First, I shall address the question of what the objective of educating management should be. Should it be a sales pitch, or to broaden their minds, or alter their expectations or something else? Having chosen a suitable objective, I will then look at how to achieve this objective; should it be tool based, technical, lecture, workshop etc? Finally, I will discuss my own experience of presenting information on formal methods to managers, and assess their reactions.

## Why Educate Management?

Before we begin to teach management about Z, we need to know what we are trying to achieve. We have a slightly better chance of achieving our goal if we know where the goal posts are.

A few years ago formal methods got a bad name, principally through people "selling" it as a panacea of all ills. We need now to be sure that the Z community does not make a similar mistake again.

A useful way of defining our objectives is to ask the question, "what do we want a manager to *do* when she or he has just experienced our Z education?" I suggest that the answer to this question is "the manager will make a good decision about the steps to be carried out to improve software development".

There are some answers we should *not* give, such as: "the manager decides to use Z for all his or her future developments". "The manager starts writing lots of Z specifications and refinements". "The manager fires any employee with knowledge of Z".

We have some evidence that in certain circumstances the use of formal methods can, and does, lead to better software development. Here, "better" means cheaper, faster and with fewer defects. We also believe (although with less justification, I think) that in some circumstances formal methods does not bring any advantage to the development. This means that managers must not leave our education activity with a religious faith in formal methods, but enough knowledge to be able to make the right decision in his or her particular application area.

As we all know, managers don't do any actual *work*, but they do make decisions. This is why the whole education activity must be directed at the manager's *decision*.

Bringing all this together we can put forward the following objective:

> *The objective of management education is to produce a manager capable of improving software development, and motivated to make the necessary decisions.*

## How Do We Educate Management?

The objective stated above is clearly different from the objectives of a technical course of Z. We are trying to do two things; produce someone capable of making a decision, and motivate them.

To achieve these objectives we must address the issues that a manager is concerned about when making planning decisions:

a)      what is the benefit of a new approach? (financial saving, time saving, defect reduction)

b)      what is the cost of a new approach? (start up costs, e.g. training, running costs, tool costs)

c)      what is the risk? (how does success affect other developments? how likely is the cost to be more than planned? What is the chance of failing to achieve the benefits?)

d)      why should I believe you? (what justification is there, such as published success/failure, experience, technical reasoning)

This list highlights one of the problems with educating management: in order to make a business decision a manager needs financial justification. This is in short supply.

The list attacks the decision making side of the objective, but doesn't tackle the motivation side. System development manages have enough day to day problems to deal with without risking some newfangled approach. We need to motivate the manager to want to know more, to investigate the risks, to track developments and to want *improvement* (rather than the status quo).

Motivation can be achieved through well presented real experience, technical involvement, and "flashing lights". It's a sad fact that gee-whiz gizmos seem to be an important motivation for many managers, but I suppose we must admit that managers are, after all, human. Provided that the manager has sufficient mathematical expertise, working through some small technical examples can give a clue to how formal methods can help, and help to increase motivation.

Management education must therefore include a balance of financial and risk analysis, justification, and technical motivation.

## How Do Managers Respond?

Some of the reactions of managers to the education activities I have been involved in are:

a)          The approach only tackles some of the problems, and hence is of no use to me.

This is a difficult one to overcome, because it is the symptom of a generally dissatisfied manager.  This person will always be able to find an area where you can't help, and will decide that this area is critical.  You cannot tackle this problem head on, because any realistic technique will have holes in it --- it can't be a panacea.  Someone who reacts this way is really looking for an excuse to keep their head buried in the sand.  Therefore, to overcome this the manager must be led to understand that trying something new can have benefits, and if it is managed properly the risks can be handled.

b)          No one will understand these notations.

To a non-mathematician notations like Z are frightening.  This is one of the reasons why you do have to go through a simple (very simple) example in detail.  Once people see that behind the incomprehensible notation there is a nice, simple, clean idea, they warm to it.

Practical experience has shown that these notation are picked up relatively easily by software staff.  But the manager needs a way of keeping track of progress without necessarily being able to read the technical detail.  Therefore the stages of the formal development (such as abstract specification, concrete specification, retrieve schema, verification proofs, etc.) must be presented in the language the manager already knows.

c)          But we use --- 4GLs, SA/SD, Yourdon, Ada etc.--- and so we can already do all you say Z can!

Really?  This is usually a symptom of a conservative who doesn't like to hear about change.  Nothing will be gained by trying to prove them wrong.  Technical motivation with hard evidence of financial gain is the only hope.

d)          What about tools?

Industrial use of formal methods only needs simple tools: principally to be able to edit and print documents, and to be able to put them under automated control.  We do have simple tools, so don't be afraid to say that these are sufficient.

e)          But what do I do now?

Be bold; tell them what steps they can take, what decisions they must make, how to make those decisions, how to gain support from above, and so on.  Managers appreciate these comments, because it deals with the things very close to their hearts.

## Conclusion

Teaching managers is different from teaching technologists.  We need to tell them what to do (make decisions), how to do it (what to base their decisions on) and make them want to do it (motivate them).

# THE KNUTH-BENDIX COMPLETION ALGORITHM AND ITS SPECIFICATION IN Z

Alf Smith
RSRE Malvern

Address:  RSRE, St Andrews Rd, Great Malvern, Worcs WR14 3PS
Tel: (0684) 894846

## Abstract

Proving that something is a consequence of a set of axioms can be very difficult. The Knuth-Bendix completion algorithm attempts to automate this process when the axioms are equations. The algorithm is bound up in the area of term rewriting, and so this paper contains an introduction to the theory of term rewriting, followed by an overview of the algorithm. Finally a formal specification of the algorithm is given using the language Z [7, 8].

## 1. Introduction

When carrying out a formal proof, the need frequently arises to carry out substitutions, for example, of a construct for its definition. If what is substituted in a theorem is simpler than the term being substituted, the theorem can be simplified, and in many cases proved. This process of substitution is called **term rewriting**, and the **Knuth-Bendix completion algorithm** is concerned with the **mechanical** application of rewrite rules as an aid to automatic proof.

Any set of equalities may be used to provide the rewrite rules, for example the set $E$ of equations

$$e \, \$ \, x = x \qquad \text{(equation 1)}$$
$$(inv \, x) \, \$ \, x = e \qquad \text{(equation 2)}$$
$$(x \, \$ \, y) \, \$ \, z = x \, \$ \, (y \, \$ \, z) \qquad \text{(equation 3)}$$

define a group. Here, $e$ is a constant (the identity element of the group), $inv$ is a function which finds the inverse of any element $x$, and $\$$ is an infix operator which composes two elements of the group.

These equations may be turned into a set of **rewrite rules**, $R$

$$e \$ x \longrightarrow x \qquad \text{(rule 1)}$$
$$(inv\ x) \$ x \longrightarrow e \qquad \text{(rule 2)}$$
$$(x \$ y) \$ z \longrightarrow x \$ (y \$ z) \qquad \text{(rule 3)}$$

which may be used from left to right and **never** the other way. This important point is the distinction between an equation and a rewrite rule; an equation can be used in either direction, whereas a rewrite rule can only be used from left to right. Clearly if rewrite rules are to be applied automatically, we would not want both directions of the original equations to be represented as rewrite rules, since this could cause the computer to loop.

For example, from **equation 2**, we have $(inv\ x) \$ x = e$ and $e = (inv\ x) \$ x$ but from **rule 2**, we only have $(inv\ x) \$ x \longrightarrow e$, which reads $(inv\ x) \$ x$ **rewrites** to $e$.

The variables of the rules, $x$, $y$, and $z$, can be substituted with any well formed expressions made from $e, x, y, z, inv$ and $\$$. Such expressions are called **terms**.

For example, from rule 3 $(e \$ z) \$ (x \$ x) \longrightarrow e \$ (z \$ (x \$ x))$, where the term $e$ has been substituted for the variable $x$ of the rule, the term $z$ for $y$, and the term $x \$ x$ for $z$.

Rewrite rules are widely used in computing, since rewriting is an ideal task for a computer. Manipulating equations could lead to a computer "looping", since it could use an equation one way, then the other, and so on. Careful choice of rewrite rules can overcome this problem.

The use of rewrite rules instead of equations can cause a loss of power. This may be illustrated by considering the analysis tool **MALPAS**[1, 5] which has an automatic term rewriting engine. This tool can be used to formally verify existing software. In MALPAS, rewrite rules are called replacement rules, and the three group theory rules would be introduced as follows:

```
TYPE group;

FUNCTION inv (group) : group;
INFIX $ (group, group) : group;

CONST e : group;

REPLACE (x : group) e $ x BY x;
REPLACE (x : group) (inv x) $ x BY e;
REPLACE (x, y, z : group) (x $ y) $ z BY x $ (y $ z);
```

MALPAS has an algebraic simplifier which carries out term rewriting in an attempt to simplify expressions. For example, for the expression

$$(x \ e) \ y \ = \ e \ (x \ y) \qquad \text{(expression 1)}$$

the simplifier will yield the expression *true* since both sides can be rewritten to $x \ y$. This is because the LHS can firstly be rewritten to the term $x \ (e \ y)$ using rule 3, and then this term can be rewritten to the term $x \ y$ using rule 1 on the subterm $e \ y$. The RHS of expression 1 can be rewritten directly to the term $x \ y$ using rule 1.

Now suppose the simplifier is called to simplify the expression

$$(inv \ x) \ (x \ e) \ = \ e \ e \qquad \text{(expression 2)}$$

Since no rule can be applied to the LHS (such a term is called **irreducible** with respect to the rules), and only rule 1 can be applied to the RHS, the expression $(inv \ x) \ (x \ e) = e$ will be produced. However, using the original **equations**, $E$, namely

$$e \ x \ = \ x \qquad \text{(equation 1)}$$
$$(inv \ x) \ x \ = \ e \qquad \text{(equation 2)}$$
$$(x \ y) \ z \ = \ x \ (y \ z) \qquad \text{(equation 3)}$$

we have

$$(inv \ x) \ (x \ e)$$
$$= \ ((inv \ x) \ x) \ e \qquad \text{(using equation 3)}$$
$$= \ e \ e \qquad \text{(using equation 2)}$$

and thus expression 2 should really simplify to *true*.

This loss of power that results from using rewrite rules instead of equations can sometimes be recovered using the **Knuth-Bendix completion algorithm** [3,4]. Suppose a set of equations $E$ is turned into a set of rules $R$, as in the example, then the algorithm takes $R$ and produces a new set of rules $R'$ such that $t = u$ , where $t$ and $u$ are terms, is a consequence of $E$ precisely when both $t$ and $u$ can be rewritten to the same term using $R'$. This rewriting of $t$ and $u$ is carried out as far as possible, using the rules in any order, and the terms that result are known as the **normal form** of $t$ and $u$ with respect to $R'$; denoted $t \downarrow R'$ and $u \downarrow R'$. Any term is guaranteed to have a unique normal form with respect to $R'$, which is not necessarily the case with respect to $R$.

As an example, Knuth-Bendix completion on the three group theory rules, $R$, gives the ten rules $R'$ as below.

| | | | | |
|---|---|---|---|---|
| $e \$ x \longrightarrow x$ | (1) | $inv\, e \longrightarrow e$ | (6) |
| $(inv\, x) \$ x \longrightarrow e$ | (2) | $inv(inv\, x) \longrightarrow x$ | (7) |
| $(x \$ y) \$ z \longrightarrow x \$ (y \$ z)$ | (3) | $x \$ (inv\, x) \longrightarrow e$ | (8) |
| $(inv\, x) \$ (x \$ y) \longrightarrow y$ | (4) | $x \$ ((inv\, x) \$ y) \longrightarrow y$ | (9) |
| $x \$ e \longrightarrow x$ | (5) | $inv(x \$ y) \longrightarrow (inv\, y) \$ (inv\, x)$ | (10) |

With these rules, troublesome expressions such as expression 2, namely $(inv\ x) \$ (x \$ e) = e \$ e$, simplify to *true* since $(inv\, x) \$ (x \$ e) \downarrow R' = e$ and $e \$ e \downarrow R' = e$.

The algorithm can also be said to automate deduction, by making it automatic in deciding whether a given expression should simplify to *true* with respect to the original equations, $E$. This can be illustrated by considering another troublesome expression with respect to $R$, namely

$$e \$ x = x \$ e \qquad \text{(expression 3)}$$

With respect to $R$, this expression simplifies to $x = x \$ e$. But with respect to $E$

| | | |
|---|---|---|
| | $e \$ x$ | |
| $=$ | $(inv(inv\, x) \$ (inv\, x)) \$ x$ | (using equation 2) |
| $=$ | $inv(inv\, x) \$ ((inv\, x) \$ x)$ | ( "      "     3) |
| $=$ | $inv(inv\, x) \$ e$ | ( "      "     2) |
| $=$ | $inv(inv\, x) \$ (e \$ e)$ | ( "      "     1) |
| $=$ | $inv(inv\, x) \$ (((inv\, x) \$ x) \$ e)$ | ( "      "     2) |
| $=$ | $(inv(inv\, x) \$ ((inv\, x) \$ x)) \$ e$ | ( "      "     3) |
| $=$ | $((inv(inv\, x) \$ (inv\, x)) \$ x) \$ e$ | ( "      "     3) |
| $=$ | $(e \$ x) \$ e$ | ( "      "     2) |
| $=$ | $x \$ e$ | ( "      "     1) |

and so expression 3 should really simplify to *true*, and indeed it does with respect to $R'$. The above proof using the equations is by no means obvious (nine steps !) and really highlights the advantage of generating $R'$, since expression 3 then simplifies to *true* by the **automatic** application of these rules.

## 2. Termination of rewrite rules

A bad set of rewrite rules can still cause the computer to loop. Consider the rule

$$x \otimes y \longrightarrow y \otimes x \qquad \text{(rule A)}$$

Since **any** terms can be substituted for the variables of a rule then

$$y \otimes x \longrightarrow x \otimes y$$

giving the infinite rewrite sequence

$$x \otimes y \longrightarrow y \otimes x \longrightarrow x \otimes y \longrightarrow \ ....$$

So any set of rewrite rules containing rule A could cause the computer to loop.

A set of rules supplied to the Knuth-Bendix algorithm must not cause this problem. A set of rules that do not cause this problem is called **terminating** [2]. To show termination of a set of rules $R$, there must exist an ordering $>>$, on terms, which is

1. **transitive**
   $t >> u \wedge u >> v \Rightarrow t >> v$   for all terms $t$, $u$, and $v$

2. **irreflexive**
   $\neg\ (t >> t)$ for all terms $t$

3. **closed with respect to substitution**
   $t >> u \Rightarrow S(t, \sigma) >> S(u, \sigma)$
   for all terms $t$ and $u$, and substitutions $\sigma$ of the variables for terms
   ($S(t, \sigma)$ denotes the term $t$ after the substitution $\sigma$ has been carried out)

4. **monotonic**
   $t >> u \Rightarrow f( .. ,t, .. ) >> f( .. ,u, .. )$
   (Both $t$ and $u$ form the $n^{th}$ argument for $f$ for some $n$)
   for all terms $t$, $u$, all functions $f$, and all $n \in 1 .. deg\,f$

5. **well founded**
   there are no infinite (strictly descending) sequences of terms
   $t >> u >> v >> w >> ....$

and that $l >> r$ for each rule $l \longrightarrow r$ in $R$.

With a terminating set of rules $R$, the successive application of rules to any term $t$, in any order, will eventually produce an irreducible term.

Property 1 is needed to ensure that as rules are applied one after another, the terms get consistently smaller. Without property 2, there could be the infinite sequence $t \longrightarrow t \longrightarrow t \longrightarrow$ .... for some term $t$. Property 3 is needed because a rule is used in its substituted form. For example, from the rule $e \$ x \longrightarrow x$ then $e \$ (inv\ y) \longrightarrow inv\ y$ can be obtained, and so it is not good enough to know that $e \$ x >> x$; it must also be the case that $e \$ (inv\ y) >> inv\ y$. Property 4 is needed because subterms can be rewritten. For example as $inv(e \$ x) \longrightarrow inv\ x$ by using the rule $e \$ x \longrightarrow x$ on the subterm $e \$ x$ of $inv(e \$ x)$, it is not good enough to know that $e \$ x >> x$; it must also be the case that $inv(e \$ x) >> inv\ x$. Property 5 is needed to ensure that as a term is rewritten to smaller and smaller terms, the rewriting must eventually stop.

Such an ordering $>>$, is input into the Knuth-Bendix algorithm along with the set of rules. This ordering not only ensures termination of the existing rules, but is needed in forming new rules as described in section 3.1.

The original three group theory rules form a terminating set of rules. This can be shown using the Knuth-Bendix Ordering (KBO) as described in their original paper[4]. In general it considers a simpler term to be smaller than a complicated term. Essentially it regards the complexity of a term to be the number of symbols appearing in the term, but it also weights the function symbols (in the literature, constants are regarded as functions which take no arguments, and so these too are given a weight). It is also necessary to label each function in the form $f_i$. What follows is the result of letting $f_1 = e$ have weight 1, $f_2 = \$$ have weight 0, and $f_3 = inv$ have weight 0.

The weight $w(t)$, of a term $t$, is then the number of occurrences of variables in $t$ plus the number of occurrences of $e$ in $t$. For example the weight of the term $(x \$ y) \$ inv(e \$ x)$ is 4. Let $n(v, t)$ be the number of occurrences of the variable $v$ in the term $t$. For example $n(x, (y \$ x) \$ x) = 2$.

The ordering $>>$ on the terms, is then defined as follows:

$t >> u$   if and only if

**either**   ( $w(t) > w(u)$  **and**   $n(v, t) \geq n(v, u)$  for all variables $v$ )                    (O 1)

   **or**   ( $w(t) = w(u)$  **and**   $n(v, t) = n(v, u)$  for all variables $v$   **and**                    (O 2)

       **either**   $t = inv^m\, v$  **and**   $u = v$   for some $m \geq 1$ and variable $v$          (O 2.1)

          **or**   $t = inv\, p$   **and**   $u = e$                    (O 2.2)

          **or**   $t = inv\, p$   **and**   $u = q\,\$\, r$                    (O 2.3)

          **or**   $t = p\,\$\, q$  **and**   $u = r\,\$\, s$  **and**  $p \neq r$  **and**  $p >> r$          (O 2.4)

          **or**   $t = p\,\$\, q$  **and**   $u = p\,\$\, r$  **and**  $q \neq r$  **and**  $q >> r$          (O 2.5)

          **or**   $t = inv\, p$   **and**   $u = inv\, q$  **and**  $p \neq q$  **and**  $p >> q$ )          (O 2.6)

       where $p$, $q$, $r$ and $s$ are terms

It can be shown that the above ordering satisfies the 5 conditions required, so now just the rules themselves need to be checked that they obey $>>$.

**rule 1**   $e\,\$\, x \longrightarrow x$

       $w(LHS) > w(RHS)$ and $n(x, LHS) = n(x, RHS)$. So $LHS >> RHS$ by O 1 .

**rule 2**   $(inv\, x)\,\$\, x \longrightarrow e$

       $w(LHS) > w(RHS)$ and $n(x, LHS) > n(x, RHS)$. So $LHS >> RHS$ by O 1 .

**rule 3**   $(x\,\$\, y)\,\$\, z \longrightarrow x\,\$\, (y\,\$\, z)$

       $w(LHS) = w(RHS)$ and $n(v, LHS) = n(v, RHS)$ for $v = x, y$ and $z$, so O 2 holds.
       Also O 2.4 holds with $p = x\,\$\, y$ and $r = x$, since $p >> r$ by O 1 .
       So $LHS >> RHS$ by O 2 and O 2.4 .

202

## 3. An overview of the Knuth-Bendix algorithm

Using the original set of rewrite rules for a group, it was not possible to establish the equality of *(inv x) $ (x $ e)* and *e $ e*. This was because the intermediate term *((inv x) $ x) $ e* could not be derived using the rewrite rules, because it would have involved using rule 3 backwards. There was no problem when the original equations were used since equations can be used in either direction. This directionality problem is illustrated in figure 1.

### 3.1 New rules

The Knuth-Bendix completion algorithm replaces all these problem "peaks" as in figure 1 with "troughs" as in figure 3 by introducing new rules. Figure 3 shows how with a new rule

$$(inv\ x)\ \$\ (x\ \$\ y) \longrightarrow y \qquad \text{(rule 4)}$$

in addition to the other rules, both *(inv x) $ (x $ e)* and *e $ e* can be rewritten to the same term *e*, and thus be shown equal using rewrite rules.

The problem therefore is to derive the new rules. Figure 1 shows how the peak term was rewritten using two different rules; rules 2 and 3. Rule 3 was used on the whole term while rule 2 was used on just the subterm *(inv x) $ x*. Knuth and Bendix found that this was characteristic of all problem peaks; that two different rules are used to rewrite the term; one on the whole term, the other on a subterm.

They realised that these peak terms could be generated automatically by **superimposing** the LHS of one rule onto a subterm of the LHS of another (provided this subterm is not simply a variable). It is then guaranteed that the whole term can be rewritten with one rule and a subterm with another. The two resulting terms, known as a **critical pair**, are, if possible, made into a new rule, thus removing the need for a problem peak.

As an example, rule 4 will be constructed from rules 2 and 3. Figure 2 shows the generation of a critical pair, $cp_1$ and $cp_2$, from rules 2 and 3. Notice how figure 2 is a general version of figure 1, with the peak of figure 2 using the variable z with that of figure 1 using the constant e. The general case is considered because then other problem peaks of a similar form will be covered by this general case. Thus **general unification**[6] is used to superimpose one rule onto another.

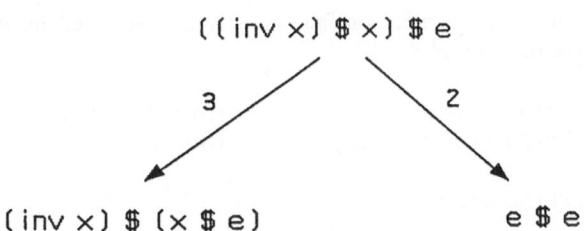

Figure 1   The problem of showing the equality of
(inv x) $ (x $ e)    and    e $ e    using the original rewrite rules.

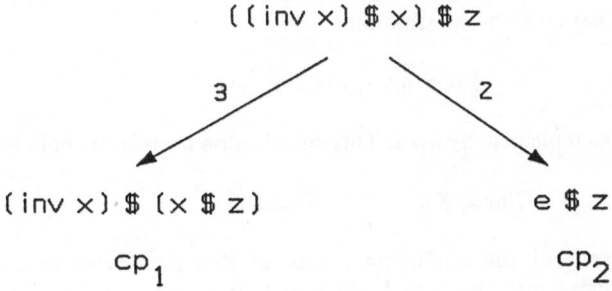

Figure 2   A critical pair of rules 2 and 3

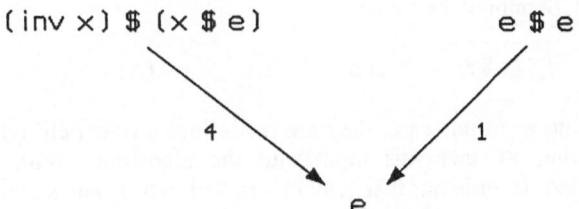

Figure 3   The "peak" of fig 1 replaced by a "trough"

This process of superposition and general unification is best explained by continuing the example which involves rules 2 and 3.

$$(inv\ x)\ \$\ x \longrightarrow e \qquad \text{(rule 2)}$$
$$(x\ \$\ y)\ \$\ z \longrightarrow x\ \$\ (y\ \$\ z) \qquad \text{(rule 3)}$$

The variable x in rule 3 is changed to w

$$(inv\ x)\ \$\ x \longrightarrow e \qquad \text{(rule 2)}$$
$$(w\ \$\ y)\ \$\ z \longrightarrow w\ \$\ (y\ \$\ z) \qquad \text{(rule 3)}$$

so that the rules have no common variable. This in no way changes the meaning of a rule since the variables of a rule are local to that rule and so may be changed.

We want to superimpose the LHS of rule 2 onto the subterm $w\ \$\ y$ of the LHS of rule 3. So general unification is carried out on the terms $(inv\ x)\ \$\ x$ and $w\ \$\ y$. This means finding the most general substitution of the variables for terms that will make both terms the same. In this case it is the substitution

$$\{\ w \mapsto inv\ x, y \mapsto x\ \}$$

where $w \mapsto inv\ x$ means replace $w$ by $inv\ x$. This substitution transforms both terms to

$$(inv\ x)\ \$\ x \qquad \text{(term 1)}$$

Also it is the **most general** substitution in the sense that for any other substitution which makes the two terms the same, say $\{\ x \mapsto e, w \mapsto inv\ e, y \mapsto e\ \}$, then the term that this gives, $(inv\ e)\ \$\ e$, can be obtained from term 1 by means of another substitution, $\{\ x \mapsto e\ \}$. The process of general unification can be carried out automatically using the **general unification algorithm** [6].

Having obtained a critical pair, each is rewritten to its normal form with respect to the current set of rules. In the case of the critical pair of figure 2, this means with respect to rules 1, 2 and 3, obtaining the terms

$$(inv\ x)\ \$\ (x\ \$\ z) \qquad \text{and} \qquad z \qquad \text{(A)}$$

If these terms are different, as in this case, they are made into a **new rule** making sure that it obeys the ordering $>>$ that was input into the algorithm. With the KBO described in the last section, it turns out that $(inv\ x)\ \$\ (x\ \$\ z) >> z$ and so the new rule is

$$(inv\ x)\ \$\ (x\ \$\ z) \longrightarrow z$$

Thus rule 4 has been derived since z can be changed for y. The current set of rules is thus

$$e \$ x \longrightarrow x \qquad \text{(rule 1)}$$
$$(inv\ x) \$ x \longrightarrow e \qquad \text{(rule 2)}$$
$$(x \$ y) \$ z \longrightarrow x \$ (y \$ z) \qquad \text{(rule 3)}$$
$$(inv\ x) \$ (x \$ y) \longrightarrow y \qquad \text{(rule 4)}$$

If, for some other two rules, the terms at stage (A) above are the same, then no new rule is made and the new rule process is started again with another two rules. Also if ever the terms at stage (A) cannot be ordered under >> then the whole algorithm fails. If for all rules and all possible superpositions the terms at stage (A) are the same, then the algorithm terminates successfully with the current set of rules.

## 3.2 Simplifying the set of rules

Each time a new rule is generated, the entire new set of rules is checked to ensure that each rule is made up only of irreducible terms with respect to the other rules. For example, this is true of the new set of four rules, since for any rule neither side can be reduced with respect to the other rules.

But this is not always the case. If there is a rule where either (or both) sides can be reduced with respect to the other rules, then one of the following can occur:

(1) If the normal forms (with respect to the other rules) of each side are equal then the rule is removed, and the simplification process is started again with the new set of rules. So rules can disappear as well as being created !

(2) If the normal forms (with respect to the other rules) of each side are not equal then the rule is replaced by a new rule made from these normal forms, provided they can be ordered under >>. The simplification process is started again with the new set of rules.

(3) If in (2), the normal forms can not be ordered under >> then the whole algorithm fails.

When all the rules consist only of irreducible terms with respect to the other rules, then the simplification has finished and another new rule is generated from this latest set, as in the last section, and so on.

As an example of the simplification process, the example of the last section will be continued. The current set of four rules do not need simplifying, and this continues to be the case until rule 7 has been generated.

| | |
|---|---|
| $e \$ x \longrightarrow x$ | (rule 1) |
| $(inv\ x) \$ x \longrightarrow e$ | (rule 2) |
| $(x \$ y) \$ z \longrightarrow x \$ (y \$ z)$ | (rule 3) |
| $(inv\ x) \$ (x \$ y) \longrightarrow y$ | (rule 4) |
| $(inv(inv\ x)) \$ e \longrightarrow x$ | (rule 5) |
| $(inv\ e) \$ x \longrightarrow x$ | (rule 6) |
| $(inv(inv\ x)) \$ y \longrightarrow x \$ y$ | (rule 7) |

Now rule 5 can be simplified with respect to the other rules, since the LHS of rule 5 can be rewritten using rule 7 to yield the expression $x \$ e$. It turns out that $x \$ e >> x$ and so rule 5 is simplified to $x \$ e \longrightarrow x$, and the set of rules becomes

| | |
|---|---|
| $e \$ x \longrightarrow x$ | (rule 1) |
| $(inv\ x) \$ x \longrightarrow e$ | (rule 2) |
| $(x \$ y) \$ z \longrightarrow x \$ (y \$ z)$ | (rule 3) |
| $(inv\ x) \$ (x \$ y) \longrightarrow y$ | (rule 4) |
| $x \$ e \longrightarrow x$ | (rule 5) |
| $(inv\ e) \$ x \longrightarrow x$ | (rule 6) |
| $(inv(inv\ x)) \$ y \longrightarrow x \$ y$ | (rule 7) |

## 3.3  Some points about the algorithm

(1) For a finite set of rules, the complete set could be infinite and so the algorithm will never terminate (unless it fails because of >>).

(2) The algorithm is very dependent on the ordering >>. For the same set of rules, the algorithm can succeed with one ordering, and not with another.

(3) As described in section 2, the algorithm cannot handle rules of the form $x \otimes y \longrightarrow y \otimes x$, since any rewrite system that contains such a rule will not be terminating. Another example is the rule $x @ (y @ z) \longrightarrow y @ (x @ z)$. Rules of this form are known as permutative rules, because one side can be obtained from the other by a simple permutation of the variables. There are ways of dealing with some of these rules, with different techniques needed for different situations. These techniques are beyond the scope of this report, which concerns itself only with the original Knuth-Bendix algorithm as described in [4].

## 4. A specification of the Knuth-Bendix completion algorithm in Z

Throughout the specification, examples from the original three group theory rules will be given.

$$e \$ x \longrightarrow x \qquad \text{(rule 1)}$$
$$(inv\ x) \$ x \longrightarrow e \qquad \text{(rule 2)}$$
$$(x \$ y) \$ z \longrightarrow x \$ (y \$ z) \qquad \text{(rule 3)}$$

### 4.1 Terms

The set of variables *VAR* must include not only the variables contained in the initial set of rewrite rules, but all the extra variables needed during the construction of new rules. For example, the rules above use the variables $x$, $y$ and $z$ and so these are in *VAR*. Also, when constructing rule 4 the variable $w$ was used (see section 3.1) and so $w$ must be in *VAR*. Other variables are used during the construction of the other rules and so these too must be in *VAR*.

[*VAR*]

The set of functions $F$ together with the variables make up the set of terms. Any constants are regarded as functions which take no arguments. For example, $F = \{\ e, inv, \$\ \}$.

[*F*]

The degree of each function is the number of arguments it takes. For example, $deg\ e = 0$, $deg\ inv = 1$ and $deg\ \$ = 2$.

$deg : F \rightarrow \mathbb{N}$

The set of terms are constructed from VAR and F. For example, $z \$ (inv\ x)$ is in *TERM*.

[*TERM*]

$CONSTANT == \{f : F \mid deg\ f = 0\}$

```
┌─ Constructed_term ─┐
│ f : F
│ s : seq₁TERM
├────────────────────
│ #s = deg f
└────────────────────
```

$TERM ::= con《CONSTANT》 \mid var《VAR》 \mid construct《Constructed\_term》$

## 4.2 Subterms

Any term *t* can be represented by a tree structure. Also the points on its tree structure can be labelled with sequences of numbers. For any term *t*, *subterm t* is a function which associates each sequence with the subterm from that point. For example, if *t* is the term *(inv y) $ (y $ (inv x))* as in figure 4 then *subterm t* is the function

$\{ \langle\rangle \mapsto t, \langle 1\rangle \mapsto inv\ y, \langle 2\rangle \mapsto y\ \$\ (inv\ x), \langle 1,1\rangle \mapsto y, \langle 2,1\rangle \mapsto y, \langle 2,2\rangle \mapsto inv\ x, \langle 2,2,1\rangle \mapsto x \}$

---

*subterm : TERM* $\rightarrowtail$ *(seq* $\mathbb{N}$ $\nrightarrow$ *TERM)*

---

$\forall\ t : TERM\ \bullet$

  $t \notin ran\ construct\ \Rightarrow\ subterm\ t = \{\langle\rangle \mapsto t\}$

  $t \in ran\ construct\ \Rightarrow$
  $subterm\ t = \{\langle\rangle \mapsto t\}\ \cup$
  $\bigcup\{\ n : dom\ s_1 \bullet \{\ p : dom\ (subterm\ (s_1\ n)) \bullet \langle n\rangle \frown p \mapsto subterm\ (s_1\ n)\ p\ \}\ \}$
  *where*
    $s_1 == (construct^{-1}\ t).s$

The function *replace* replaces a subterm of a term with another term. *replace(t, u, p)* is the result of replacing the subterm of *t* from the point *p* with the term *u*. For example if *t* is the term *(inv y) $ (y $ (inv x))* as in figure 4, *p* is the the point ⟨2,2⟩ and *u* is the term *e $ z* then *replace(t, u, p)* is the term *(inv y) $ (y $ (e $ z))*.

---

*replace : (TERM × TERM × seq ℕ) ↦ TERM*

---

*replace =* λ *t, u : TERM; p : seq* ℕ | *p* ∈ *dom(subterm t)* •

    μ *v : TERM* |

        *(t* ∈ *ran con* ∧ *v = u)*
        ∨
        *(t* ∈ *ran var* ∧ *v = u)*
        ∨
        *(t* ∈ *ran construct* ∧ *p =* ⟨⟩ ∧ *v = u)*
        ∨
          *t* ∈ *ran construct*
          *p ≠* ⟨⟩
          *v* ∈ *ran construct*
          $f_2 = f_1$
          $s_2 = s_1$ ⊕ { *hd p* ↦ *replace(s_1(hd p), u, tl p)* }
          *where*
            $f_1 ==$ *(construct⁻¹ t).f*
            $s_1 ==$ *(construct⁻¹ t).s*
            $f_2 ==$ *(construct⁻¹ v).f*
            $s_2 ==$ *(construct⁻¹ v).s*

    • *v*

t = ( inv y ) $ ( y $ ( inv x ) )

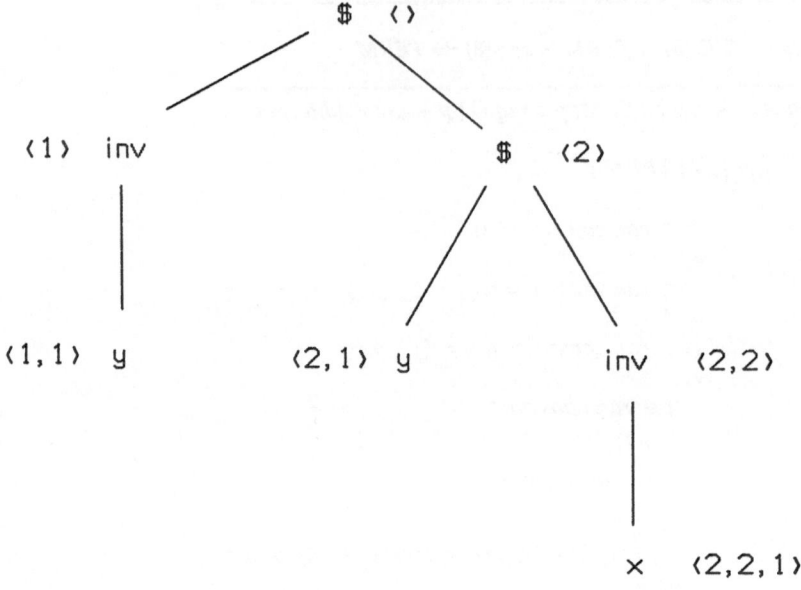

**Figure 4   The tree representation of a term**

## 4.3 Substitutions

A substitution is any function from variables to terms, for example $\{ x \mapsto y \$ e, \ z \mapsto e \}$.

*SUBSTITUTION == ran var $\nrightarrow$ TERM*

The function $S$ actually performs a substitution on a term. Given a term $t$ and substitution $\sigma$, $S(t, \sigma)$ is the result of carrying out $\sigma$ on $t$. For any variable $v$ in the domain of $\sigma$, all occurrences of $v$ in $t$ are repaced by $\sigma(v)$. Also the substitution of all the variables in the domain of $\sigma$ that appear in $t$, are carried out simultaneously. For example, if $t$ is the term $(y \$ y) \$ x$ and $\sigma$ is the substitution $\{ x \mapsto y \$ e, \ y \mapsto x \}$ then $S(t, \sigma)$ is the term $(x \$ x) \$ (y \$ e)$.

$S : (TERM \times SUBSTITUTION) \rightarrow TERM$

$S = \lambda\, t : TERM;\ \sigma : SUBSTITUTION \bullet$

$\quad \mu\, u : TERM \mid$

$\qquad (t \in ran\ con \land u = t)$
$\qquad \lor$
$\qquad (t \in ran\ var \land t \in dom\ \sigma \land u = \sigma\, t)$
$\qquad \lor$
$\qquad (t \in ran\ var \land t \notin dom\ \sigma \land u = t)$
$\qquad \lor$

$\qquad\quad t \in ran\ construct$
$\qquad\quad u \in ran\ construct$
$\qquad\quad f_2 = f_1$
$\qquad\quad \forall\, n : dom\ s_2 \bullet s_2\, n = S(s_1\, n, \sigma)$
$\qquad where$
$\qquad\quad f_1 == (construct^{-1}\, t).f$
$\qquad\quad s_1 == (construct^{-1}\, t).s$
$\qquad\quad f_2 == (construct^{-1}\, u).f$
$\qquad\quad s_2 == (construct^{-1}\, u).s$

$\quad \bullet u$

## 4.4 Terminating rewrite system

As described in section 2, to show termination of a set of rewrite rules there must be an ordering >> on terms which satisfies five conditions. It must then be shown that the rules themselves obey >>. Below are these five conditions, with the definition of a terminating rewrite system afterwards.

$$\_>>\_ : TERM \leftrightarrow TERM$$

$\forall\ t, u, v : TERM \bullet t >> u \wedge u >> v \Rightarrow t >> v$

$\forall\ t : TERM \bullet \neg\ (t >> t)$

$\forall\ t, u : TERM;\ \sigma : SUBSTITUTION \bullet t >> u\ \Rightarrow\ S(t, \sigma) >> S(u, \sigma)$

$\forall\ t, u : TERM \bullet$
   $t >> u\ \Rightarrow\ (\forall\ v, w : ran\ construct;\ n : \mathbb{N} \mid$
       $(construct^{-1}\ v).f = (construct^{-1}\ w).f$
       $n \in dom\ (construct^{-1}\ v).s$
       $(construct^{-1}\ v).s\ n = t$
       $(construct^{-1}\ w).s\ n = u$
           $\bullet\ v >> w)$

$\forall\ t : TERM \bullet \exists\ n : \mathbb{N} \bullet t \notin dom\ (\ (\_>>\_)^{n}\ )$

Given a set of terms and an ordering >> on terms, then a rule is any pair of terms, and a terminating rewrite system is any set of rules that obey >>.

$RULE == (TERM \times TERM)$

$TERMINATING\_REWRITE\_SYSTEM == \mathbb{P}\ \{\ rule : RULE \mid (fst\ rule) >> (snd\ rule)\ \}$

## 4.5 Normal form

Given a terminating rewrite system $R$, then a term $t$ rewrites to another term $u$, in one step, if and only if there is a rule in $R$ that rewrites a subterm of $t$ (possibly $t$ itself), so that $t$ becomes $u$. If this is the case then $t$ (--> $R$) $u$ . For example, if $R$ is the original set of three group theory rules then $(e \$ y) \$ (e \$ x)$ rewrites in one step to either $y \$ (e \$ x)$ or $(e \$ y) \$ x$ or $e \$ (y \$ (e \$ x))$.

$-->$  ==  $\lambda$ *trs : TERMINATING_REWRITE_SYSTEM* •

    { *t, u : TERM* | ∃ *rule : trs; p : dom(subterm t);* σ *: SUBSTITUTION* •

        *subterm t p = S(fst rule,* σ*)*
        *u = replace( t,  S(snd rule,* σ*),  p )*

    }

Given a term $t$ and a terminating set of rules $R$, then $t \downarrow R$ is the normal form of $t$ with respect to $R$ and is obtained by applying rules from $R$, to $t$, one after another until no more apply. In general the normal form is not unique. For example, if $R$ is the original set of three group theory rules then the normal form of $((inv\ x) \$ x) \$ e$ is either $e$ or $(inv\ x) \$ (x \$ e)$.

$\downarrow$ ==  $\lambda$ *trs : TERMINATING_REWRITE_SYSTEM* •

    { *t, u : TERM* |

        $t \in dom(--> trs) \Rightarrow u \notin dom(--> trs) \wedge (t, u) \in ((--> trs)^{+})$
        $t \notin dom(--> trs) \Rightarrow u = t$

    }

## 4.6  Unification

The function $v$ gives the variables that appear in a term. For example if $t$ is the term $(x \$ y) \$ (x \$ e)$ then $v(t)$ is the set $\{x, y\}$.

$$v == \lambda\, t : TERM \bullet \{\, x : ran\ var \mid \exists\, p : dom(subterm\ t) \bullet subterm\ t\ p = x\ \}$$

Given two terms $t$ and $u$, a substitution $\sigma$ is a most general unifier of $t$ and $u$ if it makes $t$ and $u$ the same and is most general as described in section 3.1. The most general unifier of two terms is not unique; for example the two terms $x$ and $y$ have most general unifier $\{x \mapsto y\}$ or $\{y \mapsto x\}$.

$mgu : (TERM \times TERM) \leftrightarrow SUBSTITUTION$

$\forall\, t, u : TERM;\ \sigma : SUBSTITUTION \bullet$

    $mgu((t, u), \sigma)$
$\Leftrightarrow$
  $v(t) \cap v(u) = \{\}$
  $unify \neq \{\}$
  $\sigma \in unify$
  $\forall\, \tau : unify \bullet \exists\, \rho : SUBSTITUTION \bullet S(\, S(t, \sigma), \rho) = S(t, \tau)$

$where$

  $unify == \{\, \tau : SUBSTITUTION \mid (\forall\, x : dom\ \tau \bullet x \notin v(\tau\ x) \wedge S(t, \tau) = S(u, \tau))\, \}$

When *mgu* is used, during the generation of critical pairs, we need to make sure that the two rules have no common variable. For example, in section 3.1, when a critical pair of rules 2 and 3 was being formed, rules 2 and 3 were transformed from *(inv x) \$ x* —> *e* and *(x \$ y) \$ z* —> *x \$ (y \$ z)* to *(inv x) \$ x* —> *e* and *(w \$ y) \$ z* —> *w \$ (y \$ z)*.

---

*var_change : (RULE × RULE) ↔ (RULE × RULE)*

---

∀ *rule$_1$, rule$_2$, r$_1$, r$_2$ : RULE •*

  *var_change( (rule$_1$, rule$_2$), (r$_1$, r$_2$) )*
⇔
  *(v(fst r$_1$) ∪ v(snd r$_1$)) ∩ (v(fst r$_2$) ∪ v(snd r$_2$)) = {}*
  ∃ σ, τ : *ran var* ↠ *ran var* •
    *dom σ = v(fst rule$_1$) ∪ v(snd rule$_1$)*
    *dom τ = v(fst rule$_2$) ∪ v(snd rule$_2$)*
    *S(fst rule$_1$, σ) = fst r$_1$*
    *S(snd rule$_1$, σ) = snd r$_1$*
    *S(fst rule$_2$, τ) = fst r$_2$*
    *S(snd rule$_2$, τ) = snd r$_2$*

## 4.7 Critical pairs

As described in section 3.1, critical pairs are used in the generation of new rules. In the schema below, $cp_1$ and $cp_2$ are a critical pair. The actual formation of new rules occurs in the function *knuth_bendix* in section 4.9.

---

*Critical_pair*

*trs* : *TERMINATING_REWRITE_SYSTEM*

$cp_1$, $cp_2$ : *TERM*

---

$\exists\ rule_1, rule_2 : trs;\ r_1, r_2 : RULE;\ p : seq\ \mathbb{N};\ \sigma : SUBSTITUTION \bullet$

$\quad var\_change(\ (rule_1, rule_2),\ (r_1, r_2)\ )$

$\quad p \in dom\ (\ subterm\ (fst\ r_1)\ )$

$\quad subterm\ (fst\ r_1)\ p \notin ran\ var$

$\quad mgu(\ (\ subterm\ (fst\ r_1)\ p,\ fst\ r_2\ ),\ \sigma\ )$

$\quad cp_1\ =\ S(snd\ r_1, \sigma)$

$\quad cp_2\ =\ replace(\ S(fst\ r_1, \sigma),\ S(snd\ r_2, \sigma),\ p\ )$

---

## 4.8 Simplifying the set of rules

The function *simplify* corresponds to the simplification of the set of rules as described in section 3.2. Failure has been handled by outputting the empty set of rules. The result of *simplify* is a set of rules where each rule consists only of irreducible terms with respect to the other rules.

$$simplify : TERMINATING\_REWRITE\_SYSTEM \rightarrow TERMINATING\_REWRITE\_SYSTEM$$

---

$\forall\ trs_1 : TERMINATING\_REWRITE\_SYSTEM \bullet$

$trs_1 = \{\} \wedge simplify\ trs_1 = trs_1$

$\vee$

$(\ \forall\ rule : trs_1 \bullet$
  $fst\ rule \notin dom(\ \text{-->}(trs_1 \backslash \{rule\})\ )$
  $snd\ rule \notin dom(\ \text{-->}(trs_1 \backslash \{rule\})\ )$
$)$
$\wedge\ simplify\ trs_1 = trs_1$

$\vee$

$(\ \exists\ rule : trs_1 \bullet$
  $v \neq fst\ rule \vee w \neq snd\ rule$
  $v = w \Rightarrow simplify\ trs_1 = simplify\ trs_2$
  $v >> w \Rightarrow simplify\ trs_1 = simplify\ (trs_2 \cup \{(v, w)\})$
  $w >> v \Rightarrow simplify\ trs_1 = simplify\ (trs_2 \cup \{(w, v)\})$
  $\neg(\ v = w \vee v >> w \vee w >> v\ ) \Rightarrow simplify\ trs_1 = \{\}$
$where$

> $v, w : TERM$
> $trs_2 : TERMINATING\_REWRITE\_SYSTEM$
>
> ---
>
> $trs_2 = trs_1 \backslash \{rule\}$
> $(fst\ rule, v) \in\ \downarrow trs_2$
> $(snd\ rule, w) \in\ \downarrow trs_2$

$)$

## 4.9 The algorithm

The function *knuth_bendix* generates a complete set of rules as described in the introduction. It does this recursively by generating new rules from critical pairs, simplifying the set of rules and so on. Once again, failure has been handled by outputting the empty set of rules.

$knuth\_bendix : TERMINATING\_REWRITE\_SYSTEM \rightarrow$
$\qquad\qquad\qquad TERMINATING\_REWRITE\_SYSTEM$

---

$\forall\ trs_1 : TERMINATING\_REWRITE\_SYSTEM \bullet$


$\quad trs_1 = \{\} \wedge knuth\_bendix\ trs_1 = trs_1$

$\quad \vee$

$\quad (\ \forall\ Critical\_pair \mid trs = trs_1 \bullet$
$\qquad t = u$
$\qquad where$
$\qquad\quad \mid\ t, u : TERM$
$\qquad\quad \overline{\quad\quad\quad\quad\quad\quad\quad\quad}$
$\qquad\quad \mid\ (cp_1, t) \in\ \downarrow trs_1$
$\qquad\quad \mid\ (cp_2, u) \in\ \downarrow trs_1$
$\quad )$
$\quad \wedge knuth\_bendix\ trs_1 = trs_1$

$\quad \vee$

$\quad (\ \exists\ Critical\_pair \mid trs = trs_1 \bullet$
$\qquad t \neq u$
$\qquad t >> u\ \Rightarrow\ knuth\_bendix\ trs_1 = knuth\_bendix\ (\ simplify\ (trs_1 \cup \{(t, u)\})\ )$
$\qquad u >> t\ \Rightarrow\ knuth\_bendix\ trs_1 = knuth\_bendix\ (\ simplify\ (trs_1 \cup \{(u, t)\})\ )$
$\qquad \neg (\ t >> u\ \vee\ u >> t\ )\ \Rightarrow\ knuth\_bendix\ trs_1 = \{\}$
$\qquad where$
$\qquad\quad \mid\ t, u : TERM$
$\qquad\quad \overline{\quad\quad\quad\quad\quad\quad\quad\quad}$
$\qquad\quad \mid\ (cp_1, t) \in\ \downarrow trs_1$
$\qquad\quad \mid\ (cp_2, u) \in\ \downarrow trs_1$
$\quad )$

# 5. Conclusions

Rewrite rules are widely used in computing since rewriting is an ideal task for a computer, and also manipulation of equations could cause a computer to loop, since it could use an equation one way and then the other and so on. Careful choice of rewrite rules can overcome this problem since they can only be used in one direction.

Simply converting equations into rewrite rules by replacing the "equals" sign by a "rewrite" sign can cause a loss of power, with expressions that simplify to *true* using the equations, not simplifying to *true* using the rewrite rules. This report illustrates this point using the MALPAS system which contains an algebraic simplifier which in turn contains a term rewriting engine.

The user could try manually to add extra rules to compensate for this loss of power but runs the risk of adding inconsistencies and non-termination, and even then not being sure that all the power had been recovered. The Knuth-Bendix completion algorithm can, for certain sets of rewrite rules, recover this power automatically without running these risks. If the algorithm terminates successfully then it is guaranteed that the new set of rules it produces is terminating, does not contain inconsistencies, and recovers all the power lost.

The algorithm can also be said to automate deduction, by making it automatic in deciding whether a given expression should simplify to *true* with respect to the original equations. In the MALPAS system, the algorithm would make the algebraic simplifier more powerful.

# References

1. B. D. Bramson  "Tools for the Specification, Design, Analysis and Verification of software". RSRE report number 87005 (1987)

2. N. Dershowitz  "Termination of Rewriting"
   pp 69 - 115 in Journal of Symbolic Computation, Vol 3 (1987)

3. A. J. J. Dick  "Automated Equational Reasoning and the Knuth-Bendix Algorithm: An Informal Introduction"
   Rutherford Appleton Laboratory  report number RAL-88-043 (1988)

4. D.E. Knuth and P.B. Bendix  "Simple Word Problems in Universal Algebras"
   pp 263 - 297 in Computational Problems in Abstract Algebra, ed J. Leech, Pergamon press (1970)

5. MALPAS Intermediate Language (Version 4.0).  Rex, Thompson and partners (1987)

6. J. A. Robinson  "A Machine-Oriented Logic Based on the Resolution Principle"
   pp 23 - 41  in Journal of the Association for Computing Machinery, Vol 12, No 1 (1965)

7. C. T. Sennett  "Review of Type Checking and Scope Rules of the Specification Language Z". RSRE report number 87017 (1987)

8. J. M. Spivey  "The Z Notation: A Reference Manual"
   Prentice-Hall International, Series in Computing Science (1988)

# A Message Passing System.
# An example of combining CSP and Z.

M.Benjamin.
British Aerospace Sowerby Research Centre,
FPC 267, PO BOX 5,
Filton, Bristol.
BS12 7QW.


Phone (0272) 366198

## Abstract

Z is good at describing state and logical conditions. CSP is well suited to talking about communication and parallelism. These are potentially complementary notations. It would be useful if a method existed for relating a CSP specification of a system to a more detailed specification of its component processes written using Z.

This paper suggests a possible solution. A CSP specification can be interpreted as describing a state machine. This state machine can then be specified using Z, thus completing a translation from CSP to Z. The structure of a Z specification helps to identify possible problems which may have been overlooked, for example showing where operations are only partially defined. These can readily be remedied as translation may also involve refinement. The resulting design is still dependent on the CSP model of communication, however this dependence could be eliminated by further refining the design.

The technique is described by means of a specific example. This describes how the specification of a message passing system in CSP can be translated to give an abstract design of its component parts written using Z.

The paper concludes that the advantages of the two notations may best be exploited by using CSP to perform the top level specification, then Z for the detailed design of the component processes. It points out that the method needs to be placed on a sound theoretical footing. This might also include investigating whether the method could be extended to timed systems by using timed CSP. Finally it emphasises the importance of good proof assistance if such methods are to be usefully applied to developing real systems.

# Introduction.

Research into formal methods has spawned a host of specification languages intended to meet many different objectives. For instance CSP[1] is intended to describe communication and parallelism whilst Z describes state and logical conditions. These are potentially complementary notations. What is required is a method of relating a CSP specification of an abstract system to more detailed specifications of the component processes developed using Z. This paper introduces such a method.

Work at Oxford[2] has described a method of specifying communicating processes by state transition systems. This paper takes the opposite viewpoint and interprets a CSP specification as describing a state machine which can then be specified using Z. This provides a relationship between processes and events on the one hand, and states and operations on the other.

Rather than develop the theory in a rigorous fashion this paper illustrates these ideas by means of an example, a message passing system. This hopefully serves both to prove the utility of the method and make it comparatively accessible.

# A Specification in CSP.

A message passing system is intended to connect together a group of users.

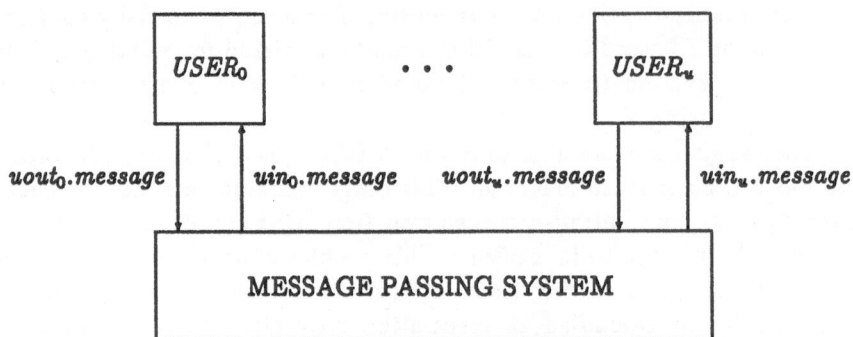

Figure 1: The Message Passing System.

A user is equally happy to send or receive a message.

$$\alpha(USER_n) = \{\ uin_n?message, uout_n!message\ \}$$
$$USER_n = (uin_n?message \rightarrow USER_n)\ |\ (uout_n!message \rightarrow USER_n)$$

The message passing system is envisaged as consisting of a group of independent messengers who carry messages between users.

$$\alpha(SYSTEM) = \bigcup_{n \in 0..u} \{\ uout_n?message, uin_n!message\ \}$$
$$SYSTEM = |||_{i \in 0..m}\ MESSENGER_i$$

Each messenger can interact with any user, hence:-

$$\alpha(MESSENGER_i) = \alpha(SYSTEM)$$

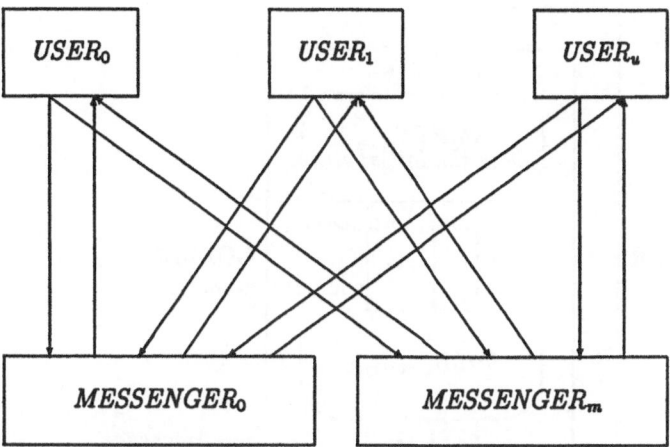

Figure 2: Users and Messengers.

A messenger will spend its time accepting messages then delivering them.

$$MESSENGER_i =|_{j\in 0..u} (uout_j?message \rightarrow (|_{k\in 0..u} uin_k!message \rightarrow MESSENGER_i))$$

This CSP specification can be investigated to discover system properties including deadlock[1] and livelock.

# An Abstract Design in Z.

The message passing system could alternatively be specified using Z. Such a specification can be derived via the intermediate step of interpreting the CSP specification as describing a state machine. State can be regarded as being a function, or in the case of a non-deterministic system a relation, of past events. State may thus be treated as corresponding to a process, while the input required for a change of state corresponds to an event. The transition between successive positions in a state machine equates to an operation in the Z specification. Processes thus equate to state while events represent schema inputs or outputs.

To show how this works let's consider an individual messenger. Translation is assisted by rewriting the CSP specification to make explicit the process which follows each event.

$$EMPTY_{< >} =|_{j\in 0..u} (uout_j?message \rightarrow FULL_{<message>})$$
$$FULL_{<message>} =|_{k\in 0..u} (uin_k!message \rightarrow EMPTY_{< >})$$

This state machine can then be specified using Z, hence completing the translation from CSP to Z.

---

[1]See appendix.

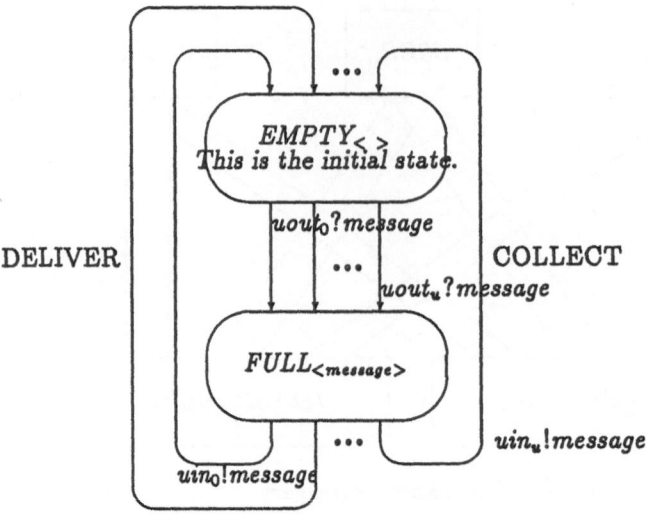

Figure 3: A Messenger Viewed as a State Machine.

The state machine involves passing messages. These are otherwise undefined, hence they need to be introduced as an abstract data type.

[*MESSAGE*]

Just as in the CSP specification, users are identified by integers.

$$| \quad USER == \mathbb{P}\, \mathbb{N}$$

Any information which is implicit in the CSP specification should be made explicit during translation. For example there must be some method of discovering a message's destination.

$$| \quad DESTINATION : MESSAGE \rightarrow USER$$

Some considerations are undefined in the CSP specification, but should be resolved in the Z specification. Translation thus involves refinement as well as a change of notation. With this in mind it is reassuring to note that refinement, and translation from CSP to Z, should commute. For example if for any reason a message can not be accepted it should be returned to its sender. This means that we need to be able to determine a message's source.

$$| \quad SOURCE : MESSAGE \rightarrow USER$$

The possible positions of the state machine are defined in the Z specification as a user enumerated type.

$$POSITION ::= EMPTY \mid FULL$$

The abstract state defined in the Z specification can now be derived by examining the state machine. It must include a flag to record position. In addition there must also be a message buffer. Not every user may be connected by the message passing system. A messenger must know who are the valid users, so as to avoid trying to deliver a message to a non existent user!

```
┌─ MESSENGER_i ────────────────────────────────
│ FLAG_i : POSITION
│ BUFFER_i : MESSAGE
│ USERS : USER
└──────────────────────────────────────────────
```

From the state machine we can see that a messenger is initially in the EMPTY position.

```
┌─ INIT_MESSENGER_i ───────────────────────────
│ MESSENGER'_i
├──────────────────────────────────────────────
│ FLAG'_i = EMPTY
└──────────────────────────────────────────────
```

The system's configuration of users will remain static.

```
┌─ ΔMESSENGER_i ───────────────────────────────
│ MESSENGER_i
│ MESSENGER'_i
├──────────────────────────────────────────────
│ USERS' = USERS
└──────────────────────────────────────────────
```

A messenger receives then delivers messages. The value of FLAG in the these operations reflects the corresponding positions of the state machine.

```
┌─ COLLECT_{i,j} ──────────────────────────────
│ ΔMESSENGER_i
│ uout_j? : MESSAGE
├──────────────────────────────────────────────
│ FLAG_i = EMPTY
│ BUFFER'_i = uout_j?
│ FLAG'_i = FULL
└──────────────────────────────────────────────
```

A message is delivered to the destination stated in the message, provided this is valid.

```
┌─ DELIVER_ok_{i,j} ───────────────────────────
│ ΔMESSENGER_i
│ uin_j! : MESSAGE
├──────────────────────────────────────────────
│ FLAG_i = FULL
│ FLAG'_i = EMPTY
│ j = DESTINATION(BUFFER_i)
│ j ∈ USERS
│ uin_j! = BUFFER
└──────────────────────────────────────────────
```

The Z specification can be checked for completeness and consistency. Delivering messages is only a partial operation. We need to define the error cases!

$$\begin{array}{|l}
\_DELIVER\_message\_returned_{i,j,k} \underline{\qquad\qquad\qquad\qquad\qquad} \\
\Delta MESSENGER_i \\
uin_k! : MESSAGE \\
\hline
FLAG_i = FULL \\
FLAG_i' = EMPTY \\
j = DESTINATION(BUFFER_i) \\
j \notin USERS \\
k = SOURCE(BUFFER_i) \\
k \in USERS \\
uin_k! = BUFFER
\end{array}$$

Finally the address may have been corrupted so that the message can not be delivered or returned. The CSP specification does not permit us to throw away a corrupted message! This equates to the possibility of deadlock in the CSP specification.

$$\begin{array}{|l}
\_DELIVER\_message\_corrupted_{i,j,k} \underline{\qquad\qquad\qquad\qquad\qquad} \\
\Delta MESSENGER_i \\
\hline
FLAG_i = FULL \\
FLAG_i' = FULL \\
j = DESTINATION(BUFFER_i) \\
j \notin USERS \\
k = SOURCE(BUFFER_i) \\
k \notin USERS \\
BUFFER_i' = BUFFER_i
\end{array}$$

$$DELIVER_{i,j} \triangleq DELIVER\_ok_{i,j} \vee$$
$$(\bigvee_{k=0..u} DELIVER\_message\_returned_{i,j,k}) \vee$$
$$(\bigvee_{k=0..u} DELIVER\_message\_corrupted_{i,j,k})$$

If necessary one could now define the complete system in Z. It is formed by interleaving a number of messengers. In triple bar parallelism (|||) the state and the operations of each process are independent. However CSP does assume that no two events can occur simultaneously and this is reflected in the specification of system operations.

$$SYSTEM \triangleq \bigwedge_{i\in0..m} MESSENGER_i$$
$$INIT\_SYSTEM \triangleq \bigwedge_{i\in0..m} INIT\_MESSENGER_i$$
$$COLLECT_j \triangleq \bigvee_{n\in0..m}(COLLECT_{n,j} \wedge (\bigwedge_{i\in0..m\backslash\{n\}} \Xi MESSENGER_i))$$
$$DELIVER_j \triangleq \bigvee_{n\in0..m}(DELIVER_{n,j} \wedge (\bigwedge_{i\in0..m\backslash\{n\}} \Xi MESSENGER_i))$$

The abstract design involves a very complex interconnect structure reflecting the fact that all the messengers are independent. Further the abstract design is non deterministic, both in the way the messengers are interleaved and because it is self timed. It also still assumes the CSP model of communication. The design would thus require further refinement to produce a concrete design.

## Conclusions.

- This paper illustrates how CSP and Z may be used to complement one another. The former appears best suited to reasoning about the abstract system while the latter seems superior when considering the more detailed aspects of a design. It would be interesting to see if the method could be extended to cope with real time systems using timed CSP.

- While the underlying ideas are complete they have not been put on a formal basis. If the method proves useful then it will be important to ensure it is sound.

- While an abstract specification can be investigated to discover its properties, great care must be taken if the results are to be meaningful. In addition my subjective experience is that performing proofs, especially when using CSP, can be very tedious. Good proof assistants for Z and CSP will be very important if these notations are to be used for developing real systems.

## References

[1] C.A.R.Hoare, *'Communicating Sequential Processes.'* Prentice-Hall, 1985.

[2] Mark B. Josephs, *'A State-Based Approach to Communicating Processes.'* Distributed Computing 3:9-18, 1988.

# Appendix.

It is possible to investigate the abstract CSP specification. In particular we wish to ensure the message passing system can't deadlock.

- *GUARDED:* Firstly a rather restricted definition is introduced of what it means for a process to be guarded.

$$GUARDED : process \leftrightarrow process$$

$$\forall P, Q : process;\ x : event \bullet$$
$$\quad GUARDED(P, x \to P)\ \wedge$$
$$\quad GUARDED(P, Q) \Rightarrow GUARDED(P, x \to Q)$$

- *Lemma 1:* A process defined as a GUARDED version of itself will not deadlock.
$$\vdash \forall P : process \bullet GUARDED(P, P) \Rightarrow \neg\, DEADLOCK(P)$$

- *Lemma 2:* If a number of copies of a process are interleaved they will only deadlock if the individual processes can deadlock.
$$\vdash \forall P : process \bullet DEADLOCK(|||_{i \in 0..m}\ P_i) \Leftrightarrow DEADLOCK(P)$$

(*i*)            [Definition of a GUARDED process.]
$$\vdash GUARDED(MESSENGER_i, MESSENGER_i)$$

(*ii*)            [(i), Lemma 1.]
$$\vdash \neg\, DEADLOCK(MESSENGER_i)$$

(*iii*)            [(ii), Lemma 2.]
$$\vdash \neg\, DEADLOCK(|||_{i \in 0..m}\ MESSENGER_i)$$

(*iv*)            [Definition of RUN]
$$\vdash USER_i = RUN_{\alpha(USER_i)}$$

(*v*)            [(iv) and laws of CSP.]
$$\vdash (|||_{i \in 0..u}\ USER_i) = RUN_{\alpha(SYSTEM)}$$

(*vi*)            [Law of CSP.]
$$\vdash RUN_{\alpha(P)}\ ||\ P = P$$

(*vii*)            [(iii),(v),(vi)]
$$\vdash \neg\, DEADLOCK((|||_{i \in 0..u}\ USER_i)\ ||\ (|||_{i \in 0..m}\ MESSENGER_i))$$
$$\textbf{QED.}$$

The resulting proof is rigorous but not necessarily very formal in the sense that it relies on the readers understanding of the problem rather than the mechanistic manipulation of terms. This becomes evident when one attempts to perform such proofs using proof assistants.

It is also important to be aware of the context of the proof, in this case the CSP specification. This in effect assumed that messages can always be delivered. In that sense the above proof is a truism. In reality deadlock can occur if messages remain undelivered. This issue is partly tackled in the Z specification by making it clear that undelivered messages are returned to their sender.

# Structured methodologies & formal notations: Developing a framework for synthesis and investigation

Tony Bryant
BT Reader in Software Engineering
Division of Informatics
Leeds Polytechnic

**Abstract**

Report on the Structured & Formal Methods Workshop hosted by Leeds Polytechnic in conjunction with British Telecom as part of their collaborative research project.[1]

## Introduction

The workshop arose from activities concerned with the research project initiated by members of the department of Computing Science at Leeds Polytechnic. Starting in 1987, the project has been funded jointly with BT, and its major theme is concerned with the use of Formal and Structured Methods in the development of Information Systems.

One of the major factors preventing the widespread adoption of formal methods[2] outside research environments arises from the difficulties of comprehension which they present to a large proportion of the workforce, let alone to the general user community. On the other hand, the adoption of structured methods, particularly SSADM, arouses some hostility from within the professional software community. The methodology is somewhat cumbersome, particularly if implemented without computer support and incorporates many activities and techniques which seem redundant and time-consuming without necessarily ensuring the incorporation of the relevant qualities in the finished product.

The objective of the project is to design a way of merging or linking structured and formal methods, along the following lines:

---

[1] The proceedings of the workshop were for the most part recorded verbatim, and the following report is based on that material together with written contributions and notes made at the time. The interpretation that follows is, however, my sole responsibility, and I apologise in advance if it does not exactly correspond with other participants' recollections of the event.

[2] There is little consistency in use and understanding of terms such as methodology, method, model, notation, technique, etc. In our project we have arrived at one possible range of definitions, but I have not sought to impose them in this report, since many of the speakers and contributors used alternatives.

1. Defining the best ways of describing the semantic contents of the techniques and models incorporated in structured methods;

2. Discovering and stating in what ways formal methods can assist in developing criteria for judging progress through specified project milestones;

3. Relating formal specifications to the types of specifications demanded within structured methods;

4. Designing a 'hybrid' methodology encompassing aspects of both structured and formal approaches; incorporating the benefits and rigour of formal proofs of structured milestones in some fashion; specifying the potential for software support; and the ways in which these forms of support could provide more rigorous foundations for the diagrammatic aspects of structured methods.

Once embarked upon this project it became apparent that many other institutions and organisations were involved in similar or related ventures. In order to enhance collaboration, the workshop was called to provide an initial forum for representatives of these groups to exchange ideas and generate an agenda of interests, issues, requirements and activities. The participants were drawn from a wide range of organisations including industrial and commercial users, systems developers, and research and academic institutions (almost exclusively polytechnics rather than universities).

# 1 Invited Presentations at the Workshop

The first part of the workshop was devoted to two introductory papers aimed at setting out the objectives of the exercise and establishing some guidelines for the ensuing activities. These were then followed by a small number of invited papers embellishing key areas of interest.

### Setting the Agenda

Paul McGrath (Leeds Polytechnic) outlined the interests which, he assumed, were shared by all attending. These included an overall preoccupation with quality in systems seen from a variety of perspectives, encompassing both the process of development and the products. In addition, it was noted that those in attendance were for the most part advocates of particular perspectives, ready to discuss their approaches in a non-dogmatic fashion. The aims of the gathering were therefore to decide upon those matters on which all could agree; those about which no general agreement could be reached; an 'audit' of how things stood at present; and the bases for continued exchange of ideas amongst the community represented.

Introducing some themes developed by later contributors, it was noted that the current situation was fluid, but provided a basis for development. There were numerous case studies of methods usage, extending across a range of target systems. These had ramifications both in terms of the technology and in terms of the organisational and social aspects of systems. There was a great deal of source material relevant to be used as a basis for such exercises, but its availability was understandably restricted by commercial interests. Any attempts to advance collaboration and dialogue had to recognise these constraints. Indeed the entire methods project had to be located within the economics of systems development, although it was stressed that advances in aspects such as re-use of specification, design, or code would alter the balance currently prejudiced against significant use of formal methods and quality in general.

On the specific subject of the methods themselves there were a number of observations to be made. Structured methods could at worst be seen as a 'rather inadequate algebra of boxes and arcs', underpinned by a questionable separation of data from process. Formal methods on the other hand might be termed 'notations' rather than methods. Furthermore the problem of teaching the current workforce to use them was difficult to surmount. This was not to seek to oppose one approach against the other, but rather to highlight weaknesses in order to ask in what ways might the one complement the other in the progression from uncertainty to rigour and actuality.

## Structured & Formal Methods; Developing a Framework for Synthesis and Investigation

Tony Bryant (Leeds Polytechnic) began by noting the paradox that after two decades or more of technological advances, organisations experienced more problems than ever before in IS development and management. Given that the 1980s had witnessed a flourishing of IS development methodologies, it was pertinent to ask if the cure was worse than the disease: had the methodologies contributed to the systems malaise? One reason why they might indeed have done so lay in the 'temporal paradox' between the methodologies and the systems. Whereas systems are dynamic, complex and multi-faceted, the methodologies on offer are unyielding, inflexible, and relentless. The need is fundamentally for rigour and stability, but the methodologies offer weight and rigidity.

This was not surprising given the common assumptions of most methodologies — applications are targeted at stable, routine and predictable activities; projects begin from scratch in an autonomous fashion; the system is designed to handle well-structured information; the design process is linear; the separation of data from process is well attested.

These suppositions needed to be stated explicitly to test their adequacy. Some clearly had to be amended or even effaced in the light of experience. The desire and necessity of combining rigour with stability lay beneath much of the interest in introducing a role for formal approaches in systems development. There were, however, obstacles in the path of such solutions. The major one stemmed from the lack of response to substantive criticisms from the exponents of specific methodologies, and the tendency to channel disputation into the parameters of the market. Methodologies tended therefore to be packaged for sale rather than developed for use, and often the response to criticism was simply to add new features which exacerbated the inherent unwieldiness. These new features did not, however, encompass formal notations which were dismissed as labyrinthine and convoluted. This commodification of methodologies had effectively curtailed discussion on issues other than those designed at gaining a competitive edge. Two factors, however, would alter this.

First SSADM, in the role of (un)disputed standard bearer, would become the prime target for criticism; and this would not merely emanate from its competitors, but also from those with a greater degree of disinterestedness and detachment. Key critical questions would be raised, and the general range of discussion moved to include scrutiny of fundamental methodological issues in general.

Second many of the established methodologies in Europe were being used by experienced practitioners in non-standard ways. Methodologies were being fragmented by systems professionals, a consequence of the open-ended learning experience of using methods or methodologies. Simultaneously developments towards a 'Euromethod' were encouraging this intelligent fragmentation on the basis of recognition of need and requirements, selection based on relevant criteria, and adaptation of techniques and tools to specific tasks.

The two trends, although at first sight contradictory, aspire to a common cause: a global view of IS development incorporating a 'methodological map', a universal model. This perspective requires the application of some universal conception of IS development. This was not likely to be the outcome of the workshop! Although one of the later presentations would develop precisely these sorts of issue. In the meantime a start could be made by seeking to locate the two forms of approach: structured and formal. They could be seen to emanate from two perspectives on software development. The first of these characterised the process as a discipline based on clear objectives, tasks, and activities in a well defined framework of planning, monitoring and control. The second saw the discipline being provided by theoretical constructs, rigour and proof. These influenced the respective trends of 'structured specification' and 'formal specification'.

Projects such as the Leeds Polytechnic/BT one were aiming precisely at this goal, and in so doing were contributing to the larger undertaking of constructing a global model. As a direct result of activities comprising the early stages of that project the initial intentions had been clarified and revised, and the direction of research refined to encompass three emphases.

The first, ensuing from discussion regarding a straight-forward merging of structured and formal approaches, consists in attaching Z as a notation to SSADM at strategic points, notably the LDS, DFD and ELH[3] models. This will give rise to a 'complete' Z specification, within an SSADM context, which can subsequently provide a basis for rigorous proof and reasoning. This approach is extremely pragmatic, and is proving illustrative in the short term, although offering little to address the outstanding deficiencies identified in SSADM.

Second, a revision of SSADM will be ventured in a fashion that will permit an incorporation of Z, and potentially other formal approaches, into the methodology. This will address some of the shortcomings in SSADM and possibly overtake revisions of SSADM that are in the offing. Apprehensions here will concern the duality of models, data and process, which form the cornerstones of SSADM but which are not acknowledged by Z. Data, process and event are accessible substantive facets the analyst can grasp in the early stages of analysis and are necessary in the dialogue with end-users for specification acceptance. A possible solution could be found through the use of prototyping, permitting these separate views to merge into one coherent view. On the other hand it might be found that they should be maintained as distinct perspectives. Possibly they may exist as distinct views living off the same conceptual base being created by the analysis activity. This approach represents a

---

[3]Respectively — Logical Data Structure (Entity Relation Analysis), Data Flow Diagrams, Entity Life Histories.

substantial undertaking; certainly at a level different from the first. But it is a necessary stage in seriously addressing the problems for formulating a strategy for merging structured and formal methods.

Third, we shall examine the theoretical underpinnings of SSADM, and perhaps other methodologies, in set-theoretic terms. This will permit an evaluation of the worth of SSADM and identification of those aspects that will be worth retaining in any 'formally-based' methodology. This approach represents some initial stages in an extended and multi-faceted study of systems development methods which will be of worth in the long term by indicating which models and techniques could be accommodated in a 'completely formal' methodology. As such it contributes to the development of a methodological map.

The first strand is felt to be useful in illustrating key points of congruence between SSADM and Z: also demonstrating points in the lifecycle most readily addressed by a formal method of reasoning. The second and third ones may be viewed as complementary; the second founded upon a case-based analysis, with a longer term and more profound aim than that of the first approach; the third being a general, theoretical scheme with the objective of explicating widely applicable theoretical underpinnings.

The way forward, initially linking these latter two, will be to describe the milestones and deliverable products of SSADM in set theoretic language (specifically using Z). A distinction will be drawn between those aspects of the methodology which contribute directly to the overall specification, and those which contribute in the main to the progression of product development. This provides a basis from which the methodology can be critically analysed, and also offers a foundation for ascertaining formal criteria by which the development of a software product can be assessed in terms of specific milestones and degrees of completion.

Although there are numerous less ambitious and intermediate goals, the ultimate objective of the project is to design a way of merging or linking structured and formal approaches within the context of the putative methodological map. Posing the following sorts of questions it is anticipated that an outline design of a methodology will emerge —

1. What are the best ways of describing the semantic contents of the techniques and models incorporated in structured methods — not merely restricted to SSADM;

2. In what ways can formal methods assist in developing criteria for judging progress through and satisfactory, rigorous completion of specified project milestones;

3. In what ways can formal specifications be related to specifications demanded within structured methods;

4. Can a merged methodology be designed: if so what would it encompass from structured and formal aspects; what form would the formal proofs of structured milestones take; what forms of software support could be envisaged; could these forms of support provide more rigorous foundations for the diagrammatic aspects of structured methods;

5. Can the methodology be extended to cover other aspects of the lifecycle; can its applicability be extended to alternative lifecycle models.

Overall this will augment and benefit from initiatives aimed at explicating a more comprehensive picture of the methodological terrain; an expanse conceptualised more in declarative or functional terms rather than in procedural ones.

What must not be lost sight of in the open-minded co-operation and collaboration between different methodological approaches is the concept of an Information System Development Methodology as an organised collection of concepts, beliefs, values and normative resources, aimed at assisting the development group in successfully changing object systems. At present the structured and formal approaches have intrinsic deficiencies, although they represent significant advances in many respects. If the consolidation of the two is to prove fruitful, it must take place within the framework of an overall critical concept of the IS development process as a whole.

## Methods in the Commercial Environment

Alan Stoddart (Divisional Manager Systems & Software Engineering Division, BT Research Laboratories) located the structured and formal methods research project in BT as a whole. He is responsible for 'identifying and transferring the best technologies relevant to BT's businesses'. This implied a strong commitment to research in order to ascertain what were the best technologies, and also a recognition of the need to develop candidate technologies until they could be assessed, evaluated and transferred. Ultimately all costs are borne by the operational units of BT, outside of the Research & Technology unit, but the former tended to have specific interests in the short to medium term while the latter were also concerned with the long term (7-15 years) developments in technology.

The interest in notations and methods was seen as medium term, whilst the longer term perspective encompassed the system as a whole considered from a range of viewpoints. This would involve not only the traditional data processing activities, but also demands for on-line and real time processing as well as all the complexities of communications, networking, distribution. The presiding objective is then to ascertain the extent to which these aspects can be consolidated within a methodological framework allowing critical choice and adaptation in the specific system context.

At present, however, this is not the case. Product loyalty and ingrained practice dictate the options rather than considered judgment. In addition the methods on offer (SSADM and Yourdon predominate in DP applications) are themselves incomplete and ambiguous, with little or no guidance in terms of satisfactory levels of precision or correctness. This is aggravated by the lack of adequate tool support. Tools are non-existent or provide only poor levels of support for a method. The methods themselves are rigid, and this results in the development process being dictated by the method rather than vice-versa. Or, conversely, it leads to the misuse of techniques or methods concealed in a way that results in poor quality products or detrimental consequences that do not become apparent until it is too late.

BT's requirements of a method are that it alleviates all these problems. It must cover real time, data processing, and transaction processing aspects. There must be coverage of the complete lifecycle from initiation to obsolescence. The method must be unambiguous and there must be tool support suited both to users and developers. (The users often being highly skilled people, although not primarily working in software or information systems.) It must address the loading of upfront costs which seems unavoidable with the use of methodologies. Formal notations are seen as one route towards such a method, but there must be a seamless transition between a formal notation and the graphic or user-oriented facets of the method. BT's interest in advancing along these lines is based on their reliance on systems for competitive edge, their employment of over 6000 software engineers, the related expenditure of £500 million per year, and an estimated annual maintenance bill in excess of £200 million.

## Standardising Methods — Euromethod

Neil Glover (CCTA) charted the experience of the CCTA in selecting, developing and pioneering the use of SSADM, and also on the initiatives to develop a European method (Euromethod) aimed at the likelihood of large cross-frontier projects in the future.

SSADM itself had been aimed at increasing staff effectiveness, improving project communication between different types of personnel, obtaining user commitment and involvement throughout the duration of the project, and providing mechanisms for better management and enhanced quality. Given its record of success in the UK it might appear to have been a candidate for a pan-European method, but other countries have their own particular approaches and it is more realistic to see Euromethod not as an individual method but as a basis for procurement specification, enabling information exchange in planning and development projects, offering a target for tool builders, and facilitating skills exchange.

There are a significant number of difficulties in dealing with multifarious European software practices. There are cultural distinctions; diversity in the principal actors and bodies involved; and language problems even within the highly restricted vocabulary of IS development — e.g. a generally agreed definition of the term 'function' has proved elusive within a single method, let alone across several.

Euromethod then will provide a framework to be used as a procurement mechanism, and perhaps later might become a basis for harmonisation of key techniques. The framework itself will take the form of a series of templates defined as points of the lifecycle, with mandatory deliverables available for evaluation and review. The time frame to build the model is 1-5 years.

In response to various questions and comments it seemed that there was a tension between the necessity for a common framework for assessment and management of trans-national systems after 1992, and the perfection of a standard methodology. The shorter term objective related to the management demands, the concept of a single methodology was much longer term and consequently undefined and unresolved.

## Do we need a universal systems model ?

Professor John McDermid (York University) noted that the title of his talk was 'magnificently opaque'! By way of explanation: If you are going to try to unify formal and structured methods you do need some underlying canonical system model. Without this there is no way in which the specifications can be related and the benefits of relating them assessed. As a warning to the unwary one had only to look at the example of IPSEs. These had been 'developed' by simply throwing lots of tools into one environment, but this did not produce a magically integrated product. Similarly one could not merely lump together a variety of techniques or methods.

There are some key questions worth consideration: do we need a pair of related models or is a single model sufficient? are the static/dynamic pair of models sufficient? do they let us reason about security, safety? is the static/dynamic model pair sufficient for all types of system? how can we assess if a model is a good one? what are examples of good models? how can we evaluate proposed models?

As an example consider the use of a formal method to 'underpin' a structured one. This might operate as a relationship between say the SSADM ELH model with mappings onto CSP traces as an underlying representation acting as a frame of reference. This frame of reference might permit different forms of specification to be demonstrated to be representations of the same system, highlighting conflicts or inconsistencies. This might operate in a fashion similar to that in architecture where the static structure and the dynamic model form a complementary couple.

This principle can be illustrated with an example. The static structure can be seen in terms of objects, the dynamic aspects as transactions. Objects give a basic system structuring, with the potential for an algebraic view of individual object behaviour. This can then be supplemented by a model oriented view of the internal state of individual objects. The external behaviour of objects can be seen in terms of CSP traces or similar, producing a detailed 'set of transactions'. This transaction view offers an abstraction over traces, relating input to output for the system as a whole. Timing aspects can then be introduced as constraints over transactions.

This sort of approach proves useful in linking different notations in order to model system behaviour. This applies to techniques in structured methods. The ELH can be used to model the effects of calling the methods provided by objects on data stored in the objects.[4] This is similar to the Process Structure Diagram in Jackson Structure Design where the PSDs represent 'actions on entities'. Entity Relationship Analysis could be used to model the structure of the data objects passed between methods. This is not to claim that this object/transaction approach is the correct or only model for facilitating such linking of notations, but it certainly offers an initial framework.

## A Strategic View of Formal Methods

Anthony Hall (Praxis) took the view that to an extent it was timely to move away from levels of detail, to pose some very basic questions about methods, and to assess the responses in the context of formal and structured methods.

The most fundamental question is 'what are methods for'? If this question is not posed much of the ensuing discussion will have no focus. Once this has been discussed, one can then consider 'what should we look for in a method'? 'what problems do methods solve'? 'how do methods solve problems'?

Agreeing with Brooks, amongst others, that there is 'no silver bullet' in software development — that it is an inherently difficult intellectual task — methods exist to help people think. The process of software engineering cannot be automated or

---

[4]The use of the term 'methods' derives from the area of object oriented design; objects correspond to abstract data types, methods are then equivalent to the operations provided by the objects.

mechanised, the activity constitutes an intellectual challenge. Any method aimed at assisting the fulfilment of this must help the developer think: think about the right things, and think about the things right. And it must do these in that order.

Certain consequences emerge from this. First methods exist to enable the activity of development, they do not and cannot deskill the process. Recognising this, any choice of method will depend initially on the sorts of problems for which the method is of assistance, next on how (in what way) and how well does it provide this, and only subsequently should the extent to which a method is automated influence choice.

Prompted from the audience, it was agreed that it might also be important to recognise that methods could hinder or distract from aspects of the problem, and that this should be taken into account.

This perspective then led to two questions of relevance to structured and formal methods. What should we think about; what can we think about using the respective approaches.

In general we should think about the hardest and biggest problems, not those which can be most easily solved or for which we have good notations. This approach is embodied in Boehm's 'spiral' model of software development, which states that at the start of development one must look at the biggest risks and the biggest problems involved, and ensure that they can be reduced and resolved. Although this will vary between systems, in most cases the biggest problem will concern understanding what the user wants and not how it is to be built.

Structured methods make us think about structure. Both the structure of the environment, and the structure of the system. Formal methods help us think about function, what the system will actually do: Also what the system should not do, for reasons of safety or integrity. Many formal methods gave little or no assistance with the structure of a large software development: no structured methods shed much light on the functioning of the system. (There was some evidence of disagreement with this last statement from participants.) It was interesting to point out that prototyping similarly focuses on what the system is supposed to do, and as such it parallels formal specification, both being contrasted with structured methods.

Taking the view that a key element of any method is its notation, it is important to ask what a notation should offer. It must convey meaning, both in the sense that it intrinsically has and denotes that meaning, and that the meaning can be comprehended. Additionally the notation must be abstract. It must be user-oriented or application-oriented rather than machine-oriented. It must denote what is to be done, the effects, not how it is to be achieved, the procedures. It should have an appropriate level of detail. If the abstraction is not sufficient, it will be as difficult to say anything useful in the notation as to build the system itself.

How then do structured notations conform to this archetype? They are easily assimilated, being predominantly diagrammatic. They appear to have meaning, and usually they have a defined syntax; one can judge how well-formed an entity-relationship diagram might be. But other structured notations do not have a well defined meaning; data flow diagrams being a prime instance. Furthermore, notations such as ER diagrams and JSP structures, although having some claim to being 'formal', are simply not very expressive. ER diagrams do not say very much about either the entities or the relationships. Finally, structured notations offer little by way of abstractions of functionality apart from the code itself or perhaps a slightly higher level pseudo-code.

Formal notations, on the other hand, are superficially more difficult to understand. But their meaning, once understood, is unambiguous, well defined and they are highly expressive. For a sequential process any level of detail can be expressed; there are some problems with concurrent processes. The notation is compact, and formal specification meets the criteria of abstraction.

The two approaches then appear to differ markedly, and to be confronting different problems in different ways. Both, however, have been brought to bear on the critical early stages of the development process. In the realm of structured practices there has been a move from structured programming to structured analysis. While the formal focus has shifted from program proving to the formal specification of requirements and top level design. In general there is concentration on involving the user through operations such as prototyping and task analysis. There is an increasing need for the early definition of function, a consequence of focusing on the user rather than the builder, and this will probably lead to the adoption of formal methods even in areas where only structured ones are currently accepted.

In the future there will be a convergence between real-time systems (which increasingly need more data) and commercial systems (which are on-line). Systems in the future will often be both data intensive and processing intensive, with concomitant demands for safety and security guarantees. For technicians there will be an increasing familiarity with formal notations, the mathematics will become more accessible, and the range of practical experience of such notations in use will facilitate this trend. Also there will be a better understanding of the complementary roles of different notations, and improved notations particularly for concurrent and time-critical aspects of systems will appear.

In conclusion, just as structured methods such as SSADM are combinations of techniques, there is no reason why formal techniques should not be combined to form a single approach. Initiatives such as the present workshop will assist and foster the intellectual work required to understand the best ways in which such consolidation can be achieved in order to meet the increasingly demanding challenges ahead.

## Def Stan 00-55

The final formal presentation consisted of a brief survey of a standard in the formal realm. John Robinson (KBSL) outlined some aspects of the standard, together with some predictions based on what he considered to be the similar case of the reception and acceptance of Ada.

The standard consists of three components: safety management procedures, software engineering practices, and the safety critical lifecycle. There was, therefore, much more to the standard than merely the advocacy of use of formal methods, a false impression engendered by recent press coverage.

Although much of the standard concerned the military sector, it was recognised that not only are the needs of this sector and the civil ones similar, but also that a larger market will encourage suppliers and developers and may help to cut costs.

It could, however, still be asked if the standard is of purely academic or limited interest, particularly as it is still in draft form. The standard will have a large impact on many areas, it will stimulate the market, and changes people's ideas on the process of planning and developing systems. It will promote the demand for training and specialist support, and increase customer awareness of the importance of standards.

But will it work? Will it be enforced? This will depend on several factors including whether or not customers will be willing to pay for quality. Safety critical techniques are expensive, and if the prime criterion is 'best price' rather than 'best result', then widespread adoption of formal or similar techniques is unlikely. This has proved to be the case with Ada. It will also be affected by the willingness of people to change: attitudes, skills, experience, awareness.

To those who say 'it will never work', one can respond by pointing to the experience with Ada. In the early 1980s there were many who were sceptical about the widespread acceptance and use of the language as a standard. It has taken roughly 5 years for the standard to achieve stability through application in real projects, and only now, more than 7 years after its launch can it be seen to be starting to be 'proven in action'. If the experience is to be repeated for 00-55, it will be at least 1995 before there is any general stability and project application, and 1997 before there is a general acceptance.

There is a deal of pressure from industry to abandon or relax the standard. This could lead to the near excision of formal methods: they could either be removed altogether, or be allowed to be subject to negotiation, or become optional rather than mandatory. The speaker's view, however, was that the standard would develop, with formal methods included. This would lead to some developers and customers falling behind in the associated developments, while others will grasp the opportunity and flourish. The best route forward is not to wait for definitive decisions, but to begin using basic techniques on existing projects, looking to apply more complex ones on real or perhaps pilot projects, and, crucially, to monitor the results so that they have some basis for answering the question 'has it worked?'.

# 2   Discussion

Following the presentations, the remaining time was scheduled for discussions and the development of ideas. As a broad framework for this a number of topics and questions were posed by the organisers.

1. What is a method?
   How are formal and structured methods characterised?

2. Evolution of methods — convergence of methods

3. A Universal Systems Model
   A Methods Map — types of methods
   A Systems Map — classifying systems and classifying methods

4. Implementing Methods Why bother with methods? Is method-driven systems development merely technology-driven systems in another guise?

5. Real Time Systems — what problems do they pose in terms of methods?

The discussions took a wide variety of directions, and it would be impossible to do justice to them in entirety. All that is offered at this juncture is a very cryptic recapitulation of the major concerns of contributors.

There was some discussion of the meaning of the term 'formal', with an argument being put that structured methods are formal in certain meanings of the term. This led to attempts to distinguish between levels or types of formality, also it led to concern with motivations behind methods. Are structured methods meant primarily for managers? Who are formal methods for? It was agreed that a key, intractable, problem was that no single approach or notation could encompass the necessary range of views, skills, and interests inevitable in systems development. This requirement for the capture of meaning had also to be extended into its preservation across time and across projects and contexts. Although there was some staunch defence of particular methods, in general it was agreed that aspects apart from data structures and processes, such as non-functional requirements, real-time and concurrency, could not be addressed adequately by a single method. This was particularly true for methods which were primarily dat-oriented or process-oriented.

Another aspect was the problem which arose if one considered a general guiding principle in systems development to be the ability to generate a conception of a system at a denotational level, moving to an operational level at a subsequent stage. The current systems workforce were too ready to start from the operational level. Not only is there a need to educate in terms of new notations, but also to persuade developers to think denotationally. There also has to be scope for user participation. The denotational form must be able to deal with user questioning and prompting, in the sense that it can develop derivations of system activity within criteria of criticism of the model presented. This prompted consideration of a role for the universal model supplying context for this dialogue between notations.

It was felt that one major obstacle in the path of widespread use of formal notations is realisation of the rationale behind such approaches. The initial education of the workforce is probably attainable, but far more critical is the inculcation of the ethos underlying these advances. This might be assisted if an 'added value' in the use of such methods could be demonstrated.

# 3   Additional Material

In addition to the formal presentations, some of the other participants contributed papers or outlines of current interests and research. These included the following —

1. Ideas for a Z Methods Handbook
   Part of a larger IED project (ZIP)

2. Automatic Documentation of Z schema specifications

3. Representing Real World Knowledge at the Stage of Requirements Capture

4. Structuring Physical Design in SSADM

5. Generating Database Update Programs from ELH Analysis

6. Translating Data Flow Diagrams into Z

7. The role of intuition in systems development

# 4  Conclusion

The workshop proved a useful forum for people representing a variety of interests to exchange views. There was agreement that no single approach or notation was sufficient given the multi-faceted demands for successful system development. The growing importance of real-time and concurrency systems aspects was stated, and this added further to the range of methods or approaches across which systems abstraction could and should progress. This consideration, together with advances in object-oriented design, and reusability, strengthened the argument for initial steps to outline a universal model against which these and other strategies could be mapped. The articulation of such a research programme was beyond the immediate scope of the workshop, but if nothing else the two days of presentation and discussion had underlined the necessity for such a strategy in the future.

# Posters

# Zork: A Typechecker for Z from York

*Ian Toyn*

*Department of Computer Science, University of York, England*

*(Email: ian@uk.ac.york.minster)*

### Lexical form of input

The input to zork is a troff document, in which formal material is delimited by .ZS and .ZE, etc, in the usual style of troff. The fancy symbols of Z are denoted by ASCII long-names, for example `forall` and `lambda`, as used at York since the Alvey Aspect project.

### Syntax

The syntax required by zork is based on that defined in PRG-68 [1], adapted to the troff style.

### Toolkits and Documents

Built into zork is just the core Z language. A specification is constructed from a collection of documents, each of which can import other documents and indicate which of its definitions are to be exported. The first document in a specification is usually a toolkit that provides the standard mathematical definitions. The toolkit published in Chapter 4 of Spivey's 1989 book [2] will be provided with zork.

### Typechecking

Zork checks specifications for type correctness. A report of a type error explains the kind of error in English, gives the conflicting types, and identifies the type-erroneous term.

### Prettyprinting and Typesetting

Zork exchanges information with troff to generate prettyprinted schemas, which are then typeset with the aid of a troff macro package. All definitions in a specification can be given a format string, not just the built-in long-names. A font is provided including all the fancy Z symbols, available as a PostScript outline font or as a raster font for Imagen printers. Installation of zork involves teaching troff about the Z font.

### Availability

A $\beta$-release of zork will be available in the early part of 1990. A previewer, with bit-map screen fonts, will be available later.

### Example of a correct specification

```
.ZI toolkit
.ZG [Name, File, Value]
.ZS File_System
Directory:
        Name pfx File
Contents: File pfx
          ps Value
.ZM
ran Directory =
        dom Contents
.ZE
```

Import toolkit

[Name, File, Value]

┌─ File_System ─────────────────────
│ Directory : Name $\rightarrowtail$ File
│ Contents : File $\rightarrowtail$ $\mathbb{P}$ Value
├───────────────────────────────────
│ ran Directory = dom Contents
└───────────────────────────────────

---

1.  S. King, I. H. Sørensen and J. Woodcock, "Z: Grammar and Concrete and Abstract Syntaxes (Version 2.0)", PRG-68, Oxford University Computing Laboratory, Programming Research Group (July 1988).

2.  J. M. Spivey, *The Z Notation: A Reference Manual*, Prentice Hall (1989).

## THE Z TOOL

The Z Tool provides full support for the Z specification language.
It is a powerful environment providing comprehensive support for:-

- Editing of Z specifications
- Incremental parsing
- Type checking
- Proof editing
- Pretty-printing

The Z Tool makes the Z language accessible and provides:-

- Full language support
- A user friendly interface
- Ease of use
- Effective tools
- High quality output

The Z Tool provides structure editing for Z specifications with full
incremental parsing. Editing is thus efficient and flexible. It
provides automatic pretty-printing and formatting for the language
constructs. Typechecking can be invoked directly on the
specification.

### Proof Support for Z
The Z Tool provides a proof editor for proof checking and automatic
theorem proving. This area is the subject of intense research and
development by IST as access to proof technology is essential for
serious users of Z.

### Future Developments
IST has invested a substantial effort into keeping abreast of
current developments in the field automatic and user assisted proof
tools. IST will continue this research and market products that
represent leading edge technology to the benefit of the Formal
Methods community.

Work is presently concentrated on the development of an integrated
tactical theorem prover for the Z Tool. This has been prototyped in
ML and is currently being implemented. IST intend to release this
important tool around April/May 1990.

### Hardware and Software Requirements
The Z Tool and VDM Tool both run on Sun workstations with 12MB
memory. Users will also require a Lucid Common Lisp licence.

### Prices, Licencing and Support
Z Tool       £4,000 per workstation
VDM Tool     £4,000 per workstation
Site and academic licences are available at very favourable terms.
Maintenance for both tools is free in the first year and charged at
15% in subsequent years.

For further details contact:-

Kim O´Neil or Karam Ashoo
IMPERIAL SOFTWARE TECHNOLOGY
3 Glisson Road,
CAMBRIDGE CB1 2HA.
Tel. 0223 462 400

## USE OF Z TO SPECIFY A SECURE SYSTEM

GPT Data Systems is using Z to specify a Security Policy, user access and security functions of products based on the Secure Communications Processor SCP2.

Z is being used in the formulation of a Formal Security Policy Model for a new secure product - a Shared-Terminal Access Control System (STAX). This will securely connect user terminals to a number of application processors such that at any time, each user terminal has access to only one application processor.

The Formal Security Policy Model is required in order to obtain a UK Confidence Level 5 ( 'Rigorous Design' ) rating and a US Department of Defense B3 Security Level rating.

Specifications have been produced using the IST Genesis-Z Specification Editor. This tool includes a parser and a typechecker to assist in the construction of specifications.

The Renaming Components facility ( as described in some books but excluded from M.Spivey's 'Z Notation' ) is not included in Genesis-Z, but it would be considered useful.

Martin Shuttlewood, Secure Systems Group, GPT Data Systems, Elstree Way, Borehamwood, Herts, WD6 1RX. Tel 01 953 2030.

# ESPRIT BRA ProCoS project

The objectives of the ESPRIT-funded BRA (Basic Research Action) **ProCoS** project are to advance the state of the art of systematic design of complex heterogeneous systems, including both software and hardware; in particular, to reduce the risk of error in the specification, design and implementation of embedded safety-critical systems.

To approach this goal, we plan to develop a concrete system consisting of the following five major components:

- A specification language.

- A programming language.

- A definition of a hardware machine.

- A compiler from the programming language to instructions of that machine.

- A kernel supporting the execution of compiled programs on that machine.

The syntax and semantics of these components will be formalized, and their formal interrelationships will be established.

The project will base its work on the CSP/occam/transputer tradition. In particular, the instruction set of the hardware machine will be a subset of that of the existing transputer designed by inmos. This will be specified in Z at Oxford University and will be compatible with the instruction set used on the IED safemos project.

The project started in April 1989 and is due to run for $2\frac{1}{2}$ years. The project is being co-ordinated by DTH.

**Site Address**
Oxford University Computing Laboratory
Programming Research Group
8–11 Keble Road
Oxford  OX1 3QD
England
Tel:      +44-865-273840
Fax:      +44-865-273839
Telex:    83147 ATTN comlab
E-mail:   procos@prg.oxford.ac.uk

**Partners**
Technical University of Denmark (DTH), Denmark
Christian-Albrechts Universität zu Kiel, Germany
Oxford University, England
Royal Holloway and Bedford New College, England
Aarhus University, Denmark
University of Manchester, England

*Jonathan Bowen*
Programming Research Group
Oxford University
December 1989

# safemos

## Demonstration of the Possibility of Totally Verified Systems

The IED-funded (Information Engineering Directorate) safemos project intends to address some of the problems facing the designers and users of microprocessors and micro-controllers that are arising as the complexity and power of these devices increase. Microprocessors are being used to perform increasing complex tasks as they become more powerful so that the ability to ensure correct design by traditional design techniques, centered around experimental testing, will become problematic.

The use of formal design methods seems to offer a way out of this situation by providing a design methodology which prevents the introduction of errors into designs through the rigorous use of proof techniques to validate designs against specifications. This project intends to demonstrate the feasibility of these methods in real-time control systems. In the future such real-time controllers will increasingly consist of processors running embedded programs along with specialised interface hardware. Due to this, the project intends to address the problem of verifying mixed hardware/software systems.

The three main goals of the project are:

1. to demonstrate that it is feasible and commercially advantageous to verify systems containing both hardware and software by machine checked formal proof;

2. to develop the methodology and tools needed for performing such verifications and for estimating their costs;

3. to gain improved scientific understanding of the practical use of existing formal methods and tools, including HOL(Higher Order Logic), Z and CSP.

In particular, the instruction set and high-level architecture of the processor will be specified in Z at Oxford University. This will be compatible with the instruction set used on the ESPRIT BRA ProCoS project. The instruction set is intended to be a subset of that of the existing transputer designed by inmos.

The project has just received approval and is due to run for 3 years.

*Jonathan Bowen*
Oxford University Computing Laboratory
Programming Research Group
December 1989

# IED Research Project

INMOS Limited (I) – coordinator
SRI International Cambridge Research Centre (S)
University of Cambridge Computer Laboratory (C)
Oxford University Computing Laboratory (P)

**dti**

# ESPRIT II: REDO at Oxford

contact: *K. Lano*, Programming Research Group
11, Keble Road, Oxford, U.K.

The Programming Research Group is participating in the ESPRIT project REDO; for the ReEngineering and reDOcumentation of Cobol and Fortran programs. The project involves academic and industrial partners across Europe, under the overall management of Lloyd's Register in London. Three universities, Durham, Oxford and Limerick, five software products and services houses, Centrisa (Sp), CTC (Gr), ITS (Sp), Grumman (Ger), Marconi (UK), and two large users of application codes, Electricite de France (Fr), Delft Hydraulics (Nth), provide a lively spectrum of talents and activities.

REDO aims to provide a package of tools which will modify existing programs *and* increase their maintainability, with three main goals:

- Programs will be restructured to support maintainability properties.

- Documentation will be adduced and kept in line with code

- Features relating to the validation of code will be incorporated and enhanced

The project has passed the six-month stage. The PRG contributes expertise in formal methods to the whole project but is involved chiefly with the last of the three areas, whilst the specialist applied software houses concentrate on the restructuring of control and data flow (Grumman), and the separation of environmental dependencies (Centrisa, Delft). The Centre for Software Maintenance at Durham is cooperating with ITS on the generation and maintenance of code documentation. The enhancement of other qualities of code is also being pursued; these include the promotion of the independence of code from details of the user interface (Delft) and the underlying database design (Centrisa), and improving its parallelization properties (CTC).

Z is being exploited in various parts of the programme. A case study - the specification of a real-time system - has been conducted with Marconi, and Z is also used as the basis for formal validation activities in which Lloyds have an interest. In cooperation with the University of Limerick, an Intermediate Language for the representation of Fortran and Cobol codes has been designed and specified in Z.

# Formal Specification of Window Systems

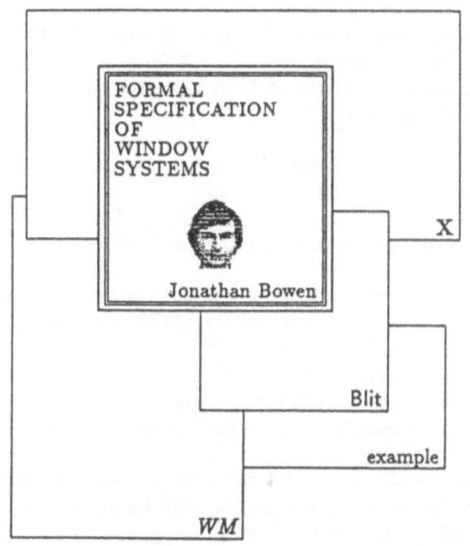

Technical Monograph PRG-74
ISBN 0-902928-56-2
88 pages
June 1989

**Abstract**

Window management systems are now used extensively for user interfaces to computer systems. Part I of this monograph introduces some of the fundamental ideas in window systems using the formal specification language Z. Part II outlines three real systems and attempts to capture the essence of each system using the same formal notation and ideas introduced in Part I. Low-level detail is avoided to keep the length to a manageable size.

In Part I, chapter 1 introduces general concepts useful for specifying pixel maps and window systems. Chapter 2 defines the raster-op function which is fundamental to many graphics operations and chapter 3 introduces a simple example window system. In Part II, chapters 4–6 detail three particular window systems, X from MIT, *WM* from Carnegie-Mellon University and the Blit from AT&T Bell Laboratories. Chapter 7 remarks on experience gained by formally specifying the three window systems.

The monograph, and others in this series, are available from the Librarian, Oxford University Computing Laboratory, 8–11 Keble Road, OXFORD OX1 3QD (telephone Oxford (0865) 273837, e-mail library@uk.ac.oxford.prg on JANET). A "Z Package" of Z-related documents is also available from the librarian. A small charge is levied to cover costs unless your organisation has a reciprocal agreement with the PRG.

*Jonathan Bowen*
Programming Research Group
Oxford University
December 1989

# PRG archive server

A computer-based archive server at the Programming Research Group in Oxford is available for anyone with access to electronic mail. This allows people interested in Z (and other things) to access various archived files. In particular, back issues of the Z FORUM electronic newsletter are available. To access the archive server, send e-mail to:

|  | archive-server@uk.ac.oxford.prg | (JANET) |
| or | ...!ukc!ox-prg!archive-server | (UUCP) |

The "Subject:" line and/or the body of the message may contain lines such as the following:

| help | – help on using the archive server |
| index | – general index of categories (e.g., "z") |
| index z | – index of Z-related files |
| send z 4.3 4.4 | – send issues 4.3 and 4.4 of Z FORUM |
| send z zbib | – send the Z bibliography |
| path *name@site* | – specify return e-mail address (optional) |

A request may contain several "send" commands. If you ask for a large number of files, or a lot of other people are also trying to access the archive, your message will be queued and sent when our machine has some free time. If you ask for a small number of files, your request is likely to be serviced more quickly. However, all being well, you should get the files back within a day or two.

If you have serious problems accessing the archive and need human help, send e-mail to:

archive-management@uk.ac.oxford.prg

Please also contact this address if you have anything which you think is worth adding to the archive.

*Jonathan Bowen*
Programming Research Group
Oxford University
December 1989

ZIP - A Unification Initiative for Z Standards, Methods & Tools

A Summary of the DTI IED ZIP Project Presented to the Meeting of Z Users, 15th December 1989, by Brian Hepworth on behalf of the ZIP Consortium comprising:

British Aerospace Plc.
BP International Ltd.
IBM UK Laboratories Ltd.
Logica Cambridge Ltd.
Praxis Systems Plc.

Rutherford Appleton Laboratory.
Oxford University Programming Research Group.

# 1 Summary

The Z notation has been shown to be effective in a number of industrial projects. Work on these projects has benefited from the descriptive power of the notation, which allows precise specifications to be developed at the early, critical stages of a project. From these pioneering applications of Z have evolved a number of Z methods and tools, which will almost certainly diverge in the absence of a coherent unification initiative such as ZIP.

The ZIP project is intended to align and standardise the development of Z methods and tools in line with a standard notation based on the Z Reference Manual [1] in order to forstall the impending divergence.

The ZIP consortium of British Aerospace (Military Aircraft) Ltd. (BAe), BP International Ltd. (BP), IBM UK Laboratories Ltd., Logica Cambridge Ltd., Praxis Systems Plc., Rutherford Appleton Laboratory (RAL) and Oxford University Programming Research Group (PRG) is well placed to effect the unification initiative for Z standards, methods and tools and is of sufficient size to align the activities of the wider Z community to advance our world lead in the development and application of model-oriented formal methods.

# 2 State-of-the-Art

As yet, formal notations are used in only a small (but important) way within industry, though they are widely taught in computing science departments. Praxis, IBM and Logica use Z in their specification work. Such notations are spreading - the increasing emphasis on safety critical applications, and the shortfall in computing staff both create pressure for their wider adoption throughout industry.

## 2.1 Z Notation

Z is a mathematical notation for expressing the specification of a computer system or program, which can also be used in the design process. A specification is the means of communication between a client (user) and a supplier (implementor); additionally it is a mode of communication between team members. To succeed it must be clear and unambiguous, which existing informal methods of specification are not. Formal notations have been developed in response to this need.

In the last few years work has proceeded apace, both at PRG and in industry, to agree a common abstract syntax for Z. With the publication of the Z Reference Manual [1], there is a basic reference for Z - the essential core of Z is now stable. Further research needs to be pursued, especially in the area of specification of concurrent systems, and this could result in extensions to the notation.

Currently there is no public standard for Z. The Z notation is now sufficiently mature for the development of a standard, and has gone through the early development stages when the language was changing rapidly but has not yet suffered from disparities. Such a standard needs to be subject to control so that changes are carefully documented and published in a regulated manner. The body to agree such a Z standard should include representatives from industry and academia.

In the past, the extent to which the involved parties had entrenched positions militated against agreement on programming language standards. That is, the standards were always too late! In the Z world, the time is ripe to agree a standard before such inflexibility develops.

If Z is to become widely adopted then a fixed point of reference is needed for the notation. Other older formal notations have suffered from a divergence in representation and use and consequently have become unwieldy, and exchange of documents has become difficult.

Most people use some form of text processing system, and it must be possible to send machine-readable formal specifications from one organisation to another. It then becomes vital that writer and reader use the same language - a standard concrete syntax for Z is needed. One additional requirement is for textual representations which can be substituted for Z symbols on devices which are incapable of displaying these symbols.

## 2.2 Research In Z

The original work on Z - conducted at the PRG - concentrated on specification, borrowing techniques from VDM to progress designs into code. More recently, two techniques have become prominent that are suited to Z. The first is due to Carroll Morgan, and is a calculus for refining specifications into code [2]. One possible criticism of this work is that the notation is not that of Z, but one chosen for convenient expression and manipulation of designs. The second technique is one developed by the IBM CICS formalisation project, and remains within the Z notation.

Carroll Morgan's calculus has a formal basis but it can be difficult to use. Contrariwise, the Z refinement ideas are easy to employ but they lack a firm theoretical foundation. It is important to have a sound technical underpinning for assured application of Z.

The work on concurrency in Z is even less mature than that on refinement. At present there are some theoretical results due to He, Josephs and Woodcock [3,4,5] on the nature of concurrent refinement in a state-based framework. There are also some unpublished case studies taken from the CICS work (for which IBM and the PRG combined forces), in which these results are put into practice. There is considerable scope for application-oriented research of the same kind as was carried out for sequential systems in the early days of the Z work.

Most of the formal methods work that has been carried out in industry has concentrated on the production of high level formal specifications, with correctness of design and code justified by reviews or informal argument. Experiments in Oxford, using Abrial's B tool, have shown that it is practicable to conduct formal proofs of industrial-sized specifications. However, it is only by conducting such experiments that we can learn how best to go about proof, and how effective it can be.

## 2.3 Methods

Although Z has a well defined notation, like many other "formal methods" there is little guidance as to the manner in which it should be used. This deficiency has been highlighted by the Systems Engineering Strategy [6] and the Alvey Formal Methods Advisory Group [7]. Z needs to have a developed method if it is to become widely used.

At present there is a great interest in Z, stimulated in part by DEF-STAN-0055, as is witnessed by the increasing number of people who attend courses in Z. Logica, Praxis and the PRG are involved in this training process, often as a co-operative venture and also with NCC. Unfortunately, these converts to Z experience difficulty in applying the notation because they cannot be sure that the language they use is correct. Moreover, they find writing Z arduous. One reason for this is that there is no available guidance on what constitutes a good Z specification, nor on how to approach specification problems.

## 2.4 Tools

The state of the art in tools supporting software development using Z is represented by a number of editors, text formatters, typecheckers and prototype proof assistants. These tools have been developed by individuals and organisations to varying degrees of quality using various machine representations of the formal notation.

### 2.4.1 Forsite

Forsite was an Alvey-funded project undertaken by Racal, Systems Designers, Oxford University Programming Research Group and Surrey University, with the objective of providing a toolset environment supporting formal specification using Z. As such it is to date the most concerted effort to provide support for Z users. The Forsite System has several major components including: Editor, Parser, Typechecker, Cross Referencer, Spelling Checker and Printer.

Forsite has been beta-tested at a number of industrial and academic sites. On the completion of Alvey, Racal proposed that the toolset would be re-designed to give greater efficiency and improved portability. Also proposed was a directive to develop tools supporting theorem proof and refinement. However as yet no clear marketing strategy has evolved for the Forsite System.

## 2.4.2 The FUZZ Package For Z Documents

The FUZZ Package incorporates a LaTeX style option text formatting macro set and typechecking program and has been developed by J.M. Spivey at PRG.

The style option allows Z specifications to be entered as ASCII text, with markup to indicate Z structures. This text can be formatted by the LaTeX system and printed on a wide range of printers and photo-typesetters.

The typechecker takes as its input the same form of text as the style option. It extracts the formal parts of specifications and checks for conformance to the scope and type rules of Z, as documented in the Z Reference Manual. Reports produced comprise a list of errors and optionally a list of all variables declared in the specification and their types.

The FUZZ package is commercially available for SUN Workstations and PCs running LaTeX and has been used to prepare numerous technical papers and text books.

## 2.4.3 BAe ZED Tool

The ZED Tool is a VAX-based environment running under VMS 4.6 on VT 200 and VT 300 series terminals, allowing for the production of Z documentation. As such its major components include: Front-End Management System, Editor, Browser, On-line Help, Spelling Checker and Printer

ZED has been integrated with BAe's CORE Workstation to support research into using Z within the framework of CORE. External to BAe, ZED is used by Program Validation Ltd. to support their development of the SPADE/SPARK toolset.

## 2.4.4 Genesis

As part of the Esprit-funded Genesis project, IST Cambridge have developed a generic tool for formal languages based on a structured editor. The Genesis toolset consists of an editor, a parser and a term rewriting system. These are all generic and can be parameterised by the language to be used and its logical system. The toolset can currently be configured for Z and VDM.

## 2.4.5 IBM Z Tools

IBM, in support of their CICS maintenance activity, have developed a text formatter and cross reference tool. Z documents are prepared using ASCII text, with markup to indicate Z structures, on IBM 3279 terminals. Documents are formatted using DCF (a text formatter) and printed on an IBM 3800 laser printer. The cross reference tool provides the function for reporting page index information similar to that of Forsite.

## 2.4.6 The ZEBRA Typechecking Environment

The ZEBRA typechecking environment has been developed by Bernard Sufrin of PRG from his experience of the Forsite development. ZEBRA is SUN Workstation based and can work with formalism-annotated QED files or with ASCII files and can be used either incrementally or in batch mode.

## 2.4.7 The B Tool

The B Tool has been developed by Jean-Raymond Abrial in co-operation with members of the PRG and BP's Research Centre at Sunbury.

There are two aspects to the work that has come out of the B Tool project:

(i)     An approach to specification and refinement based on the concept of "Abstract Machines". These machines encapsulate part of the functionality of the system. They are specified in a simple language which is an extension of Dijkstra's Language of Guarded Commands. Verification and refinement of machines is conducted using a calculus based on Dijkstra's WP Calculus.

(ii)    The tool itself - a Pascal program, which performs as a "proof assistant". It is not restricted to the Abstract Machine Notation, but has been used to develop proofs for Z and CSP.

It works by the application of inference rules which are supplied to it as "theories". By providing the appropriate rules, the tool can be used to support alternative formalisms.

## 2.4.8 Other Z Tool Developments

Various other Z tools have been developed for PC systems, and while at present they do not contribute significantly to the state-of-the-art they must nonetheless be considered as their technology may contribute to that of ZIP.

Logica Z Editor - IBM PC-based

Imperial College Z Editor - IBM PC-based

RSRE Z Editor and Typechecker - PERQ-based.

# 3 Proposed Research

## 3.1 ZIP Project Overview

ZIP is a three year project employing research and development effort from the partnership of British Aerospace (Military Aircraft) Ltd. (Lead), BP International Ltd., IBM UK Laboratories Ltd., Logica Cambridge Ltd., Praxis Systems Plc., Rutherford Appleton Laboratory and Oxford University Programming Research Group.

The work programme schedules activities for:

(i)     The standardisation of the Z notation, its mathematical toolkit, syntax and machine processable representations, taking account of further notation development resulting from research into refinement and concurrency; with deliverables:

- Proposed Z Standard - extracted from [1]
- Initial Z Standard
- Augmented Z Standard
- Report of Current Machine Processable Representations
- Machine Processable Representations
- Augmented Machine Processable Representations

(ii)    The application of Z in industry to provide case-study examples and heuristics for the methodical use of Z in a fully formal system and software development process; with deliverables:

- An Anthology of Z Case Studies
- Z Survey Report
- Z Handbook
- Report of Industrial Case Study Applying Z Refinement and Theorem Proof Techniques.
- Report on Automated Assistance for Z Refinement and Theorem Proof.

(iii)   The development of prototype tools adopting the standards of (i) and supporting the methods of (ii); with deliverables:

- Z Tools Evaluation Report
- Z Parser & Reverse-Parser
- Z Tools Conversion/Development Report
- Prototype Z Support Tools
- Prototype Tools to Assist Z Refinement and Theorem Proof.

(iv)    The basic and applied research to support (i), (ii) and (iii); with deliverables:

- Research Publications

The major products of these research and development activities will serve to promote the unification initiative and enhance the current state-of-the-art.

## 4 Expected Benefits

It is expected that the products of the ZIP project will be of great benefit to the current users of Z, where the adoption of Z standards and methods and tools supporting their applications would provide a significant improvement to their current working practice and would facilitate communication with other Z users.

The use of formal methods is likely to become a necessity in the development of high integrity systems, particularly in view of new MOD requirements, and is seen as a means of improving the general software development process. Thus it follows that the ZIP deliverables will potentially benefit the whole software development community, not least by facilitating the adoption of such methods.

It is expected that exploitation of ZIP products will follow from the publication of the Initial Z Standard six months after project start, and will continue throughout the 'lifetime' of Z and its derivative forms. This should stimulate growth in the use of Z, which will help to maintain the current U.K. world lead in model-oriented formal methods.

The Z Methods Handbook and the Z Standards are intended to be made publicly available. Property rights of the tools developed under the ZIP project will remain with the consortium. The quality of these tools will dictate the degree to which they will be exploited. In using the current state-of-the-art as a basis for tool development and aligning that development with the standardisation effort, it is expected that their adoption by Z users will follow.

## 5 References

[1]     The Z Notation, A Reference Manual
        Spivey
        Prentice-Hall, 1989.

[2]     On The Refinement Calculus
        Morgan, Robinson and Gardiner
        Oxford University 1988.

[3]     Process Refinement
        He Jifeng
        Digest Of The York Workshop On Refinement, January 1988.

[4]     State Based CSP
        M.B. Josephs
        to be published in Distributed Computing, 1989

[5]     A Strategy For The Correct Implementation Of Communicating Processes
        J.Woodcock
        Proceedings 1er Seminaire Sur Le Genie Logiciel, Oran Algeria, October 1988.

[6]     Systems Engineering - Improved Design And Construction Of Complex IT Systems, June 1988.

[7]     Formal Methods Strategy: Recommendations For IT92. The Alvey Formal Methods Advisory Group.

# A list of Z users

J E Nicholls, Oxford University PRG

16th May 1990

The attached list of Z users was originally distributed at the Z User Meeting on the 15th December 1989. Information for the list was obtained from enrolment forms for the meeting. This is an amended list, with additions based on forms distributed at the meeting.

The list shows organisations, the names of those reporting the use of Z, and four kinds of use:

| | |
|---|---|
| Development of software | D |
| Teaching and education | E |
| Tools and environment | T |
| Research | R |

It is known that there are other Z users and the PRG will compile and maintain a more complete list.

*Further details from J E Nicholls at Oxford University PRG, 8-11 Keble Road, Oxford OX1 3QD. Telephone: Oxford (0865) 272577.*

# A List of Z Users

| Organisation | Reported by | Dev | Edu | Tool | Res |
|---|---|---|---|---|---|
| AEA Technology, Harwell | W D Atkinson | | | T | |
| Acorn Computers | C Dornan | D | | | |
| | J E Redford | D | | T | R |
| | J G Thackray | D | | | |
| Admiral Management Services, Camberley | I Mearns | D | | | |
| BP Research, Sunbury | I H Sørensen | D | | T | R |
| Brighton Polytechnic | R Mitchell | | E | | R |
| British Aerospace, Filton | M J Benjamin | D | | T | R |
| British Aerospace, Warton | B Hepworth | D | E | T | R |
| | J A S Rowlands | D | E | T | R |
| British Telecom Research, Martlesham | B S Aujla | D | | T | |
| | G Balfour | D | | T | |
| | I Lawson | | | | R |
| | P Sanders | D | | T | |
| | J Wilson | | | | R |
| | P Young | | | | R |
| | S P Lee | | | | R |
| CESG, Cheltenham | J R Farr | D | | | |
| | T J Gollins | D | E | T | R |
| City University | D Till | | E | | R |
| Data Logic, Harrow | M Hanlon | | | T | |
| EFD, Milton Keynes | G Jones | D | E | T | R |
| Eindhoven University | K M van Hee | D | E | T | R |
| GEC Avionics, Rochester | J Draper | D | | | |
| | T Race | D | | | |
| GEC Marconi Research, Chelmsford | C Rees | D | | T | R |
| GPT Data Systems, Borehamwood | M Shuttlewood | D | | | |
| IBM UK Laboratories, Hursley | D A Andrews | D | E | | |
| | B P Collins | D | | | |
| | I Houston | D | | | |
| | P J Lupton | D | | | |
| | G Normington | D | | | R |
| | M Phillips | D | | | |
| | J B Wordsworth | D | | | |
| IBM UK Laboratories, Winchester | M McMorran | D | E | T | |
| ICL, West Gorton | M Elms | D | | | |
| | T Nash | D | | | |
| ICL, Wokingham | M J Homer | D | | | |

**A List of Z Users**                                    **Version 2: 16th May 1990**

| Organisation | Reported by | Dev | Edu | Tool | Res |
|---|---|---|---|---|---|
| Imperial Software Technology, Cambridge | C Paine | D | E | T | R |
| Imperial Cancer Research Fund | P J Krause | D | | | |
| Imperial College London | J Moffett | D | | | |
| Intecs Sistemi, Pisa | P L Iachini | D | | T | R |
| Knowledge Based Services, Bradford | P Allen | D | E | | |
| Leeds Polytechnic | P McGrath | | E | | R |
| | L Semmens | | | | R |
| Leicester Polytechnic | D Smallwood | | E | T | |
| | L Zarzycki | D | E | T | R |
| | H Beaumont | | | T | R |
| Lloyd's Register | M M Christian | D | | T | |
| Logica Cambridge | R Barden | D | E | | |
| | D Brazier | D | | T | |
| | J Brumfitt | D | | | R |
| | M Flynn | | E | T | R |
| | T Hoverd | D | E | T | R |
| | S Stepney | | | | R |
| | S Valentine | | E | | |
| | R Worden | | | | R |
| Logica Space and Defence | J Wilde | D | | | |
| Lucas Automotive, Solihull | N Garrett | D | | | |
| | J Millward | D | | | |
| Lynwood Scientific Developments, Alton | S Bishop | D | | | |
| | M Watkins | D | | | |
| | D Whitwell | D | | T | |
| Marconi Command & Control Systems (Leicester) | D W Pearson | D | | | R |
| | M Shenton | D | | | R |
| Michael Jackson Systems | N Simons | D | | | |
| Oxford University, PRG | (many users) | D | E | T | R |
| Oxford University Computing Service | A E Lawrence | D | | | |
| Plessey Research, Roke Manor | S Cordingley | D | E | | |
| | B Sowerbutts | D | E | | |
| Plessey Radar, Chessington | T S Virdee | D | | | |
| Plessey Defence Systems, Christchurch | T J Read | D | | T | |
| Praxis Systems, Bath | D Brownbridge | D | | | |
| Queensland University | I Hayes | D | E | T | R |
| | B P Mahony | | | | R |
| Racal Research, Reading | A J J Dick | D | E | T | R |

**A List of Z Users**                                    Version 2: 16th May 1990

| Organisation | Reported by | Dev | Edu | Tool | Res |
|---|---|---|---|---|---|
| RACE Consortium, Brussels | L Kahn | D | | | |
| RSRE, Malvern | R MacDonald | D | | T | R |
| | G Randell | D | | T | |
| | C Sennett | D | | T | R |
| | A Smith | D | | T | R |
| SD-Scicon, Fleet | C Fox | | | T | R |
| | J Robinson | D | | | |
| SD-Scicon, Milton Keynes | P Taylor | | | T | R |
| Secure Information Systems, Fleet | P Smith | D | E | | |
| STC Technology, Harlow | S Hughes | D | E | T | R |
| | B Potter | D | E | T | |
| Southampton University | G Edmunds | D | | T | |
| | A Gravell | D | E | T | R |
| Surrey University | J Cozens | | | T | |
| Tektronix Laboratories, Oregon | D Garlan | D | | | |
| | N Delisle | D | | | |
| Teeside Polytechnic | B Dummigan | | E | | |
| Transmitton Ltd | C A Garnecki | D | | | |
| Ulster University | S Gilmore | D | | | |
| Wolverhampton Polytechnic | P E Bates | | E | | |

**Individual users:**

| | | | | | |
|---|---|---|---|---|---|
| | C D Allen | D | E | | |

This document contains a list of Z references which are either available from the librarian or author at the Programming Research Group or as published papers, books or technical reports from other institutions. The bibliography is in alphabetical order by first author name.

This list is maintained in electronic form (in UNIX *refer* bibliography format). To add new references to this list, please contact Jonathan Bowen (P.R.G.) or Ruaridh Macdonald at the Royal Signals and Radar Establishment (R.S.R.E.), Malvern, preferably via electronic mail on <Jonathan.Bowen@prg.oxford.ac.uk> or <MACDONALD@hermes.mod.uk>. Please give as much information as possible so the entry could be included as a reference in future papers on Z.

> Jonathan Bowen — May 1990
> Oxford University Computing Laboratory
> Programming Research Group
> 8–11 Keble Road
> OXFORD OX1 3QD
> England
> Tel: +44-865-272574

*Z FORUM,* P.R.G. and R.S.R.E., 1986–1990. Electronic newsletter: vol. 1.1–9 (1986), vol. 2.1–4 (1987), vol. 3.1–7 (1988), vol. 4.1–4.4 (1989) vol. 5.1 onwards (1990).

A moderated electronic newsletter issued as demand dictates. Contributions should be sent to the editor via <zforum@prg.oxford.ac.uk>. Requests to join or leave the list should be sent to <zforum-request@prg.oxford.ac.uk>. A current list of back issues and other Z-related material is also available via e-mail by sending a message of "index z" to <archive-server@prg.oxford.ac.uk>. For a particular issue, send a message such as "send z 4.4". For more information on the archive server, send a message of "help". For human help, e-mail <archive-management@prg.oxford.ac.uk>.

*The Z Package,* Programming Research Group, Oxford University, UK, 1989.

The Z Package consists of a number of documents produced at the P.R.G. concerned with the specification language Z. The package provides a reference source for the Z language, supplemented with case studies of actual specifications, and self-assessment exercises with solutions. Included are a reference manual, and two easy-access reference cards for the schema and mathematical notation. Documents are updated periodically to reflect state-of-the-art Z. The price is £17.50, or £11.50 for a "Mini Z Package" + p&p. Contact the P.R.G. librarian, Gordon Riddell, on +44-865-273837 or <library@prg.oxford.ac.uk> for more details. "The Z Notation: A Reference Manual" by J.M. Spivey used to be included in the Z Package before its publication and is also recommended.

*Proceedings of the Fourth Annual Z Users Meeting,* Programming Research Group, Oxford University, UK, 14–15 December 1989.

Issued at the meeting. Includes 15 papers related to Z, a printed version of the *Selected Z Bibliography* by Jonathan Bowen and a number of one-page posters. The proceedings will be published in an updated form by Springer-Verlag.

*VDM and Z – Formal Methods in Software Development,* Lecture Notes in Computer Science, no. 428, Springer-Verlag, Berlin, Germany, 1990.

Proceedings of Third Interational Symposium of VDM Europe, 17–21 April 1990, Kiel, Germany. Edited by D. Bjørner, C.A.R. Hoare & H. Langmaack.

Abowd, Gregory, Bowen, Jonathan, Dix, Alan, Harrison, Michael, and Took, Roger, *User Interface Languages: a survey of existing methods,* Technical Report, PRG-TR-5-89, Programming Research Group, Oxford University, UK, October 1989.

Alan Dix, Michael Harrison and Roger Took are members of the Human Computer Interaction Group, Department of Computer Science, University of York. Originally produced as part of ESPRIT II project no. 2487: "REDO: Maintenance, Validation and Documentation of Software Systems." This report covers a number of methods, including the use of Z.

Abrial, Jean-Raymond, Schuman, S.A., and Meyer, B., "Specification Language," in *On the Construction of Programs: An Advanced Course,* ed. R.M. McKeag & A.M. Macnaghten, pp. 343-410, Cambridge University Press, UK, 1980.

Abrial, Jean-Raymond and Sørensen, Ib H., "KWIC-index generation," in *Program Specification: Proceedings of a Workshop,* ed. J. Staunstrup, Lecture Notes in Computer Science, vol. no. 134, pp. 88-95, Aarhus, Denmark, August 1981.

Barrett, Geoff, *Formal Methods Applied to a Floating-Point Number System,* Technical Monograph, PRG-58, Programming Research Group, Oxford University, UK, January 1987. Price: £2.35.

Barrett, Geoff, "Formal Methods Applied to a Floating-Point Number System," *IEEE Transactions on Software Engineering,* vol. SE-14, no. 5, pp. 611-621, May 1988.

Baxter, S., *Executing Z Specifications,* Research and Technology memorandum, Technical Report RT31/009/88, British Telecom Research Laboratories, Martlesham Heath, Ipswich, Suffolk, UK, 1988.

Benveniste, Marc, *Operational Semantics of a Distributed Object-Oriented Language and Its Z Formal Specification,* IRISA Technical Report, no. 532,, IRISA, Campus de Beaulieu, F-35042, Rennes Cedex, France, April 1990. To be published by INRIA.

Best, M.A., *Specification of a Z Cross-reference Facility,* IBM Technical Report, TR12.253, IBM United Kingdom Laboratories Ltd., Hursley Park, Winchester, Hampshire SO21 2JN, UK, September 1986.

Bowen, Jonathan P., "Formal Specification and Documentation of Microprocessor Instruction Sets," *Microprocessing and Microprogramming,* vol. 21, no. 1-5, pp. 223-230, Elsevier Science Publishers B.V. (North-Holland), Amsterdam, August 1987. Conference held on 14–17 September 1987 at Portsmouth, UK.

Bowen, Jonathan P., Gimson, Roger B., and Topp-Jørgensen, Stig, *The Specification of Network Services*, Technical Monograph, PRG-61, Programming Research Group, Oxford University, UK, August 1987. Price: £5.00.

Bowen, Jonathan P., *Proceedings of Z Users Meeting, 1 Wellington Square, Oxford*, Programming Research Group, Oxford University, UK, December 1987.

The 1987 Z Users Meeting was held on Friday 8 December at the Department of External Studies, Rewley House, 1 Wellington Square, Oxford. The L#TEX source of the Proceedings is available by sending the command "send z proc87.tex" to <archive-server@prg.oxford.ac.uk> via e-mail.

Bowen, Jonathan P., *The Formal Specification of a Microprocessor Instruction Set*, Technical Monograph, PRG-60, Programming Research Group, Oxford University, UK, January 1987. Price: £3.60.

The Z notation is used to define the Motorola M6800 8-bit microprocessor instruction set.

Bowen, Jonathan P., *Proceedings of the Third Annual Z Users Meeting*, Programming Research Group, Oxford University, UK, December 1988.

The 1988 Z Users Meeting was held on Friday 16 December at the Department of External Studies, Rewley House, 1 Wellington Square, Oxford. Issued with "A Miscellany of Handy Techniques" by Ruaridh Macdonald, R.S.R.E. (9 pages), "Practical Experience of Formal Specification: a programming interface for communications" by John B. Wordsworth, IBM United Kingdom Laboratories Ltd. (18 pages), and a number of posters (20 pages). Available from the Librarian at the P.R.G. The L#TEX source of the main part of the document available by sending the command "send z proc88.tex" to the P.R.G. archive server on <archive-server@prg.oxford.ac.uk> via e-mail.

Bowen, Jonathan P., Gimson, Roger B., and Topp-Jørgensen, Stig, *Specifying System Implementations in Z*, Technical Monograph, PRG-63, Programming Research Group, Oxford University, UK, February 1988. Price: £4.40.

Bowen, Jonathan P., "Formal Specification in Z as a Design and Documentation Tool," in *Proceedings of the Second IEE/BCS Conference on Software Engineering*, pp. 164-168, IEE/BCS, University of Liverpool, UK, July 1988.

Bowen, Jonathan P., "POS: Formal Specification of a UNIX Tool," *Software Engineering Journal*, vol. 4, no. 1, pp. 67-72, IEE/BCS, January 1989.

Bowen, Jonathan P., *Formal Specification of Window Systems*, Technical Monograph, PRG-74, Programming Research Group, Oxford University, UK, June 1989. Price: £4.50.

Three existing window systems, X from MIT, WM from Carnegie-Mellon University and the Blit from AT&T Bell Laboratories are covered.

Bowen, Jonathan P. and Macdonald, Ruaridh, *Z Bibliography*, Programming Research Group, Oxford University, UK, April 1990.

A master bibliography of both published and unpublished work related to Z. This is available via e-mail by sending a message containing the command "send z zbib" to <archive-server@prg.oxford.ac.uk>. (For more information on the archive server, send a message of "help".)

Bowen, Jonathan P. and Pandya, Paritosh K., *Specification of the ProCoS Level 0 Instruction Set,* SAFEMOS project report, doc. id. P-JPB-2/3, Programming Research Group, Oxford University, UK, May 1990.

Subset of the transputer instruction set in Z for the IED **safemos** project and the ESPRIT BRA **ProCoS** project.

Brown, David J. and Bowen, Jonathan P., "The Event Queue: An Extensible Input System for UNIX Workstations," in *Proceedings of the European Unix Users Group Conference*, pp. 29-52, Helsinki, Finland, May 1987.

Carrington, D. and others,, in *Proceedings of the Second International Conference FORTE '89*, ed. S. Vuong, Object-Z: An Object-Oriented Extension to Z, pp. 401-420, Vancouver, Canada, 5–8 December 1989.

Chalin, Patrice and Grogono, Peter, "Z Specification of an Object Manager," in *VDM and Z – Formal Methods in Software Development*, ed. D. Bjørner, C.A.R. Hoare & H. Langmaack, Lecture Notes in Computer Science, vol. no. 428, pp. 41-71, Springer-Verlag, Berlin, Germany, 1990.

Cohen, Bernie, "Justification of Formal Methods for System Specifications / A Rejustification of Formal Notations," *Software Engineering Journal*, vol. 4, no. 1, pp. 26-38, IEE/BCS, January 1989.

Collins, B.P., Nicholls, John E., and Sørensen, Ib H., *Introducing Formal Methods: the CICS Experience with Z*, IBM Technical Report, TR12.260, IBM United Kingdom Laboratories Ltd., Hursley Park, Winchester, Hampshire SO21 2JN, UK, December 1987.

Delisle, Norman and Garlan, David, *A Formal Specification of an Oscilloscope,* Technical Report, CR-88-13, Computer Research Laboratory, Tektronix Inc., P.O. Box 500, Beaverton, Oregon 97077, USA, October 1988.

Delisle, Norman and Garlan, David, "Formal Specifying Electronic Instruments," in *Proceedings of the Fifth International Workshop on Software Specification and Design*, May 1989.

Diepen, M.J. van and Hee, K.M. van, "A Formal Semantics for Z and the Link between Z and the Relational Algebra," in *VDM and Z – Formal Methods in Software Development*, ed. D. Bjørner, C.A.R. Hoare & H. Langmaack, Lecture Notes in Computer Science, vol. no. 428, pp. 526-551, Springer-Verlag, Berlin, Germany, 1990.

Duke, D. and Duke, Roger, "Towards a Semantics for Object-Z," in *VDM and Z – Formal Methods in Software Development*, ed. D. Bjørner, C.A.R. Hoare & H. Langmaack, Lecture Notes in Computer Science, vol. no. 428, pp. 244-261, Springer-Verlag, Berlin, Germany, 1990.

Duke, Roger and Rose, Gordon A., *A Complete Z Specification of an Interactive Program Editor,* Technical Report, 71, Department of Computer Science, University of Queensland, St. Lucia, Queensland, Australia, 1986.

Duke, Roger, Hayes, Ian J., King, P., and Rose, Gordon A., "Protocol Specification and Verification Using Z," in *Protocol Specification, Testing, and Verification VIII*, ed. S. Aggarwal & K. Sabnani, pp. 33-46, North-Holland, 1988.

Duke, Roger and Smith, Graeme, "Temporal Logic and Z Specifications," *Australian Computer Journal*, vol. 21, no. 2, pp. 62-66, May 1989.

Flinn, L. William and Sørensen, Ib H., *CAVIAR: A Case Study in Specification*, Technical Monograph, PRG-48, Programming Research Group, Oxford University, UK, July 1985. Price: £2.30.

Garlan, David and Delisle, Norman, "Formal Specifications as Reusable Frameworks," in *VDM and Z – Formal Methods in Software Development*, ed. D. Bjørner, C.A.R. Hoare & H. Langmaack, Lecture Notes in Computer Science, vol. no. 428, pp. 150-163, Springer-Verlag, Berlin, Germany, 1990.

Gimson, Roger B. and Morgan, C. Carroll, "Ease of Use Through Proper Specification," in *Distributed Computing Systems Programme*, ed. David A. Duce, Peter Peregrinus, London, UK, 1984.

Gimson, Roger B. and Morgan, C. Carroll, *The Distributed Computing Software Project*, Technical Monograph, PRG-50, Programming Research Group, Oxford University, UK, July 1985. Price: £4.25.

Gimson, Roger B., *The Formal Documentation of a Block Storage Service*, Technical Monograph, PRG-62, Programming Research Group, Oxford University, UK, August 1987. Price: £5.60.

Giovanni, R. Di and Iachini, P.L., "HOOD and Z for the Development of Complex Systems," in *VDM and Z – Formal Methods in Software Development*, ed. D. Bjørner, C.A.R. Hoare & H. Langmaack, Lecture Notes in Computer Science, vol. no. 428, pp. 262-289, Springer-Verlag, Berlin, Germany, 1990.

Gotzhein, Reinhard, "Specifying Open Distributed Systems with Z," in *VDM and Z – Formal Methods in Software Development*, ed. D. Bjørner, C.A.R. Hoare & H. Langmaack, Lecture Notes in Computer Science, vol. no. 428, pp. 319-339, Springer-Verlag, Berlin, Germany, 1990.

Halasz, Frank and Schwartz, Mayer, "The Dexter Hypertext Refernce Model," in *NIST Hypertext Standardization Workshop*, Gaithersburg, Maryland, USA, 16–18 January 1990.

Frank Halasz is at Xerox PARC, 3333 Coyote Hill Road, Palo Alto, CA 94304, USA, e-mail <halasz@xerox.com>. Mayer Schwartz is at Tektronix Laboratories, P.O. Box 500, MS 50-662, Beaverton, OR 97077, USA, e-mail <mayers@tekchips.labs.tek.com>.

Hall, J.A., "Using Z as a Specification Calculus for Object-Oriented Systems," in *VDM and Z – Formal Methods in Software Development*, ed. D. Bjørner, C.A.R. Hoare & H. Langmaack, Lecture Notes in Computer Science, vol. no. 428, pp. 290-318, Springer-Verlag, Berlin, Germany, 1990.

Hall, Pat A.V., "Towards testing with respect to Formal Specification," in *Proceedings of the Second IEE/BCS Conference on Software Engineering*, pp. 159-163, IEE/BCS, University of Liverpool, UK, July 1988.

Harrold, Clare L., *Formal Specification of a Secure Document Control System for SMITE*, R.S.R.E. Report, no. 88002, Royal Signals and Radar Establishment, Ministry of Defence, Malvern, UK, February 1988.

Hayes, Ian J., "Applying Formal Specification to Software Development in Industry," *IEEE Transactions on Software Engineering*, vol. SE-11, no. 2, pp. 169-178, February 1985.

Hayes, Ian J., *Specifying the CICS Application Programmer's Interface,* Technical Monograph, PRG-47, Programming Research Group, Oxford University, UK, July 1985. Price: £4.10.

Hayes, Ian J., *Specification Directed Module Testing,* Technical Monograph, PRG-49, Programming Research Group, Oxford University, UK, July 1985. Price: £1.50.

Hayes, Ian J., "Using Mathematics to Specify Software," in *Proceedings of the First Australian Software Engineering Conference*, Institution of Engineers, Australia, Canberra, Australia, May 1986.

Hayes, Ian J., Flinn, L. William, Gimson, Roger B., Morgan, C. Carroll, Sørensen, Ib H., and Sufrin, Bernard A., *Specification Case Studies,* International Series in Computer Science, Prentice Hall, Hemel Hempstead, Hertfordshire HP2 4RG, UK, 1987. Price: £17.95 paperback.

This book contains material from P.R.G. Technical Monographs 46–50. It is edited by Ian Hayes and written mainly by members of the P.R.G. It forms a varied collection of case studies in Z.

Hayes, Ian J., *Specifying Physical Limitations: A Case Study of an Oscilloscope,* Department of Computer Science, University of Queensland, Brisbane, Queensland, Australia, October 1989.

Hayes, Ian J., *Specification of an Oscilloscope,* Department of Computer Science, University of Queensland, Brisbane, Queensland, Australia, 1990. To appear.

Houston, I.S.C. and Wordsworth, J.B., *A Z Specification of Part of the CICS File Control API,* IBM Technical Report, TR12.272, IBM United Kingdom Laboratories Ltd., Hursley Park, Winchester, Hampshire SO21 2JN, UK, 16 February 1986.

Ince, Darrell C., *An Introduction to Discrete Mathematics and Formal System Specification,* Oxford Applied Mathematics and Computing Science Series, Oxford University Press, Oxford, UK, 1988. Price: £30.00 hardback.

INMOS Limited, "Specification of instruction set / Specification of floating point unit instructions," in *Transputer Instruction Set – A compiler writer's guide*, pp. 127-161, Prentice Hall, Hemel Hempstead, Hertfordshire HP2 4RG, UK, 1988. Price: £19.95 paperback.

INMOS document number: 72 TRN 199 05. Produced by INMOS Limited, 1000 Aztec West, Almondsbury, Bristol BS12 4SQ, UK. Tel: +44-454-616616, Telex: 444723, Fax: +44-454-617910. Appendices F & G use a Z-like notation.

Jifeng, He, *Various Simulations and Refinements,* Programming Research Group, Oxford University, UK, August 1989.

Josephs, Mark, "The Data Refinement Calculator for Z Specifications," *Information Processing Letters*, vol. 27, no. 1, pp. 29-33, 1988.

Josephs, Mark, "A State-Based Approach to Communicating Processes," *Distributed Computing*, vol. 3, pp. 9-18, Springer-Verlag, 1988.

A theoretical paper on combining features of CSP and Z.

Kemp, D.H., *Specification of Viper1 in Z*, R.S.R.E. Memorandum, no. 4195, Royal Signals and Radar Establishment, Ministry of Defence, Malvern, UK, October 1988.

Kemp, D.H., *Specification of Viper2 in Z*, R.S.R.E. Memorandum, no. 4217, Royal Signals and Radar Establishment, Ministry of Defence, Malvern, UK, October 1988.

King, Steve, Sørensen, Ib H., and Woodcock, James C.P., *Z: Grammar and Concrete and Abstract Syntaxes*, Technical Monograph, PRG-68, Programming Research Group, Oxford University, UK, 1988. Price: £2.40.

King, Steve and Sørensen, Ib H., "Specification and Design of a Library System," in *The Theory and Practice of Refinement: Approaches to the Formal Development of Large-Scale Software Systems*, Butterworths, UK, 1989.

King, Steve, "Z and the Refinement Calculus," in *VDM and Z – Formal Methods in Software Development*, ed. D. Bjørner, C.A.R. Hoare & H. Langmaack, Lecture Notes in Computer Science, vol. no. 428, pp. 164-188, Springer-Verlag, Berlin, Germany, 1990.

London, Ralph L., *Specifying Reusable Components Using Z: Sets Implemented by Bit Vectors*, Technical Report, CR-88-14, Tektronix Laboratories, P.O. Box 500, MS 50-662, Beaverton, Oregon 97077, USA, November 1988.

McDermid, John A., *The Theory and Practice of Refinement: Approaches to the Formal Development of Large-Scale Software Systems*, Butterworths, UK, 1989.

Papers from the Refinement Workshop at the University of York, held on 7–8 January 1988, including several on Z. Edited by Prof. John McDermid.

McDermid, John A., "Special section on Z," *Software Engineering Journal*, vol. 4, no. 1, pp. 25-72, IEE/BCS, January 1989.

A number of papers on Z. Introduced and edited by Prof. John McDermid.

McMorran, Mike A. and Nicholls, John E., *Z User Manual*, Technical Report, TR12.274, IBM United Kingdom Laboratories Ltd., Hursley Park, Winchester, Hampshire SO21 2JN, UK, 12 July 1989. Version 1.0

Meyer, B., "On Formalism in Specifications," *IEEE Software*, vol. 2, no. 1, pp. 6-26, January 1985.

Monahan, Brian Q., "Book Review," *Formal Aspects of Computing*, vol. 1, no. 1, pp. 137-142, Spinger International, January–March 1989.

Review of "Understanding Z: A Specification Language and Its Formal Semantics" by J.M. Spivey.

Morgan, C. Carroll and Sufrin, Bernard A., "Specification of the Unix Filing System," *IEEE Transactions on Software Engineering*, vol. SE-10, no. 2, pp. 128-142, March 1984.

Morgan, C. Carroll and Robinson, Ken A., "Specification Statements and Refinement," *IBM Journal of Research and Development*, vol. 31, no. 5, September 1987.

Also reprinted in Technical Monograph PRG-70, Programming Research Group, Oxford University.

Morgan, C. Carroll, "Data Refinement using Miracles," *Information Processing Letters*, vol. 26, no. 5, pp. 243-246, January 1988.

Also reprinted in Technical Monograph PRG-70, Programming Research Group, Oxford University.

Morgan, C. Carroll, "The Specification Statement," *ACM Transactions on Programming Languages & Systems (TOPLAS)*, vol. 10, no. 3, July 1988.

Also reprinted in Technical Monograph PRG-70, Programming Research Group, Oxford University.

Morgan, C. Carroll, "Procedures, Parameters, and Abstraction: Separate Concerns," *Science of Computer Programming*, vol. 11, no. 1, October 1988.

Also reprinted in Technical Monograph PRG-70, Programming Research Group, Oxford University.

Morgan, C. Carroll, Robinson, Ken A., and Gardiner, Paul H.B., *On the Refinement Calculus,* Technical Monograph, PRG-70, Programming Research Group, Oxford University, UK, October 1988. Price: £7.75.

Morgan, C. Carroll and Gardiner, Paul H.B., *A Single Complete Rule for Data Refinement,* Programming Research Group, Oxford University, UK, 1989. Submitted to TOPLAS.

Morgan, C. Carroll, "Types and Invariants in the Refinement Calculus," in *Proceedings of the Mathematics of Program Construction Conference*, Twente, June 1989.

Morgan, C. Carroll and Sanders, Jeff W., *Laws of the Logical Calculi,* Technical Monograph, PRG-78, Programming Research Group, Oxford University, UK, September 1989. Price: £1.00.

Morgan, C. Carroll, *Programming from Specifications,* International Series in Computer Science, Prentice Hall, Hemel Hempstead, Hertfordshire HP2 4RG, UK, 1990.

Narayana, K.T. and Dharap, Sanjeev, *Formal Specification of a Look Manager,* Department of Computer Science, Whitmore Laboratory, The Pennsylvania State University, University Park, PA 16802, USA, 1989.

Narayana, K.T. and Dharap, Sanjeev, *Invariant Properties in a Dialog System,* Department of Computer Science, Whitmore Laboratory, The Pennsylvania State University, University Park, PA 16802, USA, 1989.

Neilson, Dave, "Hierarchical Refinement of a Z Specification," in *Proceedings of the Foundations of Software Technology & Theoretical Computer Science*, Pune, India, December 1987.

Nicholls, John E., "Working with Formal Methods," *Journal of Information Technology*, vol. 2, no. 2, pp. 67-71, June 1987.

Based on a talk given at a one-day conference at Imperial College, London, UK.

Nicholls, John E., *Z in the Development Process,* Programming Research Group, Oxford University, UK, 21st June 1989.

> Proceedings of a discussion workshop held on Thursday 15 December in Oxford. With contributions by Peter Collins, David Cooper, Anthony Hall, Patrick Hall, Brian Hepworth, Ben Potter and Andrew Ricketts. Available from the Librarian at the P.R.G.

Nix, C.J. and Collins, B.P., "The use of Software Engineering, including the Z Notation, in the Development of CICS," *Quality Assurance,* vol. 14, no. 3, pp. 103-110, September 1988.

Norris, M., *Z – a Rigorous System Specification Technique,* STARTS Debrief Report, The National Computing Centre Limited, Manchester, UK, 1986.

> M. Norris works for British Telecom. Other reports in the series include: SLIM, PRICE S, ARTEMIS, VDM, SOFCHIP, JSD, SDL, SAFRA & CORE. The reports are available from: Sales Administration (Publications), NCC Limited, Oxford Road, Manchester M1 7ED. Tel: +44-61-228-633 or +44-1-353-4875. The reports are priced at £10 each + £1 p&p for 1st report and 55p for each subsequent report up to a maximum of £4.30. Orders under £100 should be accompanied by a cheque made payable to "The National Computing Centre Limited".

Reed, Joy N., "Semantics-Based Tools for a Specification Support Environment," in *Proceedings of the 3rd Workshop on Mathematical Foundations of Programming Language Semantics,* Lecture Notes in Computer Science, Springer-Verlag, Berlin, Germany, 1988.

Reed, Joy N. and Sinclair, Jane E., *An Algorithm for Type-checking Z – A Z Specification,* Technical Monograph, Programming Research Group, Oxford University, UK, 1990. To appear.

Rose, Gordon A. and Robinson, Peter, "A Case Study in Formal Specifications," in *Proceedings of the First Australian Software Engineering Conference,* May 1986.

Sampaio, Augusto and Meira, S., "Modular Extensions to Z," in *VDM and Z – Formal Methods in Software Development,* ed. D. Bjørner, C.A.R. Hoare & H. Langmaack, Lecture Notes in Computer Science, vol. no. 428, pp. 211-232, Springer-Verlag, Berlin, Germany, 1990.

Sanders, Jeff W. and Sufrin, Bernard A., *Mathematics for System Engineering: An Introduction to Z,* Prentice Hall, 1990. Book in preparation.

Sennett, Chris T., *Appendix to Development Environment for Secure Software,* R.S.R.E. Report, no. 87015, Royal Signals and Radar Establishment, Ministry of Defence, Malvern, UK, November 1987.

Sennett, Chris T., *Review of Type Checking and Scope Rules of the Specification Language Z,* R.S.R.E. Report, no. 87017, Royal Signals and Radar Establishment, Ministry of Defence, Malvern, UK, November 1987.

Sennett, Chris T. and Macdonald, Ruaridh, *Separability and Security Models,* R.S.R.E. Report, no. 87020, Royal Signals and Radar Establishment, Ministry of Defence, Malvern, UK, November 1987.

Shepherd, David and Wilson, Greg, "Making Chips that Work," *New Scientist*, vol. no. 1664, pp. 61-64, 13 May 1989.

Simcox, Lewis N., *The Application of Z to the Specification of Air Traffic Control Systems: 1*, R.S.R.E. Memorandum, no. 4280, Royal Signals and Radar Establishment, Ministry of Defence, Malvern, UK, April 1989.

Smith, Alf, *The Knuth-Bendix Completion Algorithm and its Specification in Z*, R.S.R.E. Memorandum, no. 4323, Royal Signals and Radar Establishment, Ministry of Defence, Malvern, UK, September 1989.

Sørensen, Ib H., "A Specification Language," in *Program Specification: Proceedings of a Workshop*, ed. J. Staunstrup, Lecture Notes in Computer Science, vol. no. 134, pp. 381-401, Aarhus, Denmark, August 1981.

Spivey, J. Michael, *Printing Z with LaTeX*, Programming Research Group, Oxford University, UK, January 1987.

A description of a Z style option "zed.sty" for the LaTeX document preparation system.

Spivey, J. Michael, *The fuzz Manual*, Computing Science Consultancy, 2 Willow Close, Garsington, Oxford OX9 9AN, UK, 1988.

Z type-checker and "fuzz.sty" style option for LaTeX documents. The package is compatible with the book, "The Z Notation: A Reference Manual" by the same author. Send orders to Mrs. A. Spivey, 34 Westlands Grove, Stockton Lane, York YO3 0EF. Technical enquiries can be sent to Mike Spivey at 2 Willow Close, Garsington, Oxford OX9 9AN, or by e-mail at <Mike.Spivey@prg.oxford.ac.uk>. Cost: SUN version on Cartridge tape, £300 and IBM PC version on 5.25in or 3.5in disk, £200. Cheques should be made payable to Dr. J.M. Spivey.

Spivey, J. Michael, *Understanding Z: A Specification Language and its Formal Semantics*, Cambridge Tracts in Theoretical Computer Science, 3, Cambridge University Press, UK, January 1988.

Published version of 1985 D.Phil. thesis.

Spivey, J. Michael, *The Z Notation: A Reference Manual*, International Series in Computer Science, Prentice Hall, Hemel Hempstead, Hertfordshire HP2 4RG, UK, 1989. Price: £15.95 ($26.95) paperback.

This book is currently the de facto "standard" for the Z notation.

Spivey, J. Michael, "An Introduction to Z and Formal Specifications," *Software Engineering Journal*, vol. 4, no. 1, IEE/BCS, January 1989.

Spivey, J. Michael and Sufrin, Bernard A., "Type Inference in Z," in *VDM and Z — Formal Methods in Software Development*, ed. D. Bjørner, C.A.R. Hoare & H. Langmaack, Lecture Notes in Computer Science, vol. no. 428, pp. 426-438, Springer-Verlag, Berlin, Germany, 1990.

Stepney, Susan and Lord, Stephen P., "Formal Specification of an Access Control System," *Software – Practice and Experience*, vol. 17, no. 9, pp. 575-593, September 1987.

Sufrin, Bernard A., *Formal Specification of a Display Editor,* Technical Monograph, PRG-21, Programming Research Group, Oxford University, UK, June 1981. Out of print.

Sufrin, Bernard A., "Formal Specification: Notation and Examples," in *Tools and Notations for Program Construction,* ed. D. Neel, Cambridge University Press, UK, 1982.

Example of a filing system specification, first published use of the schema notation to put together states.

Sufrin, Bernard A., "Towards Formal Specification of the ICL Data Dictionary," *ICL Technical Journal,* August 1984.

Sufrin, Bernard A., "Formal Methods and the Design of Effective User Interfaces," in *People and Computers: Designing for Usability,* ed. M.D. Harrison & A.F. Monk, Cambridge University Press, UK, 1986.

Sufrin, Bernard A., *The Zebra Typechecker,* Programming Research Group, Oxford University, UK, 1987.

Sufrin, Bernard A. and Woodcock, James C.P., "Towards the Formal Specification of a Simple Programming Support Environment," *Software Engineering Journal,* vol. 2, no. 4, pp. 86-94, IEE/BCS, July 1987.

Sufrin, Bernard A., *Using the Hippo System,* Programming Research Group, Oxford University, UK, 1989.

Hippo is a Z type-checker written in New Jersey Standard ML. It is a successor to the Zebra and Forsite type-checkers. Copies are available by sending a Sun cartridge tape to the author.

Terry, Phil F. and Wiseman, Simon R., *On the Design and Implementation of a Secure Computer System,* R.S.R.E. Memorandum, no. 4188, Royal Signals and Radar Establishment, Ministry of Defence, Malvern, UK, June 1988.

Till, David and Potter, Ben, "The Specification in Z of Gateway Functions within a Communications Network," in *Proceedings of the IFIP WG10.3 Conference on Distributed Processing,* Elsevier Science Publishers B.V. (North-Holland), Amsterdam, Holland, 5–7 October 1897.

David Till is at King's College, London, UK. Ben Potter is at STC Technology, Harlow, Essex, UK.

Todd, Brian S., "A Model-Based Diagnostic Program," *Software Engineering Journal,* vol. 2, no. 3, pp. 54-63, IEE/BCS, May 1987.

Wiseman, Simon R. and Harrold, Clare L., *A Security Model and its Implementation,* R.S.R.E. Memorandum, no. 4222, Royal Signals and Radar Establishment, Ministry of Defence, Malvern, UK, September 1988.

Wood, Andrew W., *A Z Specification of the MaCHO Interface Editor,* R.S.R.E. Memorandum, no. 4247, Royal Signals and Radar Establishment, Ministry of Defence, Malvern, UK, November 1988.

Woodcock, James C.P. and Loomes, Martin, *Software Engineering Mathematics: Formal Methods Demystified,* Pitman Publishing Ltd, London, UK, 1988. Price: £10.95 (+ £1.15 p&p) paperback. Credit card orders: +44-704-26881.

Woodcock, James C.P., "Teaching How to Use Mathematics for Large-Scale Software Development," *Bull. BCS-FACS*, July 1988.

Woodcock, James C.P., "Calculating Properties of Z Specifications," *ACM SIGSOFT Software Engineering Notes*, vol. 15, no. 4, pp. 43-54, 1989.

Woodcock, James C.P., "The Applicability of Formal Methods," in *Proceedings of the Halifax Formal Methods Workshop*, Halifax, Canada, 1989.

Woodcock, James C.P., "Z," in *Proceedings of the Halifax Formal Methods Workshop*, Halifax, Canada, 1989.

Woodcock, James C.P., "Structuring Specifications in Z," *Software Engineering Journal*, vol. 4, no. 1, pp. 51-66, IEE/BCS, January 1989.

Woodcock, James C.P., "Parallel Refinement in Z," in *Proceedings of the Workshop on Refinement*, Butterworths, The Open University, Milton Keynes, UK, January 1989.

Woodcock, James C.P., "Transaction Refinement in Z," in *Proceedings of the Workshop on Refinement*, Butterworths, The Open University, Milton Keynes, UK, January 1989.

Woodcock, James C.P., "Mathematics as a Management Tool: Proof Rules for Promotion," in *Proceedings of the 6th Annual CSR Conference on Large Software Systems*, Bristol, UK, September 1989.

Woodcock, James C.P. and Morgan, C. Carroll, "Refinement of State-Based Concurrent Systems," in *VDM and Z – Formal Methods in Software Development*, ed. D. Bjørner, C.A.R. Hoare & H. Langmaack, Lecture Notes in Computer Science, vol. no. 428, pp. 340-351, Springer-Verlag, Berlin, Germany, 1990.

Work on combining Z and CSP.

Woodcock, James C.P., *Using Z – Specification, Refinement and Proof*, Programming Research Group, Oxford University, UK, 1990. In preparation.

Wordsworth, John B., "Teaching Formal Specification Methods in an Industrial Environment," in *Software Engineering '86*, Peter Peregrinus, London, UK, 1986.

Wordsworth, John B., "Specifying and Refining Programs with Z," in *Proceedings of the Second IEE/BCS Conference on Software Engineering*, pp. 8-16, IEE/BCS, University of Liverpool, UK, July 1988.

A tutorial summary.

Wordsworth, John B., "A Z Development Method," in *Proceedings of the Workshop on Refinement*, Butterworths, The Open University, Milton Keynes, UK, January 1989.

Wordsworth, John B., "Refinement Tutorial: A Storage Manager," in *Proceedings of the Workshop on Refinement*, Butterworths, The Open University, Milton Keynes, UK, January 1989.

Young, William D., *Comparing Specifications Paradigms: Gypsy and Z*, Technical Report, 45, Computational Logic Inc., 1717 W. 6th St., Suite 290, Austin, Texas 78703, USA, 1989.

Tel: +1-512-322-9951. Presented at the 12th National Computer Security Conference, Baltimore, Maryland, USA, 10–13 October 1989.

# Z FORUM electronic newsletter

If you have access to an electronic mail address you could receive the **Z FORUM** electronic newsletter periodically. For example:

```
From: ZFORUM newsletter <zforum@uk.ac.oxford.prg>
Subject: Z Forum Issue 4.4
Message-ID: <8911201913.AA00796@uk.ac.oxford.prg.client60>
Date: 20 Nov 89 19:55:25 GMT
Lines: 403


20th November 1989          Z FORUM          Volume 4 Issue 4
------------------          -------          ----------------

                        Today's Topics
                        --------------


                   Administrivia
                   news group discussion
                   Z bibliography
                   Z Users Meeting announcement


   ------------------------------------------------------------------

   From:    Jonathan Bowen <zforum@uk.ac.oxford.prg>
   Date:    Mon, 20 Nov 89 18:28
   Subject: Administrivia

   This is to apologise for the lack of ZFORUM for the last few months.
   This is due partly to lack of messages, but also because RSRE have
   updated their computer-system and since they forgot to formally specify
   it first are now having e-mail problems. :-) Ruaridh Macdonald's new
   e-mail address is <MACDONALD@uk.mod.hermes> although the old address
   will remain available for a while.

   As a result of the above, this edition of ZFORUM is being issued from
   Oxford. We hope that Ruaridh can resume his valuable role as ZFORUM
   editor in the future. In any case, you can send items for ZFORUM to
   <zforum@uk.ac.oxford.prg> and requests to join or leave ZFORUM or
   changes of e-mail address to <zforum-request@uk.ac.oxford.prg> on
   JANET.

   --

   Jonathan Bowen (temporary ZFORUM editor), PRG, Oxford.

   JANET:   zforum@uk.ac.oxford.prg
   NSFnet:  zforum%prg.oxford.ac.uk@nsfnet-relay.ac.uk
   UUCP:    zforum@ox-prg.uucp  (...!uunet!mcvax!ukc!ox-prg!zforum)


   ------------------------------------------------------------------

   From:    Sean Matthews <sean@uk.ac.ed.aipna>
   Date:    Tue, 24 Oct 89 17:17:13 BST
   Subject: news group discussion

   ...

   ************************ END OF Z FORUM 4.4 ************************
```

If you wish to be added to the **Z FORUM** e-mailing list, please send a request by electronic mail to zforum-request@uk.ac.oxford.prg on JANET as detailed above.

*Ruaridh Macdonald*
RSRE
Malvern

*Jonathan Bowen*
Programming Research Group
Oxford University
December 1989

# Author Index